INVESTIGATING

GEOGRAPHY

BOOK 1

INVESTIGATING

GEOGRAPHY

Jenkins · Leigh · Richards

BOOK 1

Bell & Hyman

Published in 1986 by
BELL & HYMAN LIMITED
Denmark House
37–39 Queen Elizabeth Street
London SE1 2QB

British Library Cataloguing in Publication Data

Jenkins, Susanna
  Investigating geography.
  Bk. 1
  1. Geography——Text-books——1945–
  I. Title   II. Leigh, Moya   III. Richards, Susan
  910   G128
  ISBN 0 7135 2515 0

Typeset by August Filmsetting, Haydock, St. Helens
Printed in Great Britain by Scotprint Ltd, Musselburgh

Contents

Introduction

Three young yet experienced teachers working in quite different schools have pooled their ideas and expertise to create a series of three books to stimulate and excite all pupils in the 11–14 age group. They have done this because they firmly believe that Geography should be fun and enjoyed by teacher and taught.

The books are realistic in their expectations of pupils' abilities and achievements, and are designed for practical classroom use. So each unit is self-contained in resources and the homework ideas are simple and independent.

Learning is achieved through doing. Each unit offers a range of 'things to do' which increase in difficulty. An active role is assumed for pupils: observation, data collection, group work and simulation. Ideas introduced early in the book are consolidated later. This book uses Europe as the framework for ideas, while Book Two uses the developing countries, looking especially at ways forward for development, and Book Three adopts a global perspective in its search for world contrasts.

Acknowledgements

We would like to express our gratitude to Vincent Tidswell for advice and encouragement during the writing process, to our editor, Caroline Paines, to Catherine Anderson for the picture research, and to Mrs Leigh and Mrs Jenkins for typing the manuscript.

S.J.   M.L.   S.R.

The authors and publishers would also like to thank the following for permission to reproduce photographs and illustrations in this book.

Aerofilms 14.3, 17.1, 18.2, 19.2, 19.3, 19.4, 21.3, 38.3;   Austin Rover 38.4;   Patrick Bailey 20.1, 22.4, 22.6, 22.7, 25.2, 25.3;   BBC Hulton Picture Library 21.5, 40.2(**1**);   Dr Alan Beaumont 12.6;   Barnaby's Picture Library 12.4, 35.3, 37.1 (bus driver), 37.3, 38.7, 40.2(**3**) 41.3 (T.C, T.R, B.R.), 46.4, 51.3;   Blackpool Department of Tourism 51.2;   British Jeweller 42.5 (T.C.);   Bruce Coleman Ltd 12.2, 58.5;   Cadburys 41.2;   Camera Press Ltd 10.4 (B.L.), 21.2 (John Blau, 37.1 (farmer), 44.1;   Camerapix Hutchison Library 4.1, 42.5 (M.L.);   Central Electricity Generating Board 37.3 (pylons);   Crown Copyright (Countryside Commission) 57.1 (T.C.);   DAS Photo 20.2;   Dutch Dairy Bureau 16.5;   Farmers Weekly 10.3, (T.R.), 14.4, 14.6, 17.2, 18.4;   GeoScience Features 3.1, 3.2, 4.2, 4.5, 9.2, 10.2 (B.R.), 12.3, 13.5, 18.1, 20.3, 41.3 (T.L.), 42.3, 42.5 (M.C., M.R.), 45.1, 47.1 (T), 48.1 (pub), 56.2, 56.4, 57.1 (B);   Sally and Richard Greenhill 34.7, 35.3 (2 photos), 36.5, 42.2, 43.1 (R), 48.1 (golf; gardening), 49.1 (3 photos), 49.5;   IBM 46.3;   International Wool Secretariat 14;   J Allan Cash Photolibrary 5.1, 12.5, 29.2, 34.5, 37.3 (clay pit; shop), 41.5, 42.5 (T.L.), 43.1 (L), 48.2 (camping), 56.3, 56.5;   James Davis Photography 26.6, 50.2, 53.2, 53.3, 53.5, 53.6, 53.7, 53.8, 54.1, 54.2, 54.3, 58.1;   Lloyds Bank 37.3;   Macmillan Paper Co Ltd 42.5 (B.R.);   Mary Evans Picture Library 40.2(**2**);   The Meteorological Office 5.2, 5.3, 6.2, 9.2**A** (J.F.P. Galvin – Crown Copyright);   Midland Bank 37.1;   Milk Marketing Board of England and Wales 42.5 (B.L. and B.C.);   National Tourist Organization of Greece 15.6;   The Photo Source Ltd 10.2 (T.L.), 10.3 (B.L. and R.), 19.6, 21.4, 23.2, 40.4, 41.3 (B.L.),

41.5 (2 photos), 42.1, 44.2, 44.9, 46.1, 47.1 (B), 48.1 (football); The Post Office 36.1; David Richardson 37.1 (teacher); Robert Harding Picture Library 31.4; Sefton Photo Library 28.1 (3 photos), 31.2, 31.3, 41.1, 44.8; Liba Taylor 32.3; Thames Water 10.2 (T.R. and B.L.); Warrington Runcorn Development Corporation 46.6; Washington Development Corporation 30.1, 30.2, 30.3, 30.4; Josiah Wedgwood & Sons Ltd 37.3 (5 photos); Yorkshire Post 10.4 (B.R.).

Cover photograph: Pictor International
Cover design: Snap Graphics

Artwork: Tim Smith
Gary Hincks
Mike Webb
Susanna Jenkins
Nigel Paige

Designed by: Neil Sayer

Investigating geography

If you look at the photographs in this book, or out of your classroom window, you will see that all places look different. We can see the *man-made world* and the *natural world*. These two worlds are closely linked. Geography is a subject which studies the things that are the same about places and the differences between them. Look at Figure 1 and put all the things that you can see under two headings: **The Natural World** and **The Man-made World.**

Figure 1   Our world

This book is going to look at places in Europe, and in particular at the countries in *the EEC* (European Economic Community). This is a group of countries which have special trading agreements with each other.

Looking at places

The first book to look at when trying to find out about places is an atlas. If you want to find out where a place is, turn to the index. There you will find something like this.

Paris,	France	27	48° 45′ N	02° 15′ E
city or town,	country	page	latitude	longitude

To help you pinpoint exactly where a place is, world maps have lines of *latitude* and *longitude*. Two important lines are 0° latitude which is the equator and 0° longitude which is a line running through the North Pole, South Pole and Greenwich near London. (Look at Figure 2.)

As long as you can find these two lines you should be able to work out where a place is. The degrees of latitude always tell us N (North) or S (South) and the degrees of longitude tell us E (East) or W (West). One degree on the world map, however, covers a large amount of space. So the degrees have been divided into smaller sections called minutes. There are sixty minutes to one degree.

Now we can find Paris exactly. Look at Figure 3.

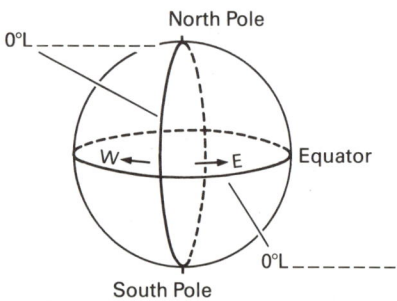

Figure 2   Lines of latitude and longitude

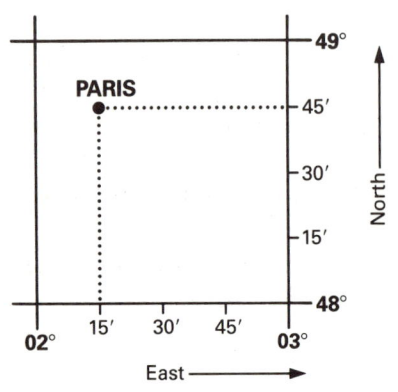

Figure 3   Locating Paris

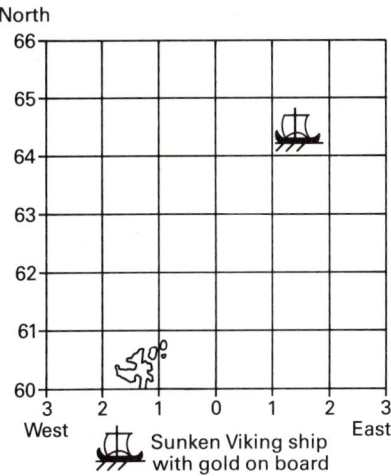

Figure 4   The seas off the Shetland Islands

Figure 5   A map of Europe

Things to do

1 Look at Figure 4. This shows the seas off the Shetland Islands where a Viking ship sank long ago. It was carrying valuable gold stolen from rich monasteries and abbeys in England. There are four teams of divers looking for the gold, but unfortunately, none of the teams has been given the right information.

  (a) Which team is the closest?
    A 62° 30′N   2° 15′W
    B 62° 30′N   2° 15′E
    C 63° 45′N   1° 30′E
    D 64° 15′N   0° 15′W

  (b) Work out the correct degrees of latitude and longitude.

2 Copy Figure 5. Use an atlas to name the countries labelled A, B, C, D, E, F, G, H, I, J, K and L. (You may find it easier to use a key.)

3 All these countries are members of the EEC. Shade them all the same colour.

4 As you can see, not all the countries in Europe are in the EEC. Europe can be divided into Eastern Europe and Western Europe. Work out the puzzles in Figure 6, and you will be able to label the rest of the countries on the map.

5 Shade all the East European countries one colour and add this to your key.

6 Find out the names of the seas and oceans around Europe numbered 1–7 on the map. Include them in your key.

7 Use your atlas to label the following capital cities. Athens, Amsterdam, Bonn, Brussels, Copenhagen, Dublin, London, Luxembourg, Paris, Rome, Lisbon and Madrid.

Western Europe
RIUSTAA
NEEDSW
YAWORN
DANNLIF
ZERLISTNDWA

Eastern Europe
AALIBNA
OLDNAP
GUNRAYH
SRUS
ARAGULBI
GASOUVILAY
CCSHKVZAAEIOOL
MERASTNEGAY

Figure 6   Word puzzle

Homework ideas

Collect pictures, stamps, postcards and newspaper cuttings of places in Europe. Mount them on a poster and show where they are on a map of Europe.

2 A close up view

Homework ideas

Draw a map showing a treasure island. Make up your own map symbols.

If you want to find your way from one place to another you will read the information you need from an Ordnance Survey (OS) map. This unit covers some of the map reading skills you will find useful when using this book. You may have to look back to these pages a number of times.

Finding places

Ordnance Survey maps are divided into squares by lines called *grid lines*. These are to help you find where places are on the map, by using *grid references*.

Look at Figure 1 to find a grid reference for ■.

Look at the bottom left hand corner of the square ■ lies in.

Follow the line that runs down the map to where you see 10.

Now go back to the left hand corner of the square and follow the line across the page to 73.

The grid reference for ■ is 1073.

A four figure reference tells you in which square to look for something. To help you remember which numbers are written down first, think of this little rhyme. 'Go along the corridor and up the stairs' (ie along the bottom of the grid and then up the side).

First read the number of the vertical line, then read the number of the horizontal line. Remember, 'along the corridor first, then up the stairs'.

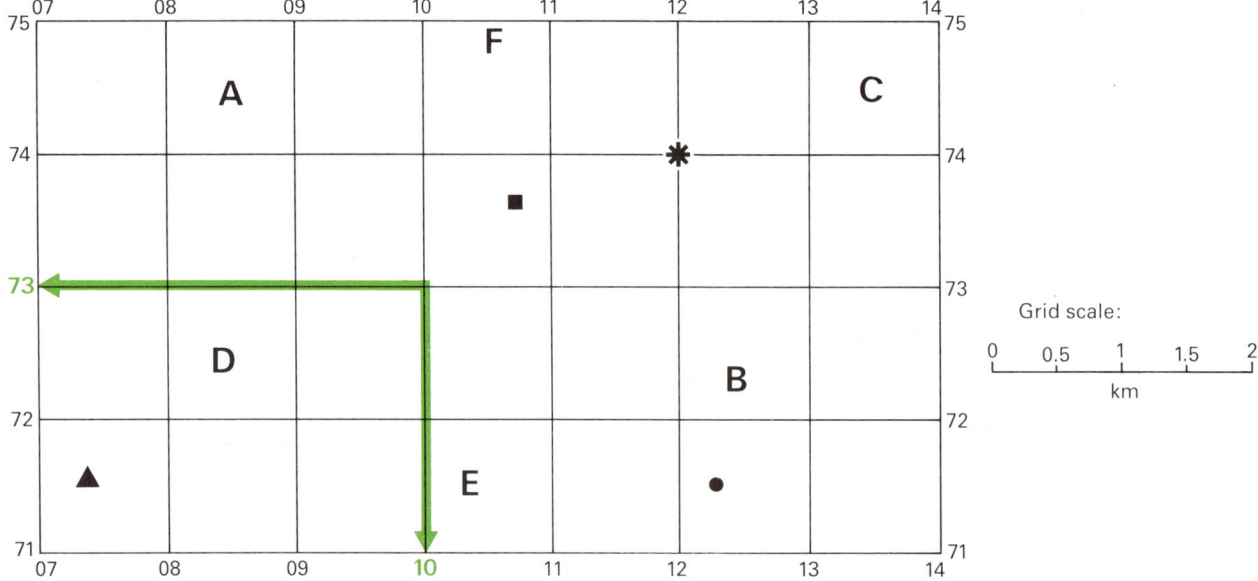

Figure 1   Grid references

Things to do

1 Find out what lies in each of these squares in Figure 1.
   (a) 0874   (b) 1272   (c) 1073
2 Work out a four figure reference for C, D and E.

To find the *exact* location of something on a map we use a six figure reference. Follow the example for ■ again.

Once we have found the square, we have to divide each line into ten parts or tenths (see Figure 2).

Grid scale:

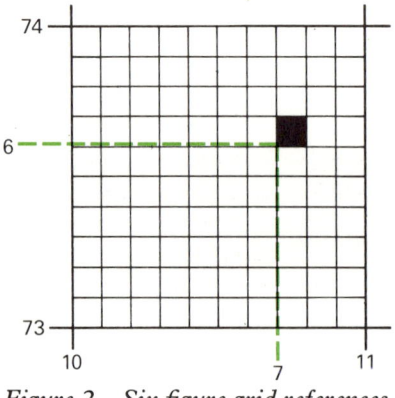

Figure 2   Six figure grid references

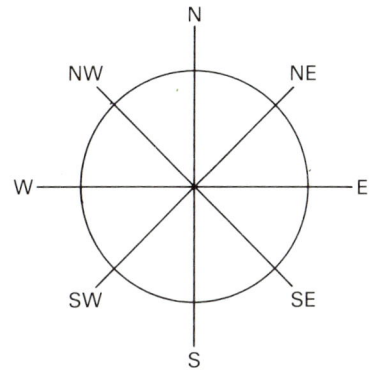

Figure 3   The points of the compass

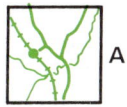

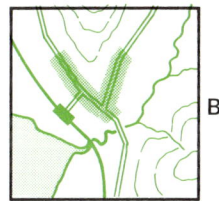

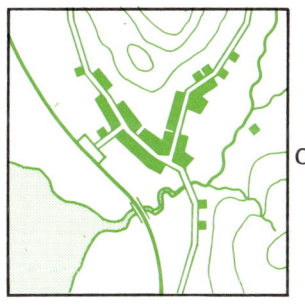

Scales:

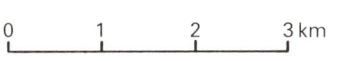

Figure 4   An area of land drawn at three scales

+ Church or chapel

& Church with a tower

& Church with a spire

& Lighthouse in use

& Railway line in a cutting

& Railway line on an embankment

P Post Office

PH Public House

CG Coastguard

Figure 5   Ordnance Survey map symbols

'Go along the corridor' until you find the left hand corner of the square at grid 10.

The point lies further along the line, so count up the tenths. This part of the reference is 107.

Now find how far up the stairs and count the number of tenths. You should find 736.

The six figure reference is 107736.

If a point lies exactly on a line this is 0 tenths and must be included in the reference.

3 Look at Figure 1 and finish the following six figure grid references.
▲ 07__ 71__   ● 12__ 71__   ✳ 12__ 74__

Which direction?

A map can be used to find the directions from one place to another. Maps are usually printed so that North is at the top of the page.

4 Use the points of the compass shown in Figure 3 to help you work out the directions below. Remember to match the centre of the compass with the point that you want to give the direction from. Make sure that N is always pointing to the top of the map. Imagine you are standing at ■, work out the directions to B, C, D, E and F.

How far?

Maps are plans of places drawn smaller than the actual size. A map would be very difficult to handle if it was drawn to actual size. Look round your classroom to see how large a map of the room would be. To solve this problem maps are drawn to *scale*.

5 (a) Look at the boxes in Figure 4. These are three outlines of the same area of land which measures 1 km by 1 km. They are all drawn to different scales. Draw the three boxes in your book.
   (b) Match up the right scale (also given in Figure 4) to each box.
   (c) Now finish these sentences
       The scale for square A is _____ cm = 1 km
       The scale for square B is _____ cm = 1 km
       The scale for square C is _____ cm = 1 km
   (d) Which square do you think will show more detail about the land?
   (e) Why do we draw maps to different scales?
   (f) Use the scale beside the grid in Figure 1 to find the distance in kilometres between the places with these symbols.
       ▲ and ■   _____ km
       ■ and ●   _____ km
       ● and ✳   _____ km
   (g) Finish this sentence.
       On the grid in Figure 1, 1 cm represents ____ km
   (h) Draw a scale plan of your classroom or a room in your house.

Map Symbols

Maps have a language of their own. To understand what they tell us we have to know what the *symbols* mean. A few symbols have been drawn for you (Figure 5). Find out some more symbols from an OS map.

3 Rocks

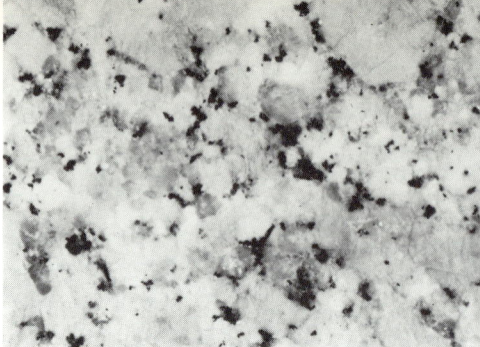
Figure 1   Granite

The rocks beneath our feet are the foundations of our buildings and roads. Where did these rocks come from? Why are rocks different?

There are three types of rock.

Igneous rocks

These rocks are very hard and are formed from very hot, molten rock, *magma*, which comes from deep inside the earth. Magma comes to the surface of the earth when a volcano erupts. The molten rock pours down the side of the cone. As the magma cools it becomes hard and forms a solid rock which is difficult to wear away. Igneous rocks frequently have crystals which make them glassy to look at. Two examples of igneous rock are granite and basalt. Look at Figures 1 and 2.

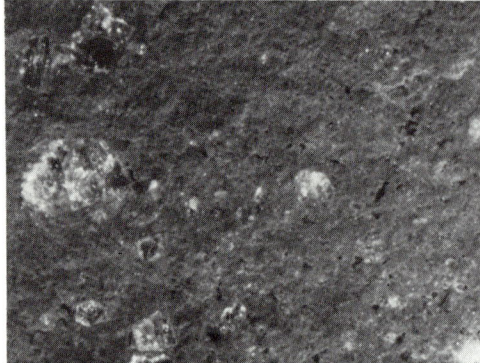
Figure 2   Basalt

Things to do

1 Copy out Figure 3 which shows how igneous rocks are formed.
2 Fill in the missing labels from these words.
   Cone, magma, granite, basalt.
3 What do you notice about the places where granite and basalt are found in Figure 3?
4 Granite can be found at the surface. How will the area of granite in Figure 3 appear on the surface?

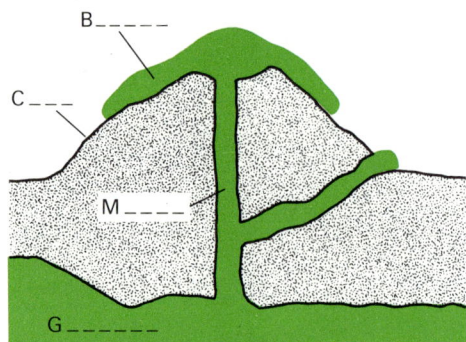
Figure 3   The formation of igneous rocks

Sedimentary rocks

Sedimentary rocks are made up from very small pieces of rock laid down in water. Rivers wear away their banks and carry a lot of material to the sea every year. What happens to the rock pieces when they reach the sea? Try the experiment below and you will find out.

This is an experiment to investigate sedimentary rocks. You will need a jar of water, one heaped tablespoon of sand and one heaped tablespoon of clay.

A Mix the sand, clay, and water together in the jar. Put the jar down and watch what happens.

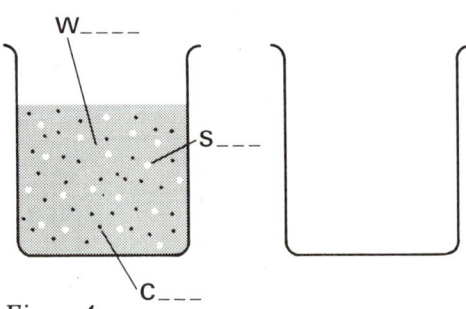
Figure 4

B Copy Figure 4. Now complete both diagrams: you need to add labels to jar 1 and draw the contents of jar 2, once the water has cleared. This will give you the final results of the experiment.

C Complete this passage from the missing words below.
   The _____ has sunk to the bottom of the jar, because it is _____ than clay. _____ settled on top of the sand because it is _____. So sediments have built up in _____.
   Missing words—heavier, layers, sand, lighter, clay.

D What would have happened if you had added small pieces of gravel to the jar? Draw a diagram to show your answer.

5 (a) Now use your knowledge to complete Figure 5 which shows the formation of sedimentary rocks.
   (b) Write a short explanation of the diagram.

Homework ideas

Look at the map showing the rocks of Great Britain (Figure 7).
1 Where in Great Britain do we find igneous rocks, sedimentary rocks and metamorphic rocks?
2 If sedimentary rocks are formed under the sea, why can we find them on the surface now?

14

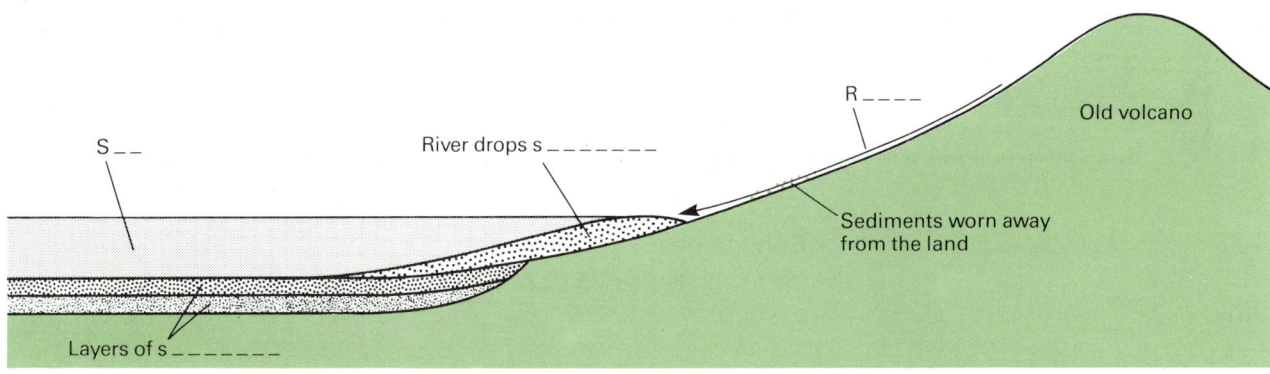

Figure 5   The formation of sedimentary rocks

Some sedimentary rocks like limestone and chalk are made from sediments that are not rocks.

6 Study Figure 6 and explain how these rocks are formed.

Metamorphic rocks

This rock can be made from sedimentary or igneous rock. The content of the rock is changed by increased heat or pressure.

7 Study Figure 8 and explain what causes the rock content to change.

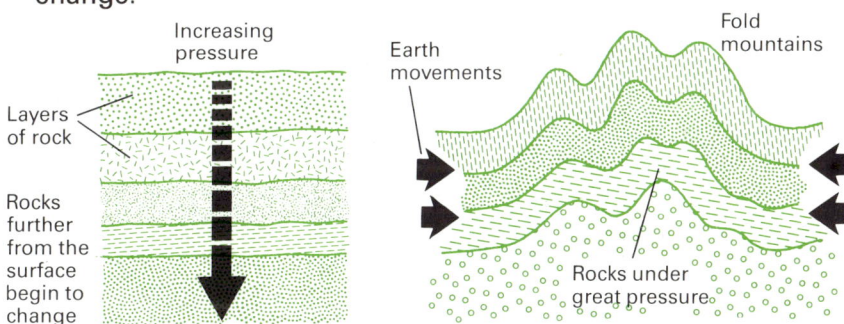

Figure 8   The formation of metamorphic rocks

Figure 6   The formation of chalk

8 Now you know how igneous, sedimentary and metamorphic rocks are formed you will be able to copy Figure 9 and label it. Match up the three rock types to the numbers on the diagram.

Figure 9

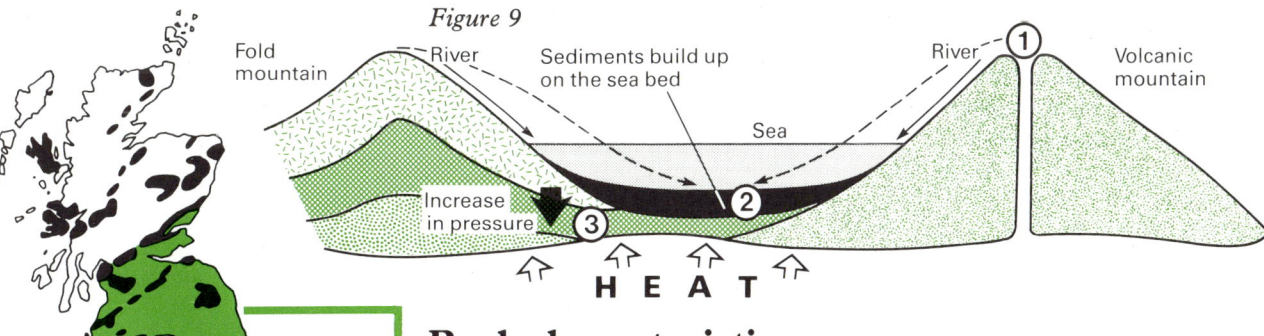

Rock characteristics

9 Look at as many samples of rock as you can, and draw up your own chart like the one below. When describing rock hardness, test the rock by seeing if you can scrape bits off with your finger nail which means it is very soft, or a coin which means it is soft, or a steel object which means it is hard.

Figure 7

Igneous

Sedimentary

Metamorphic

Rock name	Type	Colour	Weight	Hardness	Crystals (look for glassy areas)	Fossils (imprints of dead plants or animals)
Sandstone	Sedimentary	Orange/brown	Light	Hard	None	None

4 Soil—the skin of the Earth

Figure 1   This tree's roots have broken up the rock around it

Figure 2   A scree slope near Lake Wastwater in the Lake District

Where does soil come from? The photographs, Figures 1 and 2, show what happens to bare rock which is left unprotected from the weather. After a long time the rock will begin to break up because of a number of processes called *weathering*. If you are observant you will be able to see evidence of weathering all about you. The broken down bits of rock eventually form a layer of loose material we call *soil*.

Things to do

Weathering is caused by the action of different things—plants, frost, chemicals and temperature.

Plant action

1 How is the tree in Figure 1 helping to break down the rock?
2 Draw a diagram to show plant action on rocks and label the cracks.

Frost action

Figure 2 shows a highland area with a lot of fallen rocks at the foot of the slope. This loose material is called *scree*. In highland areas, temperatures are colder and there is more rainfall. Rainwater seeps into the cracks in the rock. If the temperature falls below 0°C the water freezes and expands. To see for yourselves how water expands when it freezes try putting a small open *plastic* bottle of water in the freezing compartment of a fridge. The ice makes the cracks in the rocks wider.

3 Describe the size and shape of the scree in Figure 2.
4 Copy Figure 3 and add your own labels to explain what happens.

Chemical Action

If you look at a lot of old buildings you can see the walls and statues are beginning to crumble. They are being eaten by a weak acid. Look at Figure 4 and explain why.

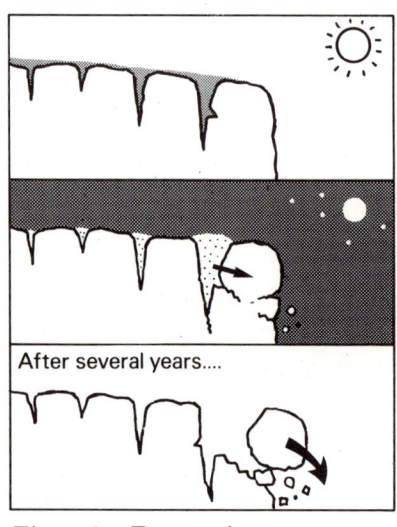

Figure 3   Frost action

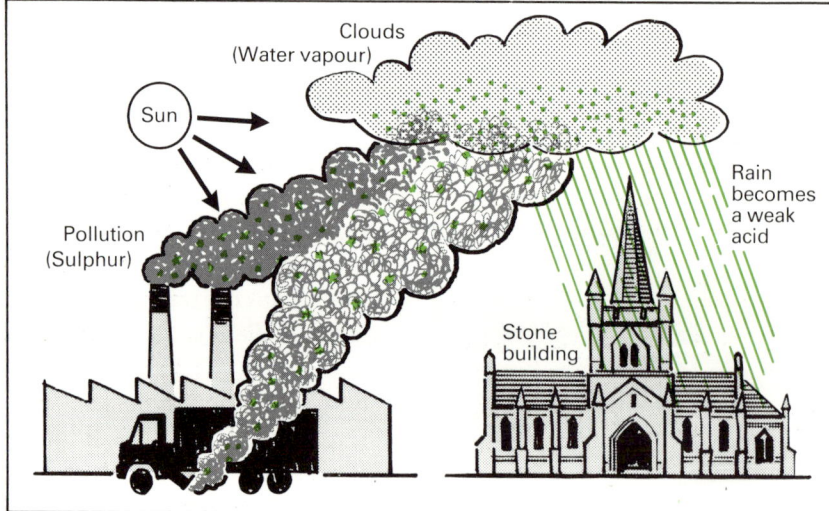

Figure 4   Chemical action on rocks

Figure 5   Onion peeling weathering

Figure 6   Soil sorters

Figure 7   A soil profile

The hot and cold effect

During the summer you often feel hot and sweaty. Some older people complain of swollen ankles and fingers. During the winter everyone is cold and the swollen joints go down.

This effect is also felt by rocks, when they become warm they expand and on cooling they contract. However not all parts of the rock do this at the same rate, so weaknesses develop. This can lead to the type of weathering shown in Figure 5 where layers of rock peel off. Sometimes this is known as *onion peeling*.

Try this experiment. Take two tin lids and paint one white and the other black. Place both of them in the sun for five to ten minutes.

5 What is the difference in temperature when you touch them?
6 How would this affect a rock if it had a mixture of colours?
7 Look back at Figure 2 in unit 3 and explain how temperature changes might alter this rock.
8 In what areas of the world do you think this type of weathering would be most effective?

Soils

The weathering processes give us some of the raw material for soil. But these loose particles do not stay still on the bedrock. They are sorted by a number of processes so as you dig deeper through the soil you will see distinct layers. Soils are easier to study if you look at a *profile* (a side on view). Sometimes soil profiles are exposed in quarries and road cuttings so that you have no need to dig one.

9 Copy Figure 6 and work out all the things which alter soils.

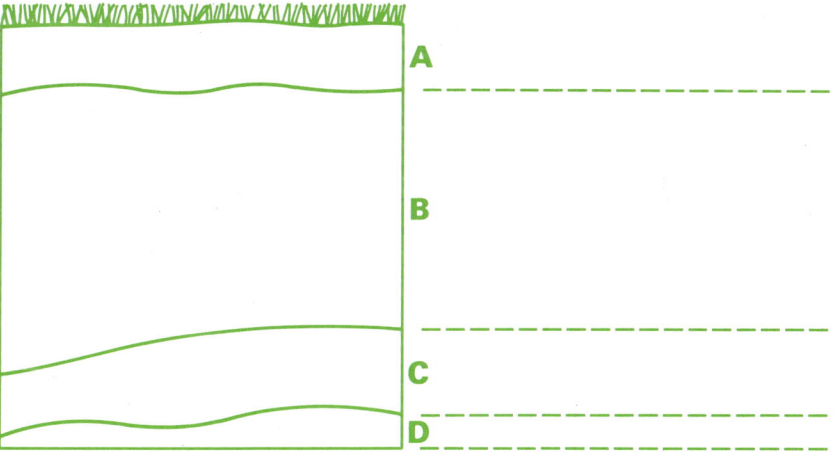
Figure 8

10 Look at Figure 7
   (a) In your exercise book draw Figure 8.
   (b) Using Figure 7 label the sections A, C, and D with the following names.
       solid bedrock
       weathered bedrock or parent material
       vegetation roots and decaying leaf litter called humus.
   (c) Section B is a special section where a lot of chemical processes take place. This layer may look different depending upon where you live.
       Add a label to describe section B.
   (d) Now you should be able to label any local profiles in a similar way. If you recognise the bedrock, add this to your profile label.

Homework ideas

Look for various types of weather around your house, school and local buildings. Fill in a chart like the one below.

Type of weathering	Place	Sketch/ description
Chemical action	Parish church	Angel wing crumbling

5 Behind the weather forecast

On television and on the radio we often hear weather forecasters predicting the weather. They are not fortune tellers but base their reports on the collection of a large amount of scientific information.

Within the British Isles there are over 100 weather stations, of which 65 make regular observations of the weather. Every hour weather reports are received from Europe and weather ships stationed in the North Atlantic ocean.

Satellites have been put into orbit around the earth to measure the amount of heat from the sun. We can see pictures from the satellites on the television. All these observations are used to produce the weather forecast.

Figure 1   A wind vane

Things to do

1 Suggest reasons why the following people may find their jobs easier if they know the weather forecast.
   (a) a farmer   (b) a builder   (c) a fisherman
   (d) an aeroplane pilot   (e) a person in charge of local highways
2 There are a number of important elements of weather that have to be measured and recorded hourly or daily.
   See if you can sort out this list. Look at the cartoons and symbols in this unit to help you sort out the puzzles.
   (a) E E E T P M A T R U R
   (b) N D I W
   (c) N R L L A F I A
   (d) O D U L C
   (e) E S N U S N H I
3 Certain elements of weather are measured by special instruments (Figures 1–3). Find the matching pairs, one word from list A matches with one word from list B.

Figure 2   A rainfall gauge

List A	List B
Thermometer	Wind direction
Anemometer	Wind speed
Wind vane	Rainfall
Rainfall gauge	Temperature

Figure 3   An anemometer

Homework ideas

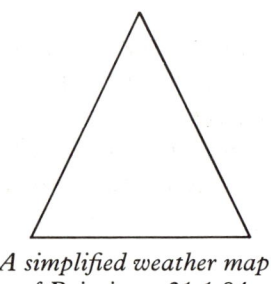

A simplified weather map of Britain on 31.1.84

1 Find a weather forecast from any of the following:
   radio
   television
   newspaper
   telephone
   Write down the forecast.
2 Use the weather symbols in Figure 5 to draw a simple weather map for Great Britain. Look at the map shown here to help you.

Figure 4   A weather map

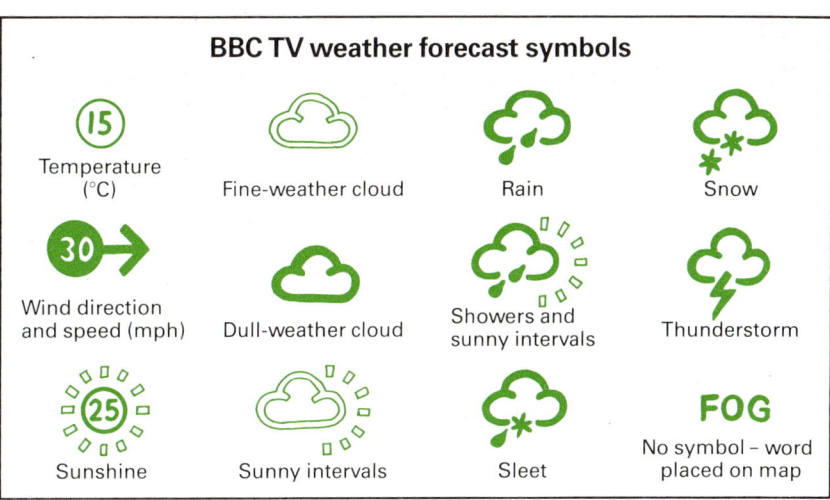

Figure 5   BBC TV weather map symbols

Television reports

4 Look at the map in Figure 4 and the symbols key in Figure 5.
   (a) What is the weather like in the Midlands?
   (b) Describe the weather over Scotland.
   (c) This is the weather report for south west England.
      'There will be sleet showers in the south west, later turning to rain. Temperatures will rise from − 1 °C to 3 °C during the day. Winds will be light (2 miles per hour).'
      Draw the map symbols to show this forecast.

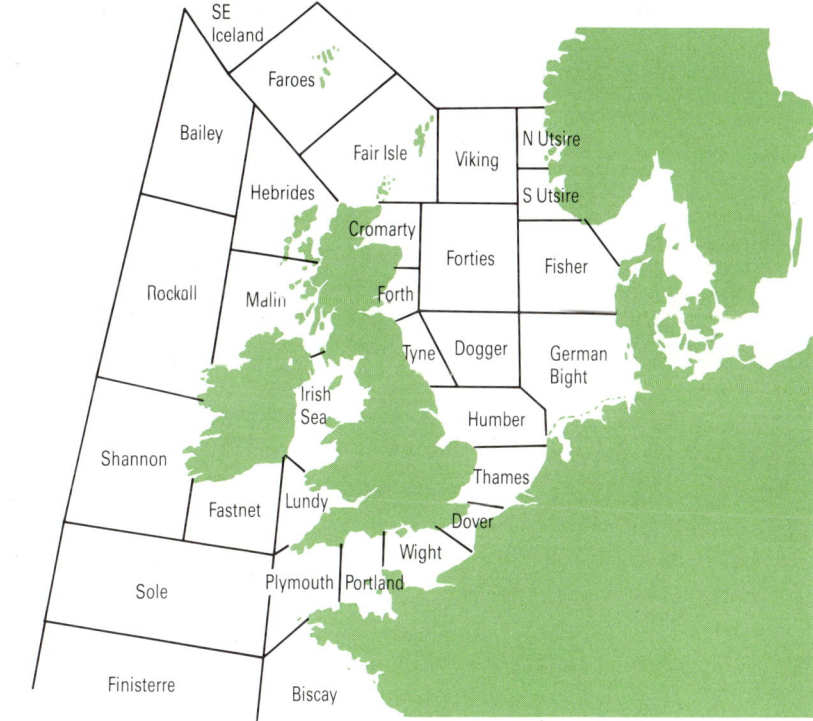

Figure 6   The sea areas of the United Kingdom

Radio weather reports—the shipping forecast

5 (a) Look at Figure 6. On your own copy of a map of Great Britain label and colour all the inshore sea areas.
   (b) Why do you think the sea has been divided into areas?
   (c) Using an atlas find out which shipping areas you would listen out for if you were sailing
      (i)   around the Isle of Wight
      (ii)   across the Severn estuary
      (iii) from the Shetland Isles to the west coast of Norway.

Folklore weather

Red sky at night –
shepherds' delight
(predicts fair weather)

Red sky in the morning –
shepherds' warning
(predicts rain)

Ash before oak –
there will be a soak.
Oak before ash –
there will be a splash.

Now find some more sayings!

6 Planning a weather station

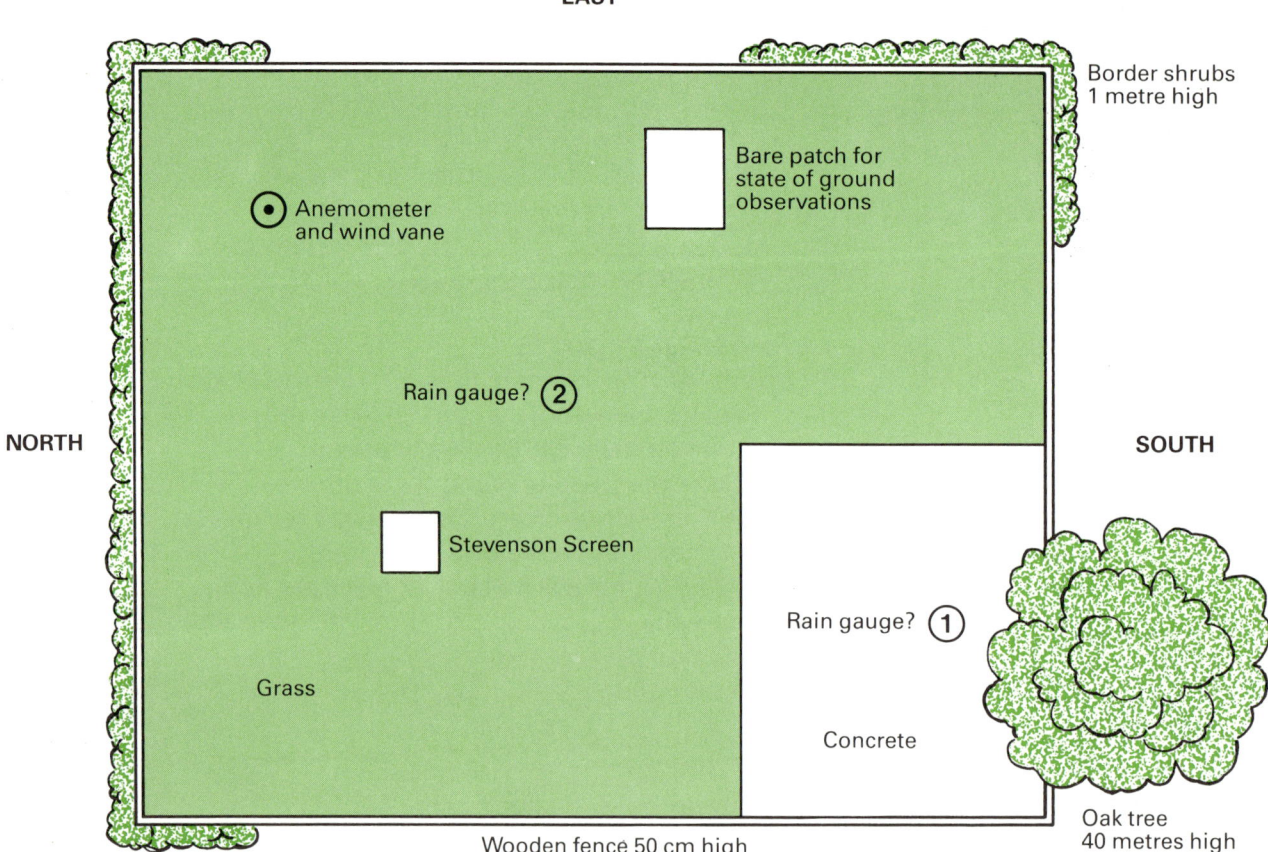

EAST

Border shrubs
1 metre high

Bare patch for
state of ground
observations

⊙ Anemometer
and wind vane

NORTH

SOUTH

Rain gauge? ②

Stevenson Screen

Rain gauge? ①

Grass

Concrete

Oak tree
40 metres high

Wooden fence 50 cm high

Figure 1   *Plan of a school weather station*   WEST

Figure 2   *A weather station*

A weather station

The plan in Figure 1 shows the ideas some pupils have for setting up their own school weather station. They need some help with siting some of the instruments. Two different places are being considered for the rain gauge.

Homework ideas

Think of a suitable place to put a weather station in your school grounds. If you already have a weather station describe the problems of its position.

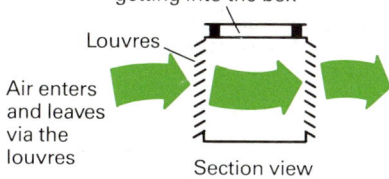

An airspace to stop extra heat getting into the box

Louvres

Air enters and leaves via the louvres

Section view

Air moving through the box allows the temperature of the shade to be measured.

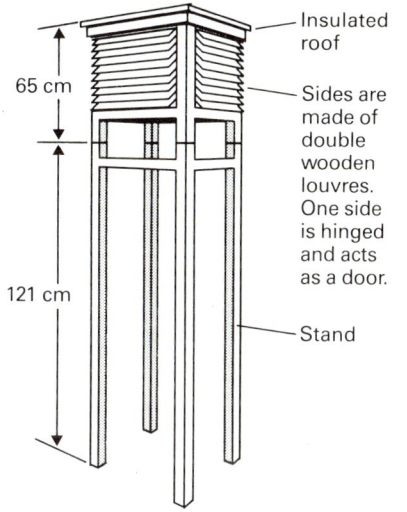

Insulated roof

65 cm

Sides are made of double wooden louvres. One side is hinged and acts as a door.

121 cm

Stand

All weather instruments have to be placed in certain positions so that they do not give false readings.

Thermometers are placed in a special screen so they measure the temperature of the shade.

Figure 3   The Stevenson Screen

Things to do

1   Here is a list of all the good and bad points about the two sites. Unfortunately the lists have become confused.

(a) Can you pick out and write down all the points for
(i) site 1   (ii) site 2
Rain splashes into the gauge from the concrete.
Rain drops soak into the ground.
Extra rain falls into the container from the oak tree's leaves.
Sheltered by the fence from the driving rain.
Not sheltered from any rain.

(b) Which site would give the most accurate readings?

(c) How high will the anemometer and wind vane have to stand so that they are not sheltered by the shrubs?

(d) Which instruments should the pupils put inside the Stevenson Screen?
wind vane   thermometer   anemometer   rainfall gauge   barometer

(e) Why should a weather station be sited in the open countryside rather than sheltered by buildings?

2 (a) Look at the picture of the Stevenson Screen (Figure 3) and write down two ways in which the box remains cool.

(b) The Stevenson Screen is painted white, can you suggest why? (Look back at question 5 in Things to do, unit 4.)

(c) These screens are placed in open spaces to get accurate readings. Think of as many places as possible where you would **not** get accurate readings if you put the screen there. Figure 4 may help you.

(d) Look at Figure 1 again. Do you think the screen is in a good position? List the reasons for your answer.

Figure 4   The best place to put a Stevenson Screen?

21

7 Recording the weather—temperature

Now it is time to take a closer look at the instruments which are used to record the weather. This unit should give you a chance to record your own local weather.

Temperature is a very important part of the weather. Most of the earth's heat comes from the sun. Look at Figure 1 and try to work out how the air is warmed.

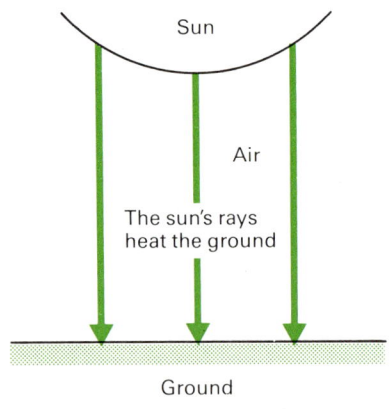
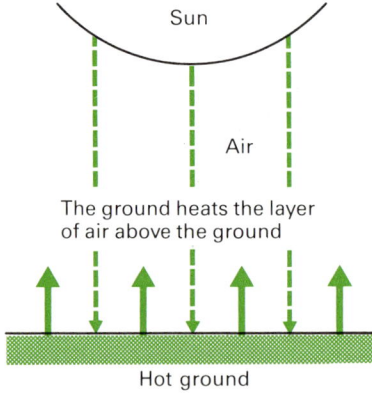

Figure 1   Heating the air

Things to do

1 Make a copy of Figure 1.
(a) Shade the diagram with cold air – blue, and the one with warm air – red.
(b) Copy out the passage below, filling in the missing words from the diagrams.
The sun gives out energy which will make objects warmer. First of all the sun will heat up the g _____. When the ground is warm it will begin to heat up the layer of a _____ next to the ground. So the air is not w _____ directly by the sun.
(c) Why does the air become cooler at night?
(d) Can you now suggest another reason for not putting the Stevenson Screen on the ground?

Maximum and minimum temperatures

It is very useful to record two temperatures. The first is the *maximum temperature* which is the highest temperature for the day, and the second is the *minimum temperature* which is the lowest temperature for the day. A special thermometer is used to record these temperatures.

The thermometer shown in Figure 3 is a U-shaped tube with mercury inside it. Each end of the mercury is marked by a metal pin. When the temperature rises the mercury rises up the maximum side and falls in the minimum side. Can you work out what happens when the temperature falls? The metal pins mark the highest point the mercury reaches in each tube. To read the temperature you look at the bottom of the pin. Each day the pins are put back on top of the mercury by a magnet.

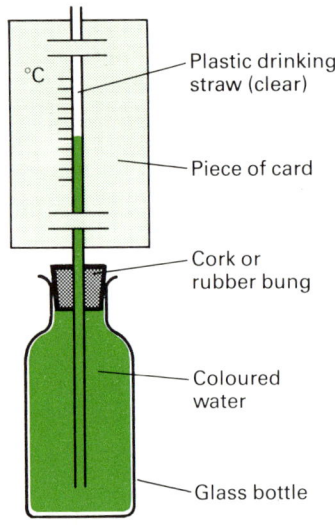

A   Collect all the items shown in the diagram. Make sure that the cork or bung fits tightly.

B   You can colour the water by adding a small amount of ink or food colouring. Some water must come up the straw when the bottle is filled.

C   To compare your thermometer with a real thermometer you must place them both in a saucepan of cold water.

D   When the coloured water stops falling in the straw, mark the level on a piece of card and write down the temperature, which you can read from the real thermometer.

E   Carefully warm the water in the saucepan until the real thermometer reads 10°C higher. Mark this level off on the card.

What has happened to the water in the home-made thermometer?

F   Divide the space between the two readings on the card into 10 equal parts. Each mark represents 1°C.

Figure 2   A home-made thermometer

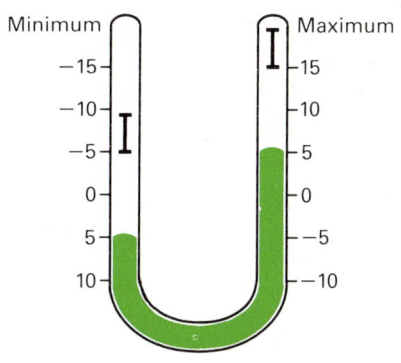

Figure 3 A maximum and minimum thermometer

Things to do

Look at Figure 3.
1 (a) What do you notice about the temperature scales on each limb?
  (b) Draw the thermometer and label the mercury, the metal pins, and the scale of temperature.
  (c) What was the minimum temperature?
  (d) What was the maximum temperature?
  (e) Why do you think the metal pin is useful? (Look at the cartoon.)

2 Here are some temperature readings for a few days in June, 1984 (Table 1).

Table 1

Location—Manchester: Date 2 to 10 June, 1984

	Sat	Sun	Mon	Tues	Wed	Thurs	Fri	Sat	Sun
Min °C	8	10	8	12	11	12	12	11	12
Max °C	17	17	19	16	17	24	23	24	18

The first three days have been plotted on the graph in Figure 4.
(a) Complete the graph.
(b) What was the minimum temperature on Sunday, 3rd June?
(c) What was the maximum temperature on Tuesday?
(d) Shade the area on the graph between the two lines (maximum and minimum).
(e) The shaded area is the *daily temperature range*. This can be worked out in °C by subtracting the minimum temperature from the maximum.
    For example Saturday 2nd June
    Max − Min
    17− 8 = 9 °C daily temperature range
    Now work out the daily range for Tuesday.
(f) Which day has the largest temperature range?

Homework ideas

1 Collect the equipment needed to make the thermometer in Figure 2, or make the thermometer at home.
2 Record the daily temperatures for a week.
3 Find out the maximum and minimum temperatures for each day. (Look in your local newspaper.)
4 At the end of the week draw your own line graph.

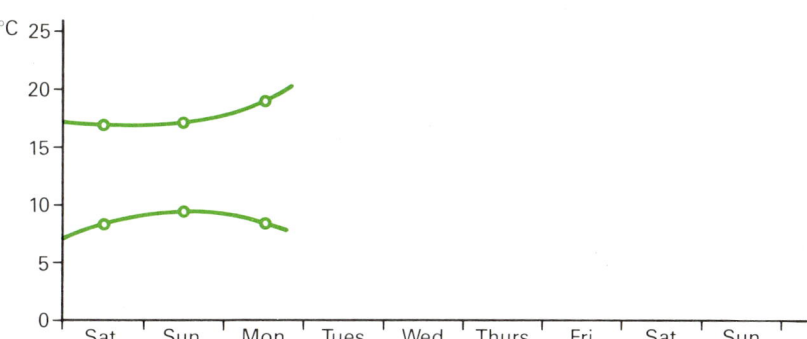

Figure 4 Maximum and minimum temperatures for Manchester, June 1984

23

8 Recording the weather—winds

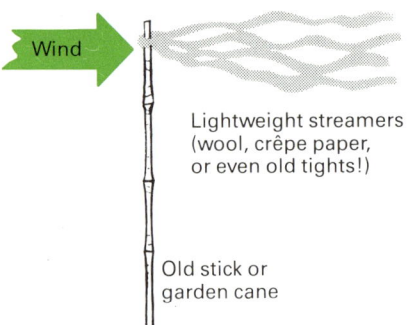

Lightweight streamers (wool, crêpe paper, or even old tights!)

Old stick or garden cane

You will need a **compass** to find the direction:

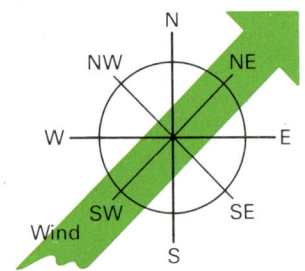

Figure 1   A simple wind vane

Table 1   *September winds recorded in a back garden in Manchester*

Direction	No. of days
N	0
NW	2
W	0
SW	12
S	0
SE	9
E	0
NE	7

Wind is air moving across the earth's surface. This air does not always move in the same direction or at the same speed. Certain winds nearly always bring the same weather during the same season. Remember the folklore rhyme 'When the north wind doth blow, we will have snow.' The weather forecaster is interested in the wind speed (or *force*) and the wind direction.

The speed of the wind is measured by an instrument called an *anemometer*. It is given a force number from the Beaufort Scale, which is often used in shipping forecasts. The direction of the wind is recorded by a *weather vane* (Figure 1).

To make a simple wind vane you need the equipment shown in Figure 1 and a compass to record the direction.

Wind directions are always given as the direction they come from. Look at the compass. If the tassels stream out in the direction of the arrow in the compass, the wind comes from the south-west and is called a south-westerly.

Things to do

1 List as many people as you can who find winds (a) useful and (b) harmful

Wind direction

Once the wind direction has been recorded it is easier to understand if it is shown in a diagram called a *wind rose*. This is really a graph in the shape of a compass like the one shown in Figure 2. Here are some results (Table 1) recorded for Manchester using the simple wind vane shown in Figure 1.

2 Finish plotting the results on the wind rose. The north-easterly winds have been done for you.

3 A wind which blows most often is called a *prevailing wind*. Which wind was the prevailing wind for the month of September in Manchester?

4 Try to record your local wind directions by using a wind vane on a building or by making a simple wind vane. Make sure you record *where* the wind comes *from*!

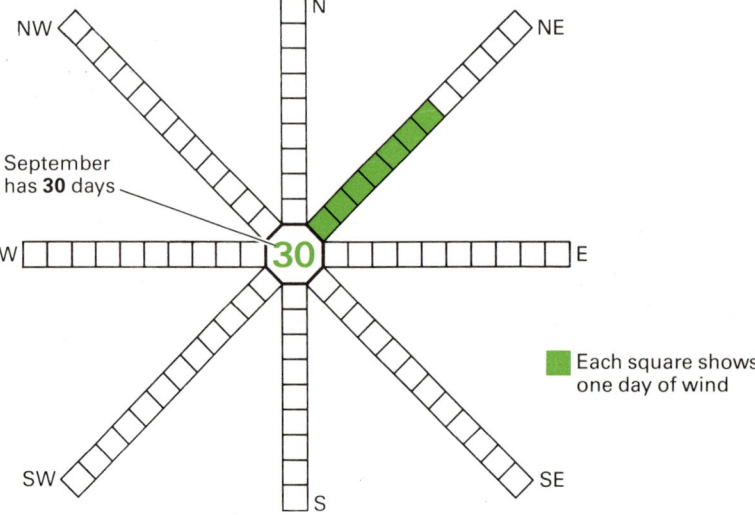

September has **30** days

Each square shows one day of wind

Figure 2   A wind rose for September

Homework ideas

1 Collect sketches and note the locations of local wind vanes.
2 Find out what a 'sou-wester' is.
3 Make the instruments in this unit.

FORCE	WIND SPEED (miles per hour)
0	less than 1
2	4 – 7
4	13 – 18
6	25 – 31
8	39 – 46
10	55 – 63

Figure 3   The Beaufort Scale

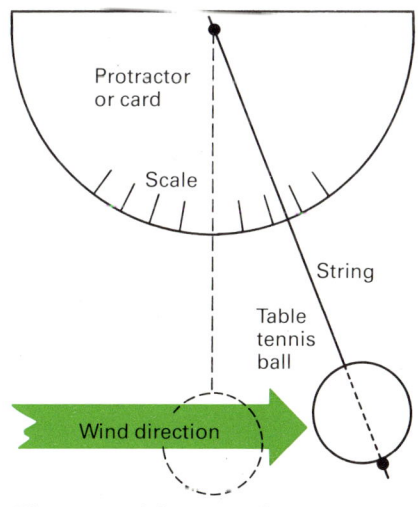

Figure 4   A home-made anemometer

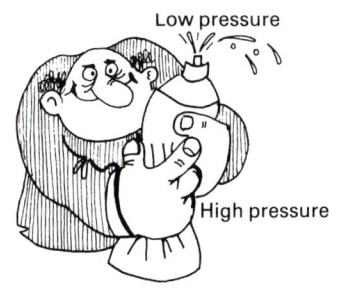

Wind force

5 Look at Figure 3 which shows the Beaufort Scale and write a short sentence describing what the wind does for each force.

6 Try to record the windspeed for a week using a simple anemometer like the one shown in Figure 4.

To make a simple anemometer you need the equipment shown in Figure 4. The scale can be marked on the instrument by watching what happens to trees and matching up the description to the Beaufort Scale (Figure 3).

Why do winds blow?

Winds blow because of differences in the weight of the air resting on the ground at different places. This is called *pressure*. Pressure varies because temperatures vary. When air is warm it rises, so there is less air pressing down (less weight) so we have low pressure. However, cold air sinks and causes high pressure because there is more air pressing down. To understand this think of a squeezy washing-up-bottle. To get the liquid out you squeeze the bottle. Squeezing applies pressure to the bottle so the liquid moves and squirts into your washing up bowl, where there is less pressure. (Look at the cartoon to help you understand this.) So winds blow from where there is high pressure to where there is low pressure.

7 Draw Figure 5 showing two different pressures at the ground, and complete the missing words.

8 Shade the colder air blue and the warmer air red.

9 Look at the squeezy bottle cartoon again.

  (a) Now add an arrow on your own copy of Figure 5 to show which way the winds blow along the ground.

  (b) What do you think would happen to the air high up in the atmosphere in columns A and B?

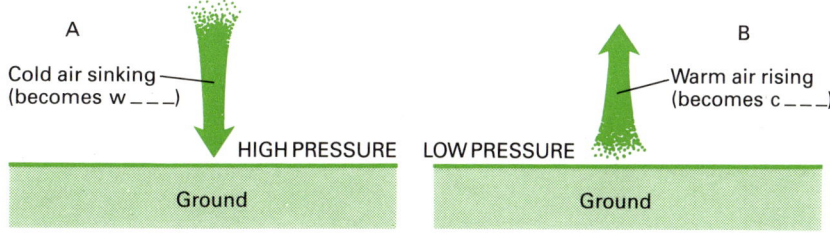

Figure 5   Moving air

9 Recording the weather— clouds and rainfall

Mr Water Vapour and Friends

Things to do

1 Read the cartoon **Mr Water Vapour and Friends**. Then in your own words write a short paragraph explaining how clouds and rain are formed. Remember to include the important words—*condensation* and *evaporation*.

2 Using Figure 1, try to find out the names of the clouds in the photographs A, B, C and D (Figure 2). Copy Table 1 and fill in all the information for each cloud.
   Cloud C has been done for you.

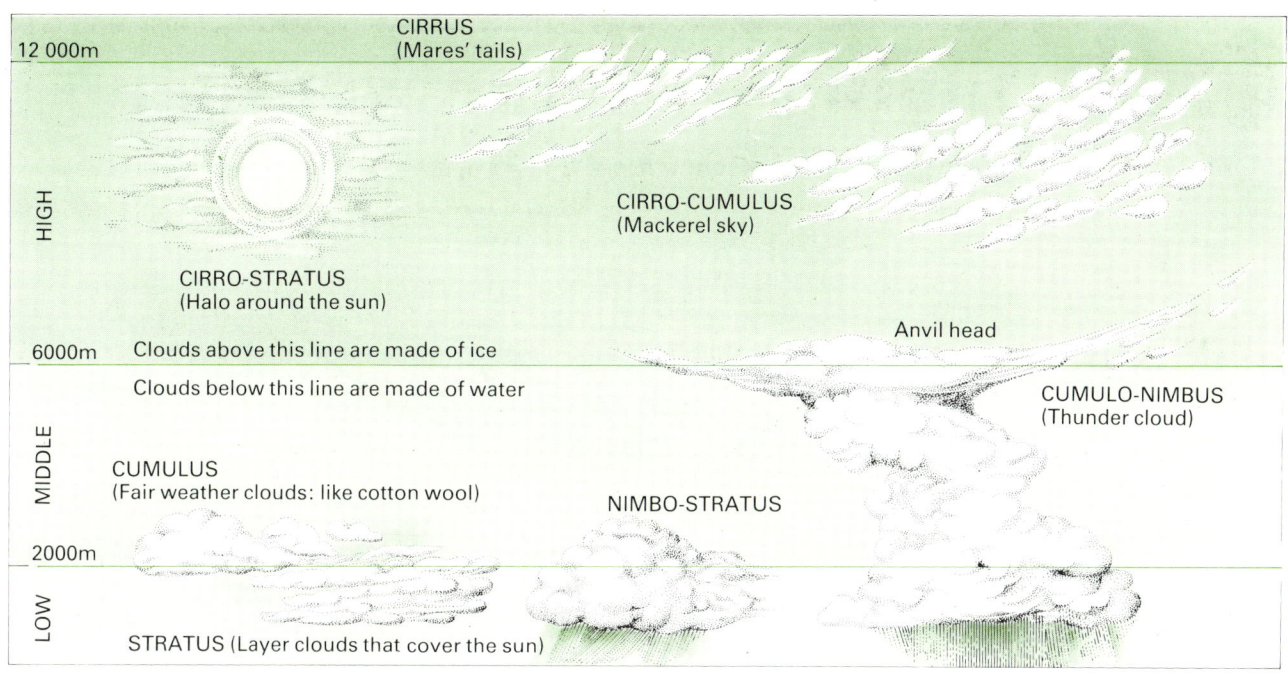

CIRRUS (Mares' tails)

12 000m

HIGH

CIRRO-CUMULUS (Mackerel sky)

CIRRO-STRATUS (Halo around the sun)

6000m — Clouds above this line are made of ice

Clouds below this line are made of water

Anvil head

CUMULO-NIMBUS (Thunder cloud)

MIDDLE

CUMULUS (Fair weather clouds: like cotton wool)

NIMBO-STRATUS

2000m

LOW

STRATUS (Layer clouds that cover the sun)

Figure 1   Naming clouds

Figure 2

Table 1

	Cloud name	Height	Made of water or ice
A			
B			
C	Stratus	Below 2000 m	Water
D			

Recording the rainfall

The weather forecaster uses a very accurate rain gauge to measure rainfall, which has to be read every day. You can easily measure rainfall by placing a jam-jar outside. Look back at unit 6, p20, to remind you of the best place to put a rain gauge. Now you can measure how much rain falls each day.

Once you have collected your data you can record it as a bar graph. Finish drawing the bar graph for a rainy week in September, 1984 (Figure 3) from Table 2.

Table 2

Date (September 1984)	8	9	10	11	12	13	14
Rain in mm	30	69	6	50	56	38	63

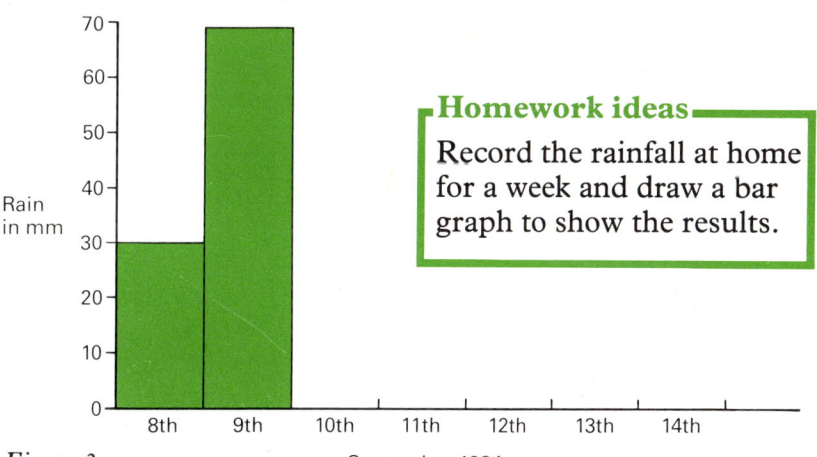

Figure 3   September 1984

Homework ideas
Record the rainfall at home for a week and draw a bar graph to show the results.

27

Living with the weather

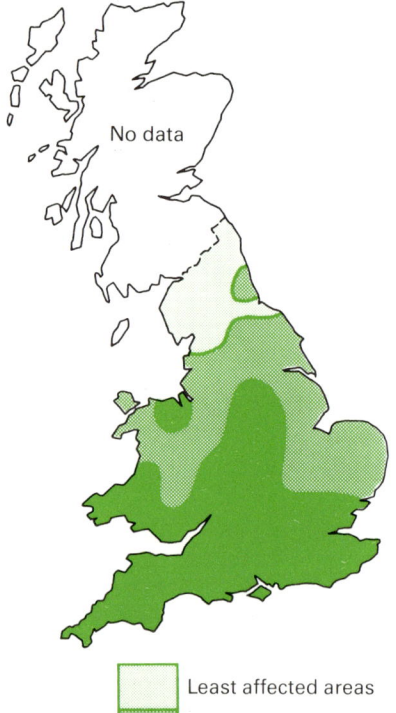

Figure 1   The 1976 drought in Britain

Least affected areas

Greatly affected areas

Worst affected areas

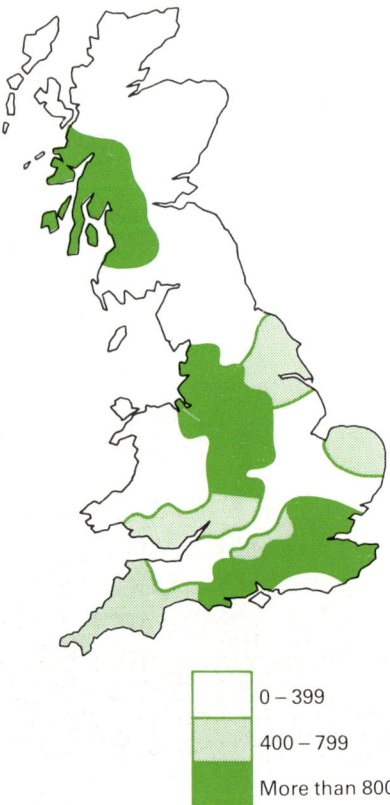

Figure 2   Fires occurring during June and August 1976

0 – 399

400 – 799

More than 800

Drought

Britain often has to cope with problems of drought during very hot summers with little rainfall. The maps (Figures 1 and 2) and photographs show areas which were badly hit by drought during the summers of 1976 and 1984.

A roadside sign in Dorset

Chelsea Reservoir, Surrey

A Water Authority poster

Sun-scorched strawberries, Kent

Things to do

Look at all the information in this unit and choose one of the events. There are a number of activities you can do.

1 Write a newspaper report.
2 Record a radio broadcast.
3 Write a diary for the time over which the event happened.
4 Design posters to warn people against the dangers and ask them to help.
5 Write a play, and then act it out in class.

Snow

Very heavy snowfall can cause many people considerable problems. The photographs and diary of notable snowfalls give you some idea of these problems.

1975	1978	1981
June 2 My brother was playing a cricket match in Buxton. It was called off because of SNOW!	**January** Uncle John phoned today from Scotland. He sells ladies' clothes. He was trapped in his car by heavy snow for 80 hours. 3 other people died, but he kept warm by wrapping up in lots of pairs of tights! **Feb 18** Mum is worried about Gran. 8m deep snowdrifts have cut off Gran's village in Devon.	**April** We went on a school trip to Stonehenge. Got stranded by a sudden heavy snowfall. Teachers were not very pleased, but good fun for us! 300 people stranded were rescued by the army.

Figure 3 (*Top right*) *Lambs wearing 'jackets' at a farm near Welshpool, Snowdrifts in Devon (left) and Kent (right).*

Floods

Rivers often burst their banks when there has been heavy rainfall or a lot of melting snow. Sometimes, near the coast, the river may flood lowland areas when high tides move up the estuary. Look at the newspaper extract of flooding in York in 1982.

Flooding in York

The River Ouse was 5 m higher than normal in York. In earlier years, 600 houses had been flooded. Villages lower downstream were also flooded. In Cawood, 100 houses were damaged and outside Selby hundreds of acres of farmland were changed into lakes. For three days, York was isolated and roads blocked.

Figure 4 Flooding in Cologne, West Germany in 1983 (left), and in York in 1982 (below).

11 A year of weather

Climate is the description of the weather we experience all the year round. This can be shown by a *climate graph*, which shows us average temperatures and average rainfall for each month.

Things to do

Look at the Heathrow data (Table 1) and the graph (Figure 1).
1 Complete the climate graph in your exercise book.
2 Name the month with the highest average temperature.
3 What is the highest temperature (___ °C)?
4 Name the month with the lowest average temperature.
5 What is the lowest temperature (___ °C)?
6 Name the wettest month.
7 How much rain falls in the wettest month?
8 Name the driest months.
9 How much rain falls in the driest months?
10 The annual temperature range is ___ °C. (Work this out by taking the lowest temperature away from the highest temperature.)
11 Now draw a climate graph for the Stornoway data (Table 2).

Table 1   Average monthly temperatures and rainfall in Heathrow

	J	F	M	A	M	J	J	A	S	O	N	D
°C	4	4	7	9	13	16	17	17	15	12	7	1
mm	48	39	39	40	50	48	58	65	52	57	63	54

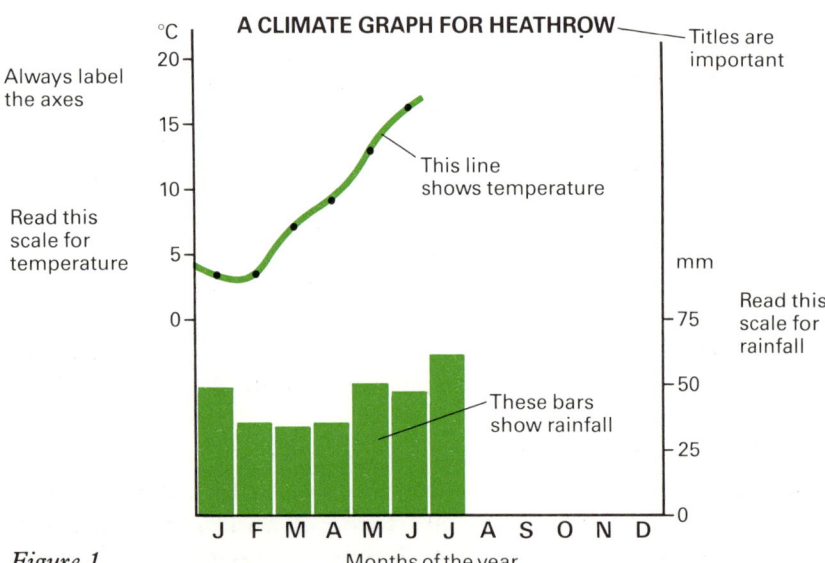

Always label the axes

Read this scale for temperature

A CLIMATE GRAPH FOR HEATHROW — Titles are important

This line shows temperature

These bars show rainfall

Read this scale for rainfall

Months of the year

Figure 1

Table 2   Average monthly temperatures and rainfall in Stornoway

	J	F	M	A	M	J	J	A	S	O	N	D
°C	4	5	6	7	9	12	13	13	12	16	6	5
mm	110	84	76	71	57	65	76	83	106	122	112	130

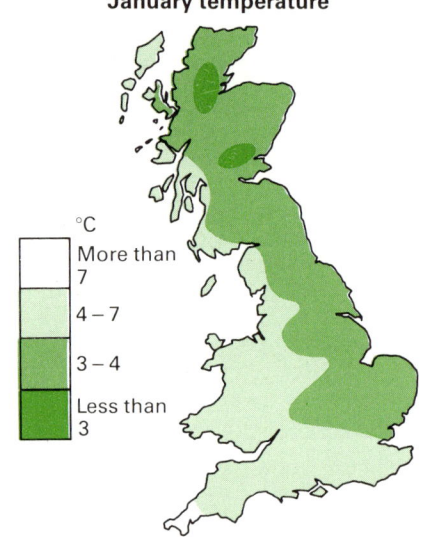

January temperature

°C
More than 7
4 – 7
3 – 4
Less than 3

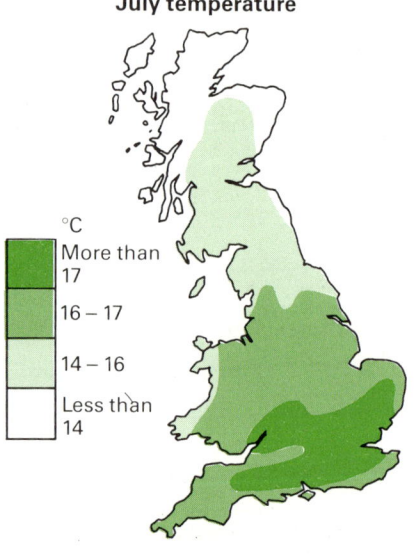

July temperature

°C
More than 17
16 – 17
14 – 16
Less than 14

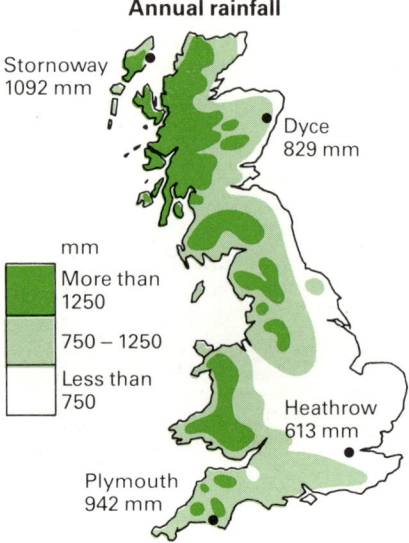

Annual rainfall

Stornoway 1092 mm
Dyce 829 mm

mm
More than 1250
750 – 1250
Less than 750

Heathrow 613 mm
Plymouth 942 mm

Figure 2   Britain's climate

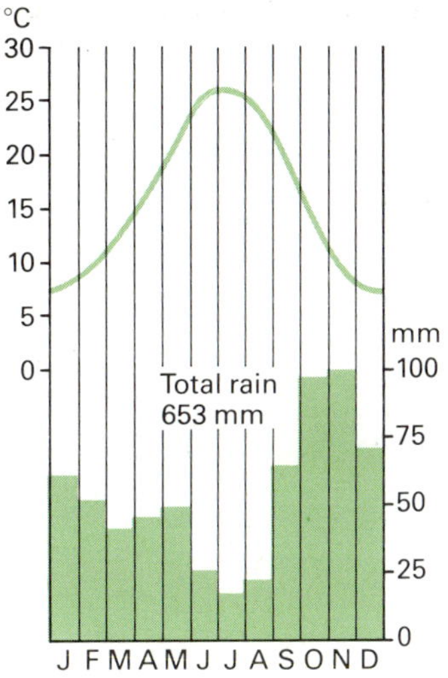

°C
30
25
20
15
10
5
0

Total rain
653 mm

mm
100
75
50
25
0

J F M A M J J A S O N D

Figure 4   Rome

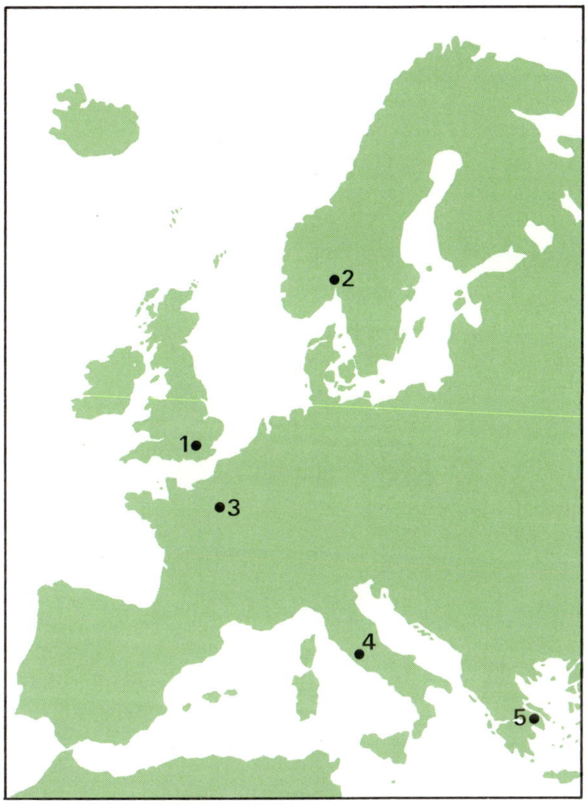

°C
30
25
20
15
10
5
0

Total rain
566 mm

mm
100
75
50
25
0

J F M A M J J A S O N D

Figure 5   Paris

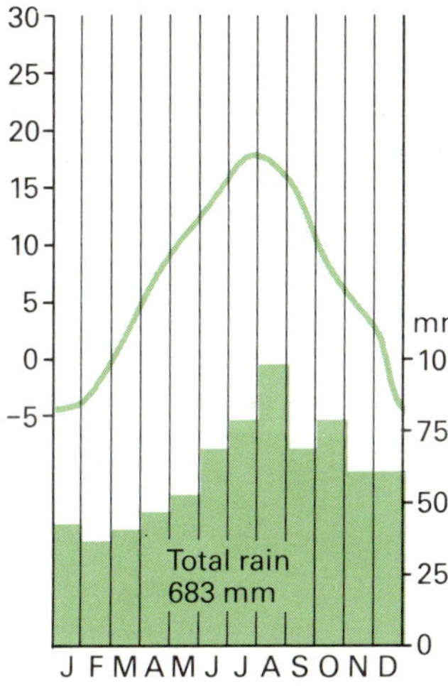

Figure 3   Europe's climate

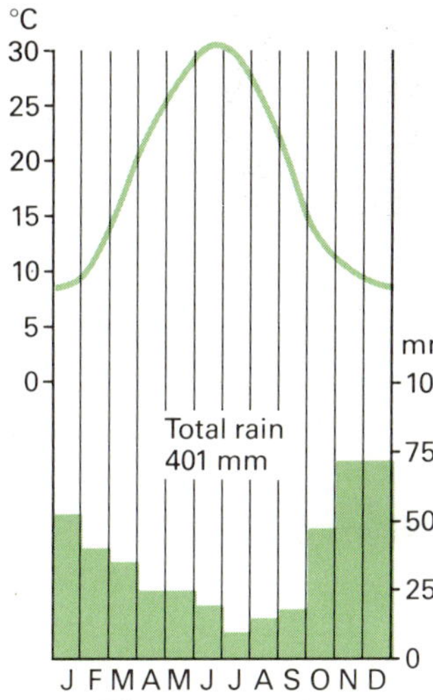

°C
30
25
20
15
10
5
0

Total rain
401 mm

mm
100
75
50
25
0

J F M A M J J A S O N D

Figure 6   Athens

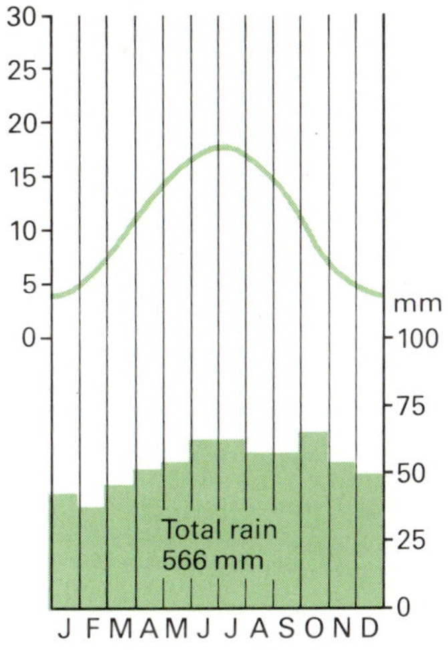

°C
30
25
20
15
10
5
0
−5

Total rain
683 mm

mm
100
75
50
25
0

J F M A M J J A S O N D

Figure 7   Oslo

1 Cool winters 4°C
   Hot summers 17°C
   Low annual rainfall 613mm

2 Mild winters 6°C
   Warm summers 16°C
   High annual rainfall 942mm

3 Cool winters 4°C
   Warm summers 13°C
   High annual rainfall 1092mm

4 Cold winters 2°C
   Warm summers 14°C
   Moderate annual rainfall 892mm

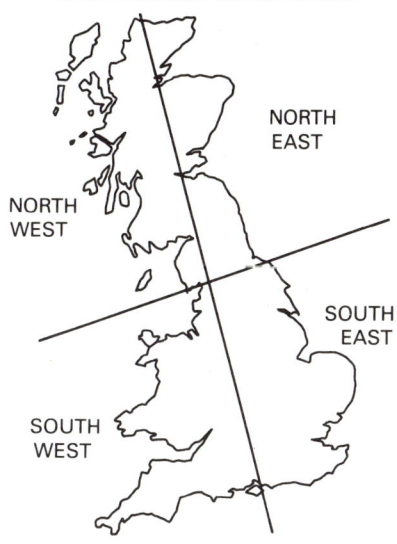

NORTH EAST

NORTH WEST

SOUTH EAST

SOUTH WEST

Figure 8   Climate areas

European climates

Look at the four climate graphs (Figures 4, 5, 6, 7), the map of Europe (Figure 3) and the climate graph you have completed for Heathrow.

1 Name the five places 1, 2, 3, 4, and 5.
2 Arrange the five places in order of rainfall received.
   Put the highest total at the top.

	Amount of rainfall in mm	Place
Highest	_____	_____
	_____	_____
	_____	_____
	_____	_____
Lowest	_____	_____

3 Which place has the highest July temperatures?
4 Complete this passage.
   As you travel northwards through Europe from A_____ to O____ the temperatures become (warmer/cooler). The winters are very cold in the north with temperatures of __°C and summers are only __ °C. In southern parts of Europe summers are relatively (dry/wet).
5 If you were given the chance to visit one of these places for a sunbathing holiday in August which place would you choose? Give reasons for your answer using the climate graph.
6 Divide an outline map of Britain into four, as shown in Figure 8. Using the data in Figure 2, put the labels in Figure 8 in the right places on the map.

31

12 Natural vegetation

Figure 2   Tundra

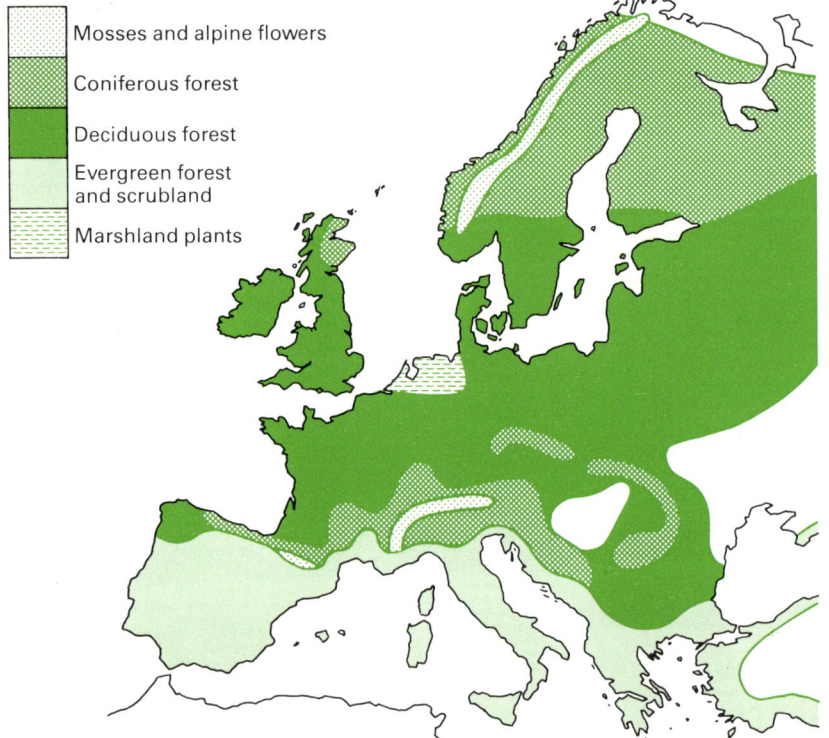

- Mosses and alpine flowers
- Coniferous forest
- Deciduous forest
- Evergreen forest and scrubland
- Marshland plants

Figure 1   Europe's vegetation

Figure 3   Coniferous forest

Figure 4   Marsh plants

Figure 5   Deciduous forest

Figure 1 shows the natural vegetation that would grow in Europe if man had not destroyed it. *Vegetation* is the name given to all types of trees, shrubs, plants, grasses, mosses, and lichens. Many trees that grow in Europe are not native vegetation, but have been imported from abroad. An example in Britain is the sycamore. Places in Europe have different types of trees because their *environments* (the area in which they live) are different. Figures 2–6 show the main vegetation types in Europe.

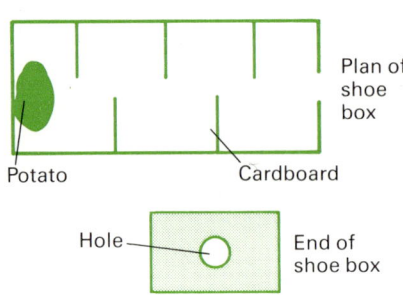

Figure 6   Evergreen forest

Plants need *sunshine, warmth* and *water. Prove it*!
What happens if you put a flowering houseplant in a dark room for a few days? What happens if you do not water a flowering house plant for a couple of weeks in the summer? What happens if you do not water a cactus for a couple of weeks in the summer? What happens if you put a flowering houseplant in the fridge for a day? Try these experiments with a number of different plants.

Now try this experiment. Put a potato with roots beginning to grow at one end of a sealed shoe box. At the opposite end cut a hole. Place pieces of cardboard half-way across the width of the box. Look at Figure 7. Leave for at least a week.

What have you learnt about plants? Record the results of your experiments in your exercise book.

Plan of shoe box

Potato

Cardboard

Hole

End of shoe box

Figure 7   Potato experiment

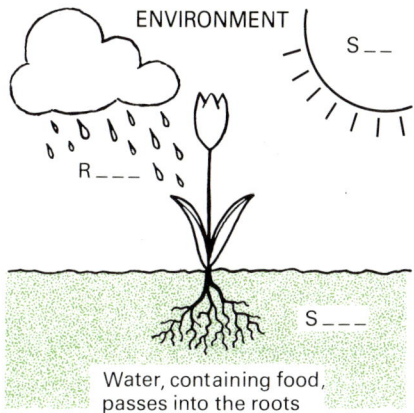

ENVIRONMENT

Water, containing food, passes into the roots

Figure 8   Plant needs

Things to do

1 Look at Figure 1 and Figures 2–6 and describe the type of natural vegetation for the areas below. You will need to use an atlas to find the places.

Northern Norway   _____   France   _____
Northern Scotland   _____   Southern Greece   _____
The Netherlands   _____

2 (a) Draw Figure 8 and add the missing labels. Then write a sentence to explain what is meant by *environment*.

(b) Try some of the 'prove it' activities to see if you can prove that plants need sunshine, warmth and water.

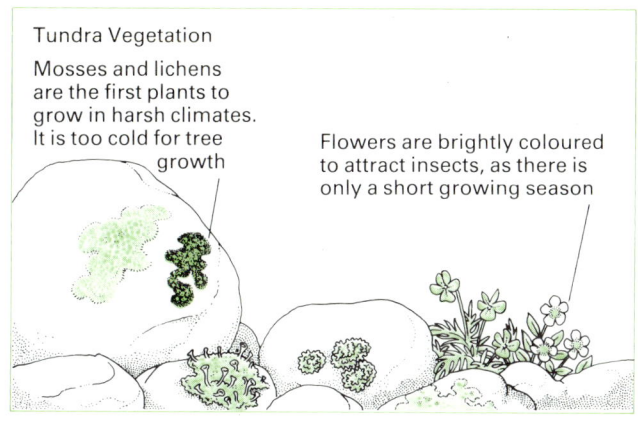

Tundra Vegetation

Mosses and lichens are the first plants to grow in harsh climates. It is too cold for tree growth

Flowers are brightly coloured to attract insects, as there is only a short growing season

Coniferous forest

Softwoods: used to make paper

Trees have conical shapes so that they can shed the snow easily

Widespread roots as the soil is shallow. It is easier to collect water with roots that are near the surface.

Branches bend readily so they do not break when full of heavy snow

Coniferous needle leaf: toughened to protect tree against the cold

Ground is permanently frozen lower down

Deciduous Forest

Hardwoods: used to make furniture

These trees have broad leaves

Trees shed leaves in winter because of low temperatures

Evergreen Forest

Some trees store water in the leaves and bark, as there is little rain in the summer

Some plants have long tap roots to reach water

Trees keep leaves all year round

Some leaves are waxy and spiny to stop water being lost from the leaves

Figure 9   Vegetation types

Homework ideas

Find out the name of three deciduous trees that grow in Britain now. Draw the leaves of each tree.

3 Study the information about each type of vegetation give in Figure 9 and try to explain why each type of vegetation grows where it does. Consider the points listed in Table 1.

4 If the climate changes, the vegetation also changes. About 10 000 years ago, much of Europe was covered by ice. When the ice melted, forests did not spring up straight away, but gradually grew up over time. Copy Figure 10 and try to work out what happened.

Table 1

Area of Europe
Climate
    summer temperature
    winter temperature
Rainfall

NORTH   SOUTH

Glacier ice

Ice melting   Climate becomes warmer ⟶

Figure 10   Changing vegetation

13 Farming

Oats

Wheat

Barley

These are cereal crops, and were originally developed from wild grasses

Sugarbeet

Turnip

Crops grown for their roots are known as root crops

A farmer who grows cereal and root crops is an arable farmer

Any crop grown to feed animals is called a fodder crop. Cattle eat barley and sugarbeet tops.

Figure 3   Types of crops

34

Farmers are very important people as they produce the food which keeps us alive. They have to make many difficult decisions to make sure that they produce enough food. Their results are very closely linked with the natural world. (Look back at unit 1 to remind yourself what we mean by the natural world.)

We can study a farm as a *system* with a number of *inputs* and *outputs*. To make it easier to understand what we mean by system, input and output, think of this example (Figure 1).

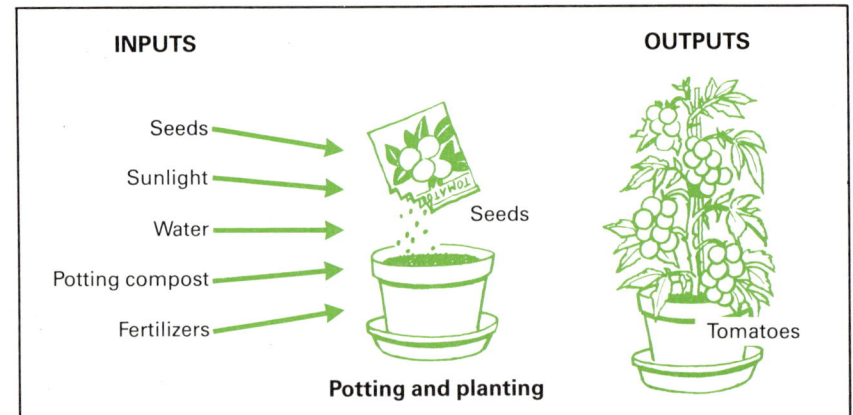

INPUTS

Seeds
Sunlight
Water
Potting compost
Fertilizers

Seeds

Potting and planting

OUTPUTS

Tomatoes

Figure 1   The pot plant system

When the Headteacher wants to grow tomatoes she does not buy new plant pots, plant holders, canes, and string every time; she already has them. So these things can be called *stores*.

For the farmer stores are very important because they help him to decide what to grow.

Things to do

1 Look at the list below and sort it into the three columns shown in Figure 2. You must decide which of the things is a store, an input or an output for the farmer. The information in Figure 3 will give you some help.

buildings, wool, land, lambs for meat, machinery, milk, seeds, soil, beef, poultry, fertilizers, livestock (pigs, hens, sheep, cows), workers, pork, eggs, fodder crops, root crops, cereal crops

Inputs	Stores	Outputs

Figure 2   The farming system

Do all the farmers have the same stores? They produce different outputs. Some farmers specialise in one product or output because their stores are most suitable for its growth. We can name farms according to their output. For example, a dairy farm produces milk.

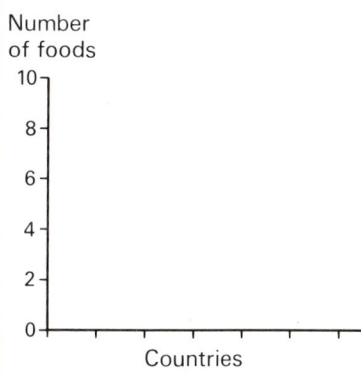

Figure 5   Glasshouses in a market garden

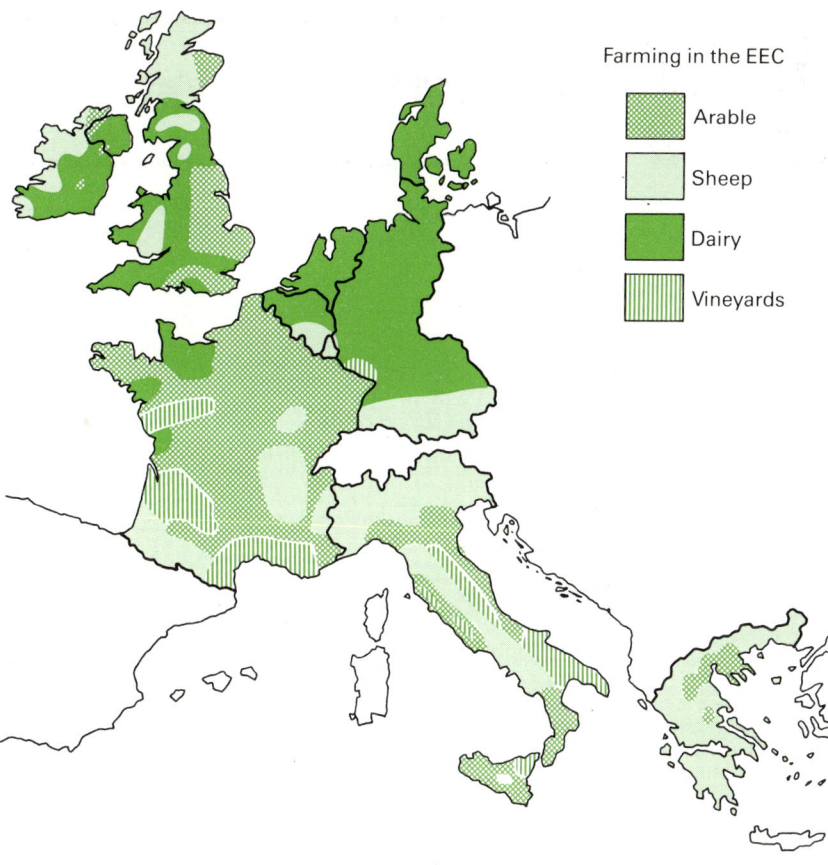

Farming in the EEC

- Arable
- Sheep
- Dairy
- Vineyards

Figure 4   Farming in the EEC

2 Look at Figure 4 which shows farming in the EEC. You may have to look at the map of Europe on pages 126/127 to help you.
  (a) Name two countries which produce mainly dairy products.
  (b) From which countries might you get wine?
  (c) What is the main type of agriculture in France?
  (d) From the list below pick out areas where you find sheep or goats grazing.

South east England	Southern Italy
West coast of Ireland	Denmark
The Netherlands	North west Scotland
Central Italy	Mainland Greece

  (e) Look at a relief map of Europe in your atlas. This shows you highland and lowland areas. Now copy out the correct sentence from the two given below.
    Sheep are found in many lowland areas of Europe.
    Sheep are found mainly in highland areas of Europe.

3 (a) The descriptions below of various types of farms have been jumbled up. Using all the information in this unit try to match up the right description with its heading.

Dairy farm	Crops are grown in glasshouses. Sometimes plants, like tomato plants, are also sold.
Sheep farm	Cereal and root crops are grown, usually in large fields.
Arable farm	A herd of cows is kept for their milk. Crops that are grown are to feed the cows.
Market garden	Usually found in upland areas where sheep are reared for wool.

  (b) What do you think a mixed farm might be?

14 Sheep farming

Figure 1   Mid Town Farm

Legend:
- —— Road
- ----- Footpath
- Craggy slope
- Fields — This is the arable land which lies below 250m. The farmer has 530 ha here.
- Peat bogs — part of the common grazing land
- DANGER AREA — Ministry of Defence land leased to local farmers

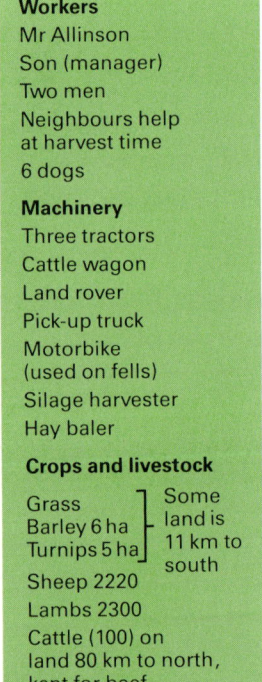

Workers
Mr Allinson
Son (manager)
Two men
Neighbours help at harvest time
6 dogs

Machinery
Three tractors
Cattle wagon
Land rover
Pick-up truck
Motorbike (used on fells)
Silage harvester
Hay baler

Crops and livestock
Grass
Barley 6 ha
Turnips 5 ha } Some land is 11 km to south
Sheep 2220
Lambs 2300
Cattle (100) on land 80 km to north, kept for beef

Homework ideas
Find out what this label means.
List all the things you can find at home made of wool.

CERTIFICATION TRADE MARK

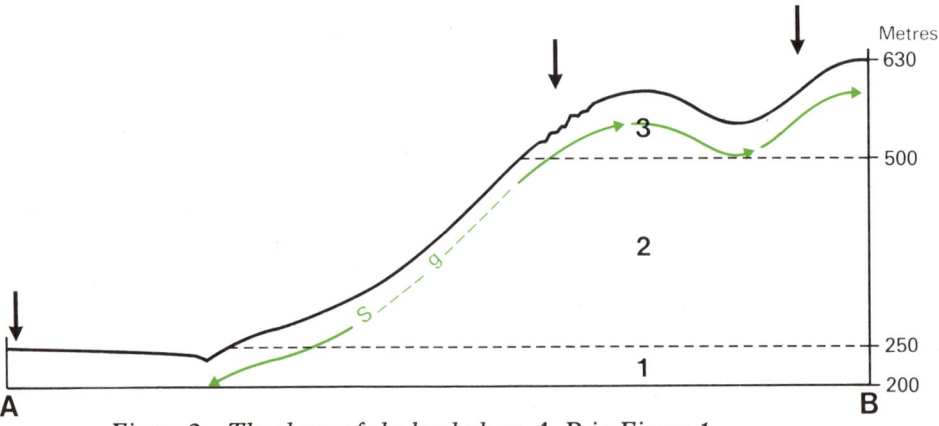

Figure 2   The shape of the land along A–B in Figure 1

Things to do

To complete all these activities you need to look carefully at all the information in this unit.

1 (a) Copy and complete this paragraph.
Mid Town Farm is in the county of Cumbria. Mr _____ owns the farm and leases some land from the M_____ O____ D_____. He is also able to graze his sheep on the f_____. All the farmers in the parish of H _____ can use the c _____ land. Not all Mr Allinson's land is in one parcel, some of his land is _____ km to the south and _____ km to the north where he keeps some beef cattle.

(b) Why does Mr Allinson have a large petrol bill?

2 (a) Make a copy of Figure 2. It shows you what land is like along the line A–B on the map.

(b) On your copy of Figure 2 add the following labels to your diagram.
sheep grazing, Hilton Fell, Mid Town Farm, craggy slope.

(c) Now shade sections 1, 2, or 3 according to where you would find (i) arable crops, (ii) peat bogs.

Figure 3   The eastern fells of Cumbria, near Appleby

Table 1   The sheep farmer's year

January	Farm repairs
February	Farm repairs
March	
April	
May	
June	
etc	

Figure 4   A Blue Leicester ram

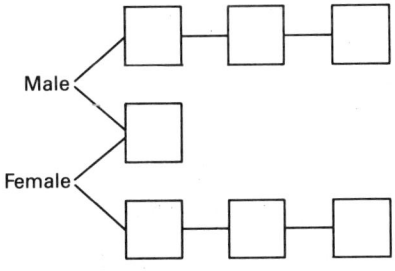

Male
Female

Figure 5   The life history of a lamb

Figure 6   A Swaledale ewe

3 Use your diagram together with Figure 3 to describe the landscape. Make sure the following words and numbers are included.

steep, peat bog, flatter, 250 m, 500 m

4 Look back to unit 11 and find out what the climate of Cumbria is like. Cumbria lies in the north west of Britain.
   (a) January temperature _____ C
   (b) July temperature   _____ C
   (c) Yearly rainfall   _____ mm

5 Read this information.

Mid Town Farm produces good quality breeding stock, which are bought by farmers to improve their sheep. Some lambs are sold for meat. Large auctions take place at Appleby, Penrith, and Lazonby. The wool shorn from the sheep in July is also taken to auctions.

List the three main outputs from the farm.

6 Mr Allinson's diary has fallen apart and the pages have become mixed up. Can you sort them out for him?

Write out the months of the year and fill in his jobs. (See Table 1.)

June	Shearing begins.
November	Dipping and dividing all the females over 1 year old into groups for mating.
April and May	Lambing. The ewes are marked when they are mated, so the farmer can bring them off the fell when they are due to lamb. During this time the farmer may work a 20 hour day. The whole family helps, sometimes bottle feeding lambs.
December	Sheep are returned to the fell. They are not given extra food out on the fell as other farmers' sheep would help themselves to Mr Allinson's food.
July	Shearing and dipping of males and females.
January February March	Mainly farm repairs.
August	Lambs removed from their mothers. Those for sale have their faces washed and trimmed. Some males are sold for meat and other males and some females sold for breeding. One year lambs dipped.
October	Preparations for sales and auctions take place.
September	Lambs for sale are dipped and kept inside. One year old ewes are kept inside for mating with the Blue Leicester rams (Figure 4).

7 Now you have sorted out the farmer's year, can you work out what happens to a lamb? Fill the following descriptions into the right boxes in Figure 5.

Sold for meat   Skins sold
Rest for a year   Sold for breeding
Wool sold   Mated when a year old

8 Hill farming is a tough job. Grants of between £4.25 and £6.25 per sheep are available from the EEC. It costs the farmer £10 to keep one sheep through the winter. During the year he will receive £1.20 for the wool removed from each sheep. The sale of lambs does not always cover all his costs.

Mr Allinson would like you to write his grant claim for this year. Remember to describe the climate, landscape, money difficulties and other problems he may have.

37

15 Farming in Greece

Greece joined the EEC in 1981. It has more people employed in agriculture (29%) than the other countries in the Community (which average 9%). Farming in Greece is very different from farming in Britain. Some Greek farmers are very traditional.

Figure 1   Tractors in Britain and Greece

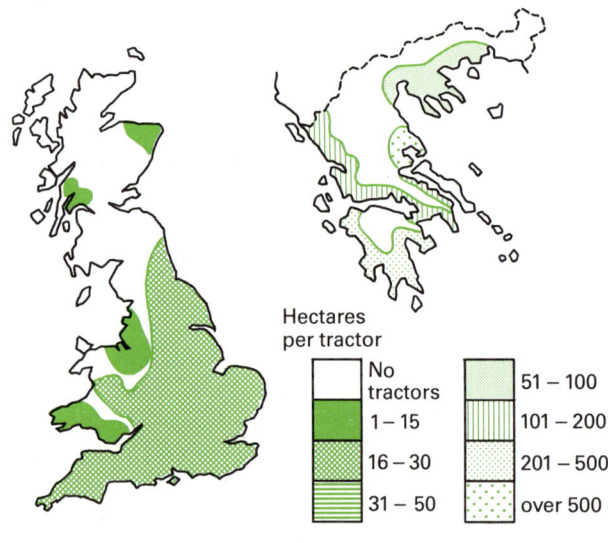

Hectares per tractor

No tractors	51 – 100
1 – 15	101 – 200
16 – 30	201 – 500
31 – 50	over 500

Figure 2   Fertilizers in Britain and Greece

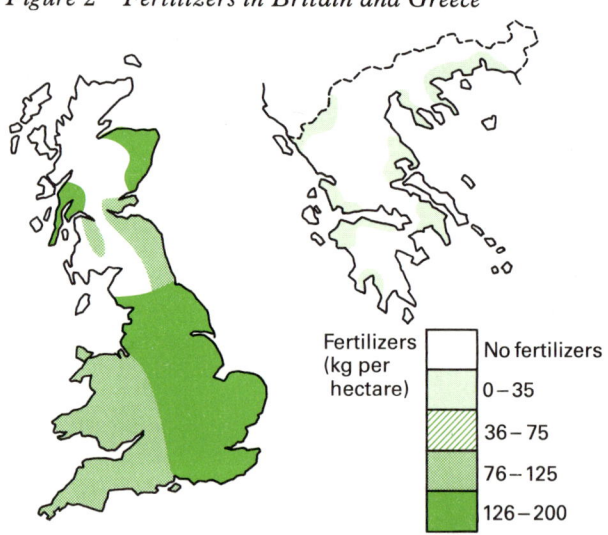

Fertilizers (kg per hectare)

No fertilizers	
0 – 35	
36 – 75	
76 – 125	
126 – 200	

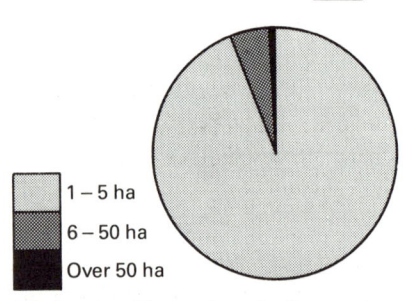

1 – 5 ha
6 – 50 ha
Over 50 ha

Figure 3   Farm sizes in Greece

Things to do

1 Look at Figures 1, 2, and 3. Choose the right answers to finish these sentences.
  (a) Most farms in Greece are
      (i) 1–5 ha   (ii) 6–50 ha   (iii) more than 50 ha
  (b) Tractors cover more hectares in (i) Greece (ii) Britain
  (c) More fertilizers are used in (i) Greece   (ii) Britain.

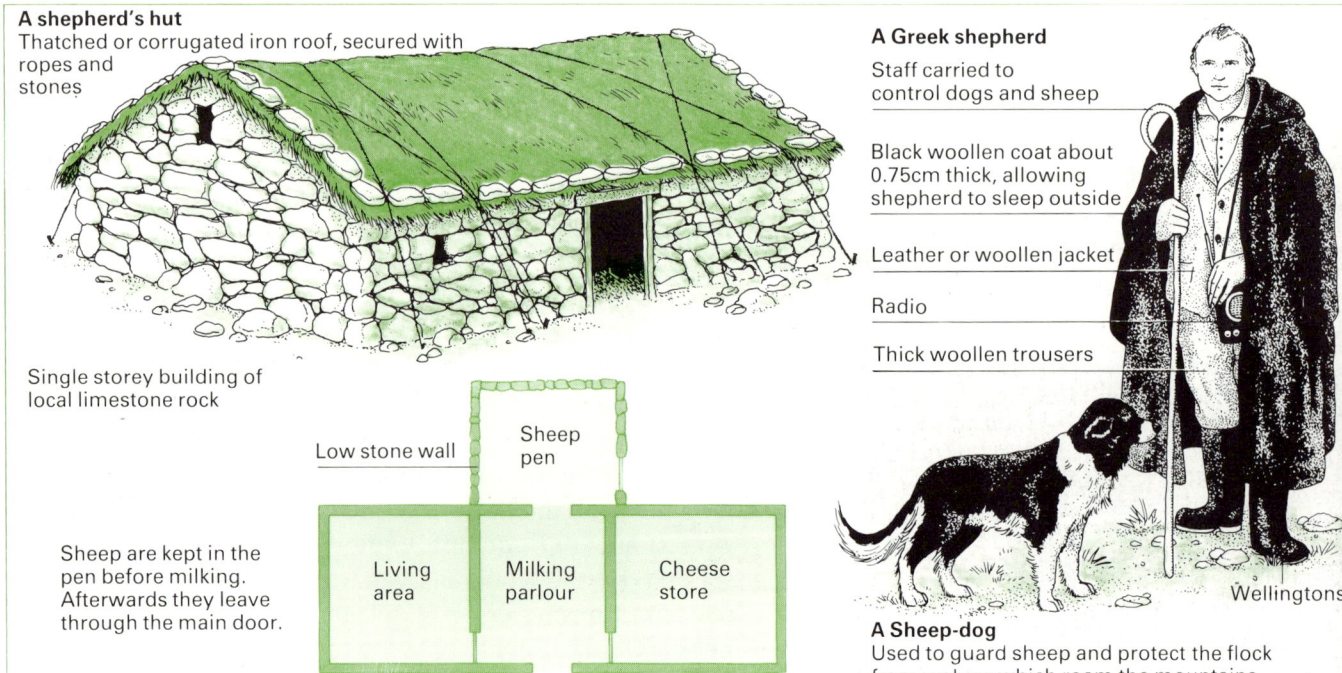

A shepherd's hut
Thatched or corrugated iron roof, secured with ropes and stones

Single storey building of local limestone rock

Sheep are kept in the pen before milking. Afterwards they leave through the main door.

Low stone wall

Sheep pen

Living area

Milking parlour

Cheese store

A Greek shepherd
Staff carried to control dogs and sheep

Black woollen coat about 0.75cm thick, allowing shepherd to sleep outside

Leather or woollen jacket

Radio

Thick woollen trousers

Wellingtons

A Sheep-dog
Used to guard sheep and protect the flock from wolves which roam the mountains

Figure 5   A shepherd's hut A typical shepherd A sheep-dog

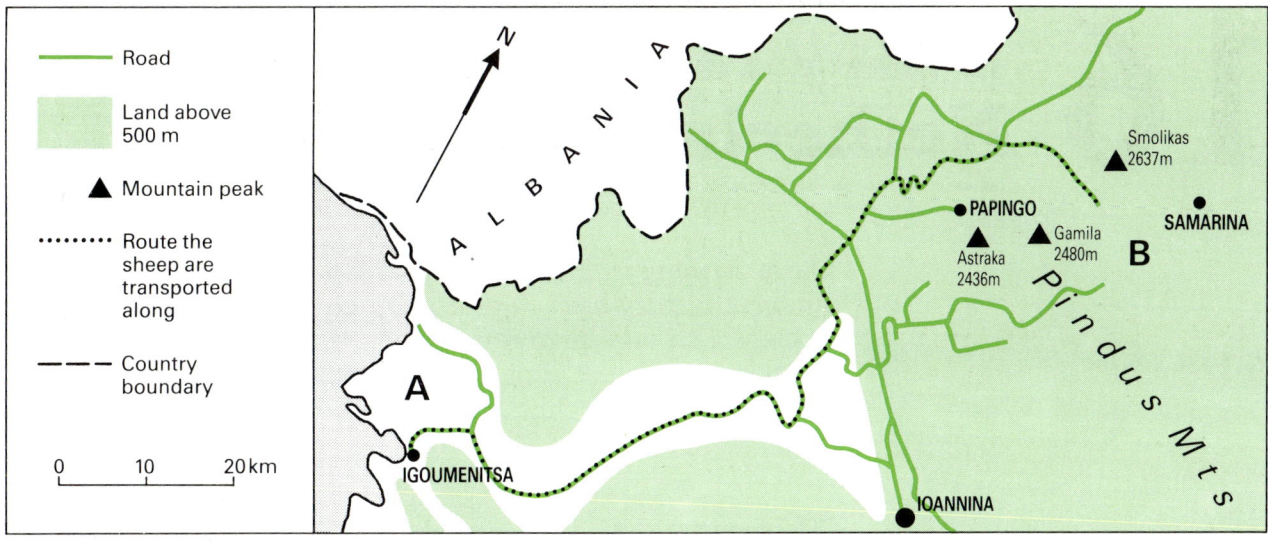

Figure 4   A sheep farming area in northern Greece

In remote parts of northern Greece there are many shepherds in the mountains. The sheep are taken up to high pastureland for four months of the year (June, July, August and September). Some shepherds transport their flocks by truck from the plains around Igoumenitsa (area A on Figure 4) to the area around Mount Smolikas (area B). Other shepherds have bought houses in Papingo and take their sheep to the area around Mounts Astraka and Gamila. The shepherds stay up in the mountains for stretches of ten days. They stay in shelters like those shown in Figure 5. After the ten days have passed, the shepherd goes back to his family and another male from the family (usually a brother) takes over for the next ten days. During his stay, the shepherd takes his flock to water and moves them to new pastures. He milks the sheep daily and uses this to make cheese, which is sent down by mule to the villages.

The shepherds remain in the mountains by themselves with only their sheep-dogs for company and perhaps a radio. Their flocks vary in size but usually range between 150–300 sheep. The sheep wear bells and are guarded carefully by sheep-dogs from roaming wolves.

Things to do

1 Look at Figure 6 and describe the landscape.
2 Work out the distance the sheep are transported by truck from Igoumenitsa to the mountain pastures. Look at Figure 4. How far does the flock have to walk to reach Samarina?
3 What happens to the roads in the mountains? Look at Figure 4. Why do you think that mule transport is used in the Pindus Mountains?
4 Use the information on this page and from p36 to complete Table 1 comparing sheep farmers in Greece with those in Britain.

Table 1	Greece	Great Britain
Landscape (height, steepness)		
Farmer's lifestyle (dress, jobs, house, Farmers' year)		
Workers		
Machinery		

Figure 6   The Pindus Mountains

16 Dairy farming in the Netherlands

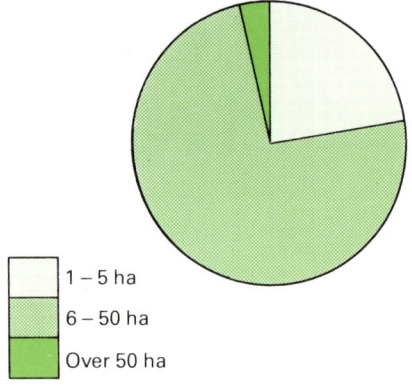

1 – 5 ha
6 – 50 ha
Over 50 ha

Figure 1   Farm sizes

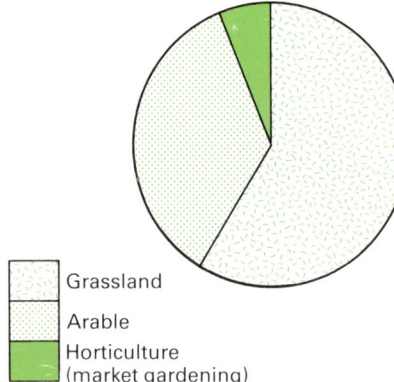

Grassland
Arable
Horticulture (market gardening)

Figure 2   Farmland use

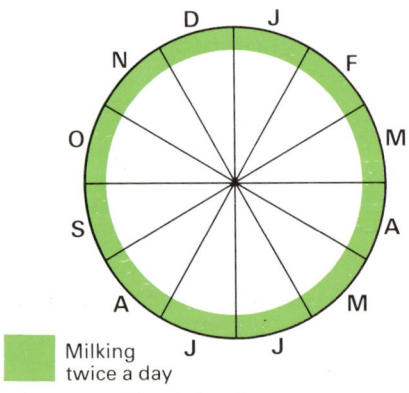

Milking twice a day

Figure 3   The dairy farmer's year

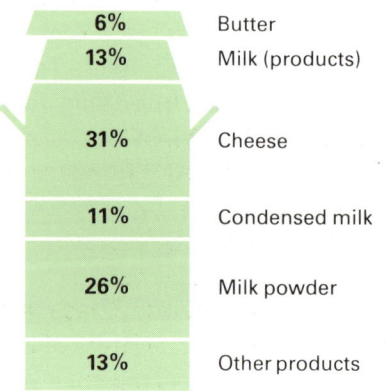

6%   Butter
13%   Milk (products)
31%   Cheese
11%   Condensed milk
26%   Milk powder
13%   Other products

Figure 4   Uses of milk

40

Dairy farming in the Netherlands is far from traditional. It is run on a factory basis. To be a Dutch farmer you have to be a manager, an administrator, an accountant and an economist. High standards are kept to make sure that the Netherlands is the world's largest cheese exporter.

Things to do

1 Complete the following sentences by using the pie charts (Figures 1 and 2).
   (a) Most of the farms in the Netherlands are _____ in size.
   (b) The cultivated land is used for _____, _____ and _____.
   (c) More than half the cultivated land (59%) is used to feed _____.

2 If there is an average of 200 cows per hectare, work out how many cows there would be on a 20 ha farm.

A dairy farmer milks his cows twice a day, once in the morning at about 5.30 am and again in the evening at 4 pm. The milk is collected by the cooperative and taken to the local dairy to be processed.

The cows are kept indoors during the winter. They are let out daily during April, and from May to September, stay outside all summer.

Some of the grassland is used for growing hay, and some for silage. However, extra fodder crops are bought in winter to supplement the hay and silage stores. The grassland is *permanent pasture* which means that it is not ploughed up every year. Occasionally it is re-sown to stop the grass becoming poorer.

A large amount of animal waste is collected throughout the year. This becomes liquid manure which can be sprayed on the fields in autumn. These farms tend to be family businesses and sons and daughters help with the milking.

3 Draw a farmer's year like the one shown in Figure 3. Use a colour key to show the jobs the farmer has to do. One job has already been done for you.

4 Figure 4 shows you what happens to milk.
   (a) Draw a bar graph to show the same information. Label the vertical scale in percentages (use 2 cm or 2 lines in your exercise book to equal 10%).
   (b) Describe what the bar graph shows.

5 Figures 5 and 6 show old and modern ways of making cheese. Make a copy of the factory way and put the labels below in the right places.

Cheese is put into moulds   Cheese is pressed
Taken by conveyor belt   Milk is prepared into curds and
It is stored   whey (the whey is removed
Soaked in a brine bath   and curd used to make cheese)

Figure 5   Traditional Dutch cheese making

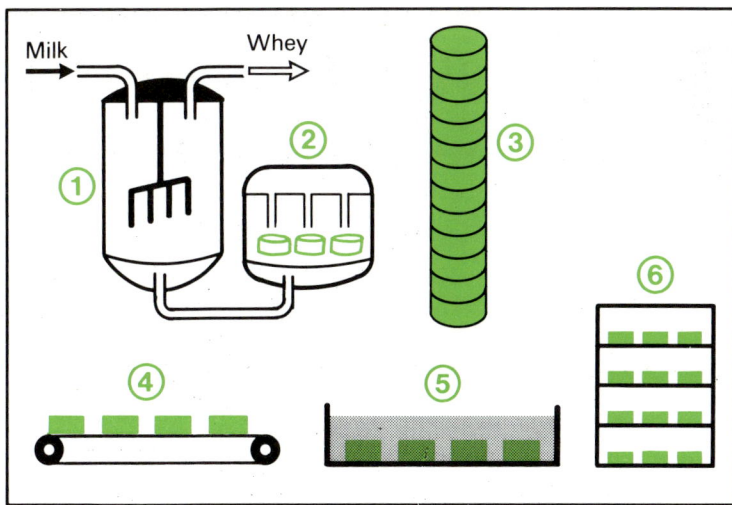

Figure 6   Modern cheese making in a factory

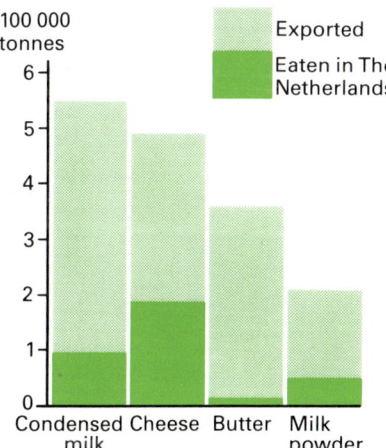

Figure 8   Dutch dairy products

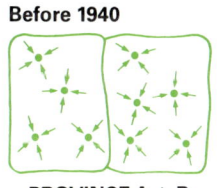

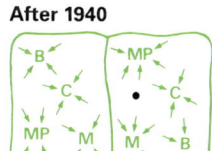

Figure 9   Changes in the dairy industry

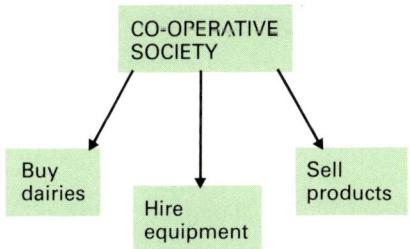

Figure 10   Help from the cooperative

6 Copy Figure 7. It shows some towns in the Netherlands which are important for cheese making. Use an atlas to fill in the gaps.

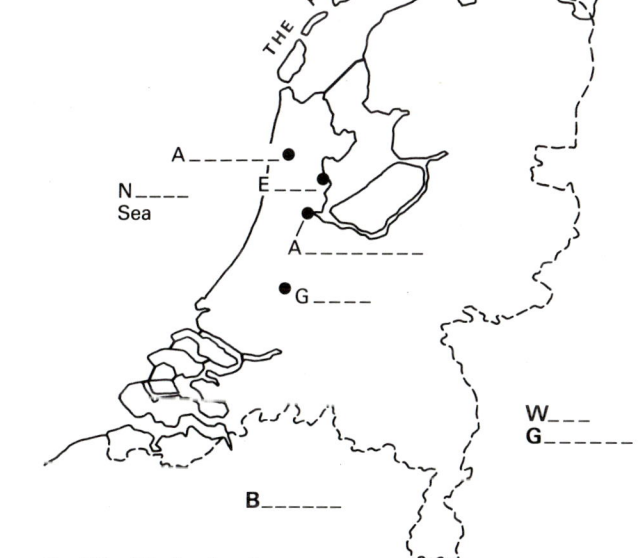

Figure 7   The Netherlands

7 The Netherlands claims to be the world's number one dairy exporter. This has not always been the case and many changes have been necessary.

(a) What does the graph (Figure 8) tell you about what happens to most of the dairy products produced in the Netherlands?

(b) Sort out the names of the countries, or blocks of countries, which the Netherlands exports to.

    PANJA   NITUDE EASTTS
    DDMLEI ESTA   MNOCOM KEMRAT

8 There have also been changes in the dairies. Look at Figure 9 and state the changes in the two provinces

(a) Before 1940 _____   (b) After 1940 _____
       _____   _____

9 Most Dutch farmers now belong to cooperatives. These are societies which help the farmers. Each farmer owns a share of the cooperative. Look at Figure 10 and say in what ways the societies help the farmer.

17 A farmer's problems

Mr Fields is a young farmer who wants to start his own arable farm. He needs a lot of advice to make sure that he chooses the right place for his farm. There are many things for him to think about: climate, soils, shape of the land, crops, machinery, farm workers, people to buy his crops, government help or rules.

He would like you to look at all the information and help him make his decision.

Figure 1   An arable farming area

Things to do

1 Look at Figure 1 which shows an arable farming area. Using the list of words below make up sentences to describe the landscape in the photograph.

flat, large, regular shapes, trees, straight roads

2 Why is it easier for the farmer if the fields are set out like those in Figure 1? (Clue: look at Figure 2.)

3 Mr Fields has decided that he would like to grow wheat, barley and sugar beet. He now has to find the best part of Britain to grow these crops. Look back to unit 11 and check the climate. Table 1 tells you the type of climate these crops like. Which area of Britain would you choose: north west, north east, south east, or south west?

Figure 2   A combine harvester at work

Homework ideas

Choose one of the following and find out how:
(a) wheat is made into biscuits,
(b) barley is made into beer,
(c) sugarbeet is made into sugar.

Table 1

Crops	Climate	Soils
Wheat	Rain less than 750 mm	Well drained
Sugar beet	Rain less than 750 mm Summer temperatures more than 15°C	Deep and well drained
Barley	Grows well in the same climate as wheat, but will grow in a cooler drier climate	Will grow in thin soils

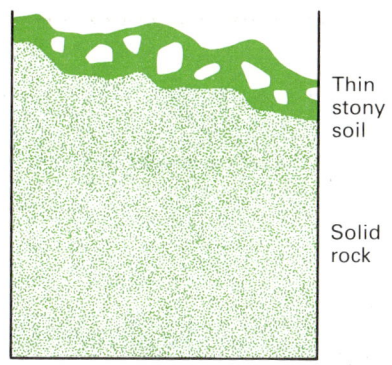

Figure 4   Soil profile for site C

Thin stony soil

Solid rock

Soils are also very important for growing crops. After Mr Fields has chosen which area to grow the crops, he must look for an actual site for his farm within this area. Figure 3 shows an area with three possible sites marked. Sites A and B have the same sort of soil but site C has a poor soil. The *soil profile* gives us an idea of the type of soil for site C (Figure 4).

4 (a) Draw a profile for site B and add these labels
        deep soil, well-drained soil, stone-free soil
  (b) Which soil do you think will be best for Mr Fields? Give two reasons for your answer. (Clue: crops, machinery.)

Table 2

Site	A	B	C
Cost of land	Expensive	Cheap	Very cheap

Table 3

Site	A	B	C
Flat land			
Deep soil			
Cheap land			
Total			

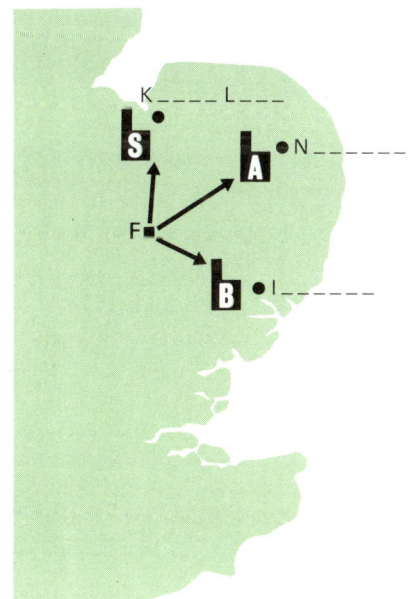

Figure 5   Farming in East Anglia

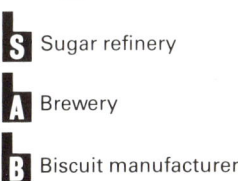 Sugar refinery

Brewery

Biscuit manufacturer

F■ Mr Field's farm

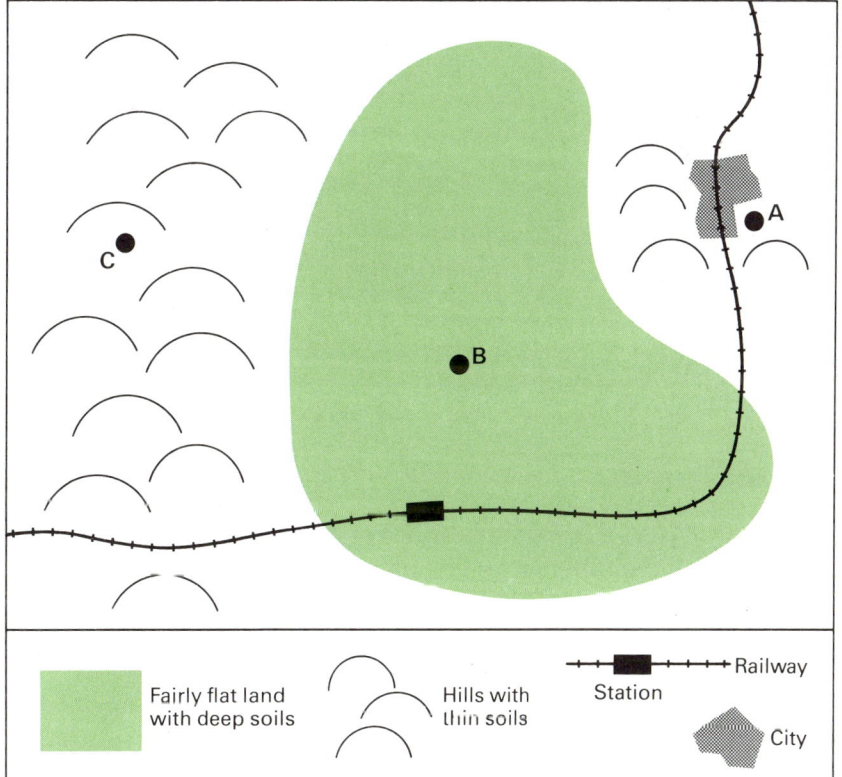

Fairly flat land with deep soils

Hills with thin soils

Station

Railway

City

Figure 3   Farmshire

5 (a) To decide the best site for the farm, look back at Figure 3 and at Table 2, then fill in Table 3 by giving each site a mark out of 3. Give 3 marks for the best site for flat land, and 1 mark for the worst site.
  (b) Explain in your own words why the site with the highest total is best.
6 Figure 5 shows a possible location for Mr Fields' farm. It also shows what products will be made from the crops.
  (a) On your own copy of the map, label the three places.
  (b) Next to each arrow draw the type of crop which will be sent to the factory. (Look back to unit 13.)
7 Draw a picture to show all the things a farmer has to think about to do his job properly. Look back to the beginning of this unit.

18 Fresh vegetables

Where do the vegetables you buy in your local shop come from? The greengrocer has to go to a market early in the morning to buy fresh vegetables. A famous fruit and vegetable market in London is Covent Garden. However, we have still not solved the problem of where these vegetables are grown! Farmers who supply vegetables like those shown in Figure 1 are known as *market gardeners*.

Figure 2   *A market gardening area, Friskney, Lincolnshire*

Figure 1   *Green groceries*

Things to do

1 Look at Figure 2, then look back at Figure 1 in unit 17.
   (a) List all the differences you can spot between the two areas.
   (b) Here are a few questions you might try to answer.
      (i)   Are the fields the same size?
      (ii) Are all the crops grown outdoors?
      (iii) Are there a lot of buildings?
      (iv) Do a lot of people live in the area?

2 From the word search (Figure 3) find out the names of ten crops grown in a market garden. Most of the crops are known as *salad crops*—but not all of them.

3 Crops grown in market gardens are *perishable*. This means that they do not stay fresh for very long and have to be packed and transported very carefully. Where do you think the best place for a market garden might be if you want fresh vegetables and fruit in towns?
   (a) 100 miles from town?
   (b) 50 miles away from town?
   (c) On the edge of the town?

4 Look at Figure 4 which shows the inside of a glasshouse. Some crops need a special climate to grow properly.
   (a) How can a glasshouse change the climate?
   (b) List all the things you can see which make this type of farming expensive.

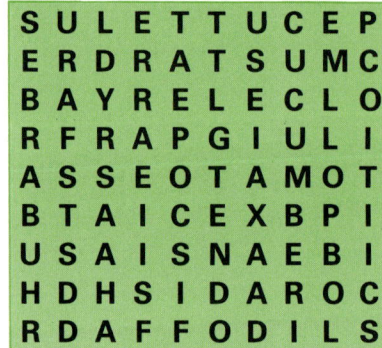

```
S U L E T T U C E P
E R D R A T S U M C
B A Y R E L E C L O
R F R A P G I U L I
A S S E O T A M O T
B T A I C E X B P I
U S A I S N A E B I
H D H S I D A R O C
R D A F F O D I L S
```

Figure 3   *Word search*

44

Figure 4   Inside a glasshouse

Homework ideas

See if you can find out about your local fruit and vegetable market.
    Or find out about Covent Garden market.

City centre

Arable

Dairy

Market gardening

Sheep

Figure 5   Farming around a city

Farming locations

Now we have looked at a number of different types of farming. Figure 5 is a map of a city and its surrounding area.

5 Copy Figure 5 and try to decide which type of farming (shown in the key) best fits each zone. Be careful to read the descriptions of each zone.

Zone 1 closest to the city centre
Zone 2 good transport links with the city centre
Zone 3 flat land and deep soil
Zone 4 area of high mountains and poor climate

(a) Where would you put the arable farm, dairy farm, market garden, and sheep farm?
(b) Fill in the key for the map.
(c) Give reasons for your answers.

Summary

The following sentences have been jumbled up. Use what you have learnt from the farming section to sort out the puzzle.

Heads	Tails
Arable farmers do not	help farmers when necessary
The government will	a lot of machinery
Arable farmers need	have a lot of workers
Perishable crops are	inputs, outputs and stores
Market gardens are found	hilly areas with a poor climate
Sheep farming takes place in	close to towns
An ewe is	wheat, barley and oats
Examples of cereal crops are	easily damaged when transported
Gouda and edam are types	a female sheep
A farming system looks at	of Dutch cheese

45

19 Where people live

*Figure 2 (top) and Figure 3
Work out the population density in
each photograph
Remember that density*
$$= \frac{number\ of\ people}{area\ in\ km^2}$$
*The area covered in Figure 2 is
1 km², and in Figure 3 is 0.5 km².
Assume that on average there are
three people in each house*

*Figure 4   Industry on the banks of
the River Wear, Sunderland*

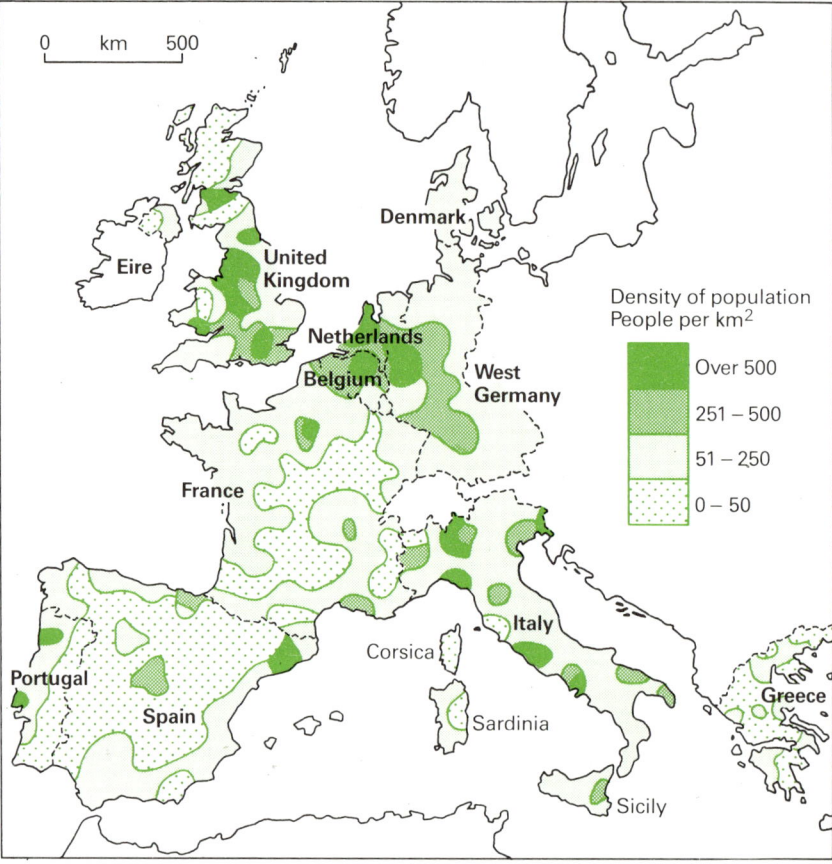

Figure 1   The density of population in the EEC

The total population of the European Economic Community—the EEC—was about 271 million in 1980, but Figure 1 shows that people are not evenly spread over the area. On the map, the dark shading shows the more densely populated areas. Some places are very *densely* populated, with many people living in one square kilometre. Other areas, like Ireland, are *sparsely* populated, and only a few people live in each square kilometre.

If an area is densely populated, with perhaps as many as 500 people to one square kilometre, people must live very close together with only a small area of land each. Which photograph (Figure 2 or 3) shows this sort of area? It must be the photograph showing the houses in a town, an *urban area*. Can you work out the population density there? In the countryside, the *rural areas*, people live much further apart, and many of them are farmers. Which picture shows a rural area?

In each country in Europe there are some crowded areas and some empty areas. The south east of England is crowded; many people live there to be near the capital city, London. North west England is also crowded; partly because many people are needed to work in the industries in that area.

Some of the empty areas of Europe—with a sparse population—are hilly or mountainous, like the north west Highlands of Scotland. Others are difficult to get to, like the island of Sardinia. These areas are on the edge of the EEC and do not attract many people to live there.

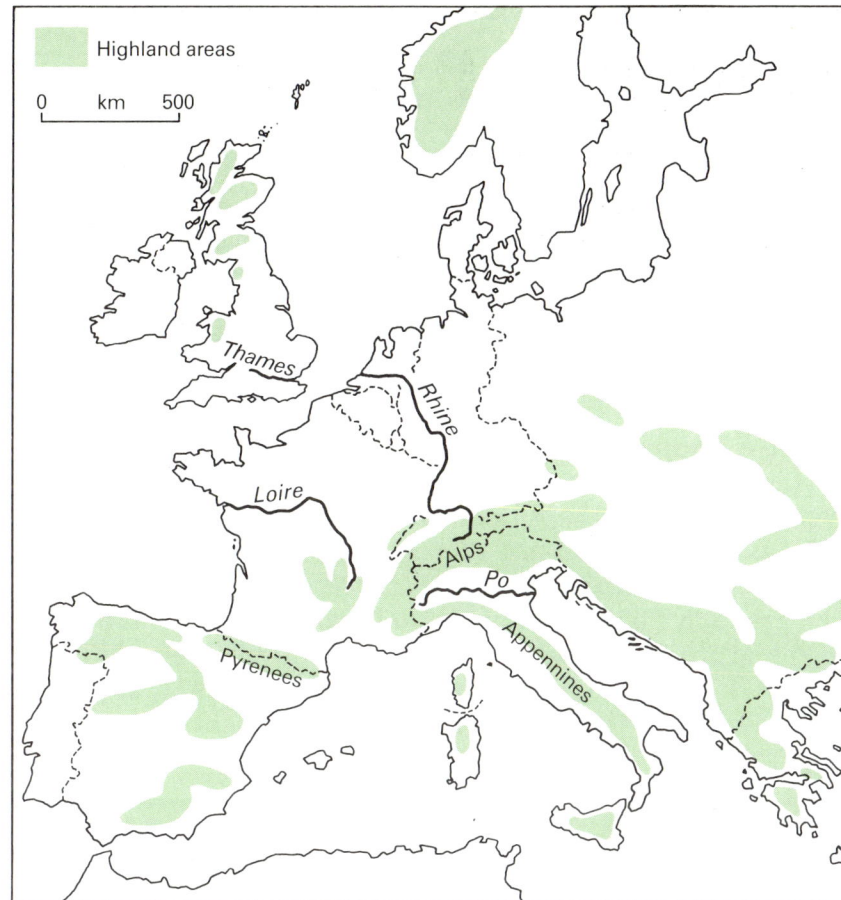

Figure 5 — Key: Highland areas — 0 km 500

Labels on map: Thames, Rhine, Loire, Alps, Po, Pyrenees, Appennines

Figure 5   A relief map of Europe

Figure 6   The European Parliament in Strasbourg

Homework ideas

The European Parliament meets in Strasbourg. Find out where this is and mark it on a traced outline of the EEC countries. Is Strasbourg in the centre of the EEC? Is it in a good position to be near where most people in Europe live?

Things to do

1 Read the following descriptions. Then looking at Figures 1 and 5, say which European country fits each of these descriptions.
   (a) A northern country which includes several islands and is sparsely populated.
   (b) A country with only a short coastline, which is most densely populated in the north.
   (c) A country with a range of mountains running down its length. This country has a low population where the mountains are highest.
   (d) A low-lying country which is most densely populated near the mouth of the River Rhine.
   (e) A large country which is nearly all sparsely populated, except for a small area in the north, surrounding its capital city.

2 Look at the valleys of the River Rhine, the River Po, the River Thames and the River Loire in Figure 5. All of these valleys except one are densely populated.
   Which is the odd one out?

3 Why do you think the valleys of large rivers are places where many people live? Think about what use these rivers would be. Figure 4 will help you.

4 Many of the islands in the EEC are sparsely populated. Use Figure 1 to find some examples of islands like this and write down their names. Can you suggest why islands often have a low population density? (Think about the problems of living on an island.)

5 Look at Figure 7. Is the biggest country in the EEC also the one with the highest population?

6 Is France more densely populated than West Germany?

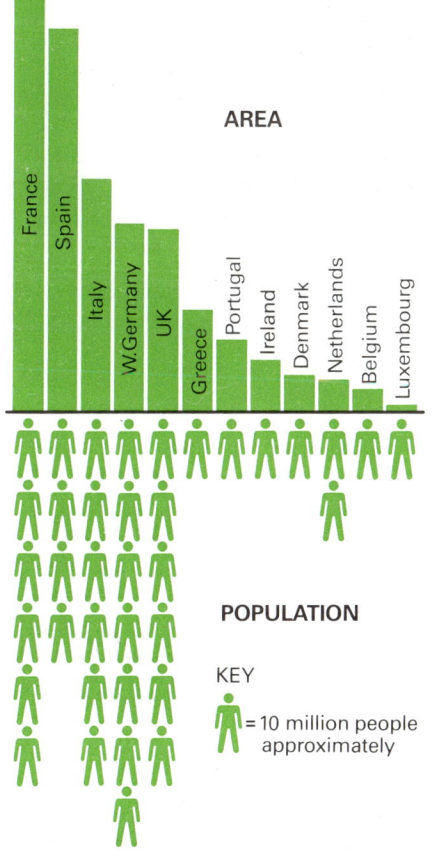

AREA

(bars labelled: France, Spain, Italy, W. Germany, UK, Greece, Portugal, Ireland, Denmark, Netherlands, Belgium, Luxembourg)

POPULATION

KEY

= 10 million people approximately

Figure 7   A graph to show the population and the area of the EEC countries

47

20 Empty areas of Europe

Figure 1 *A remote area in the highlands of Scotland*

Figure 2 *Soil erosion in southern Italy*

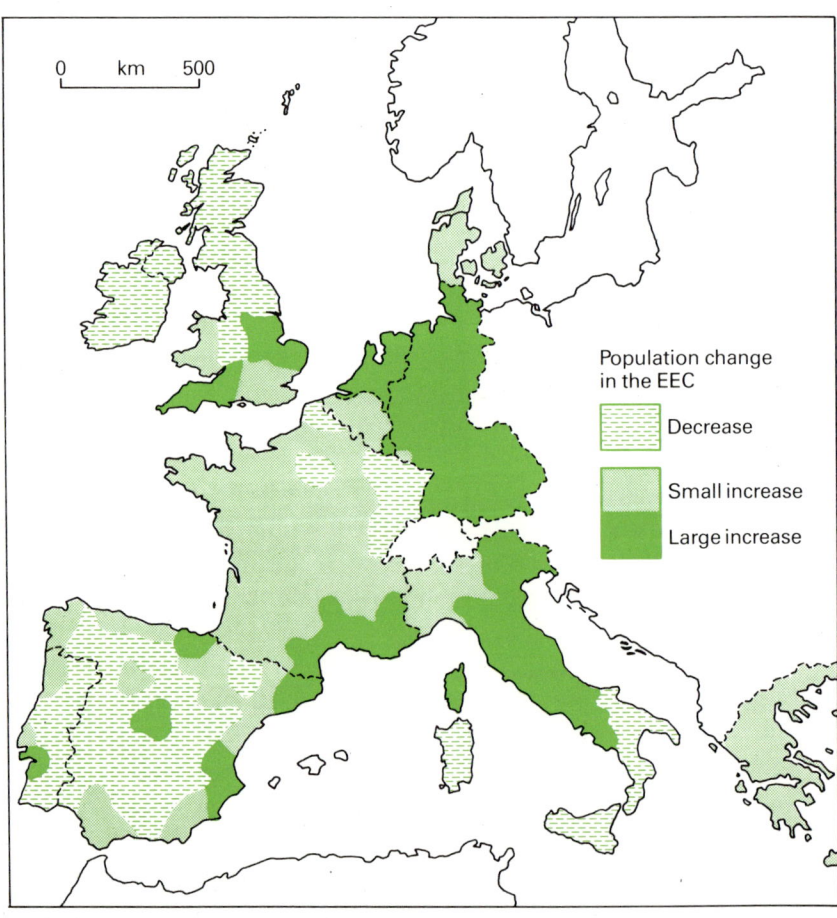

Figure 5 *Population change in the EEC*

If you look carefully at Figures 1 and 2, you can see more clearly the reasons why some areas are sparsely populated. In the Highlands of Scotland the steep slopes, bare rock, and thin soil make farming difficult. The photograph of southern Italy also shows a hilly area, but here one of the main problems is not having enough rain, especially in summer. Look carefully at what has happened to the soil in Figure 2. Figure 3 shows a village in southern Italy which has been abandoned—nobody lives there now, perhaps because farming became too difficult.

Areas like these are not very suitable for large populations and they are gradually becoming emptier as people move away. The graph in Figure 4 shows what happened to the number of people in the Highland region of Scotland between 1851 and 1971. The population decreased steadily until 1971, as people move away from the area. These people *migrated* from the Highlands.

Figure 5 shows other areas of Europe which are losing population. More people have moved out of the dotted areas than have moved in. If you find this difficult to imagine, think of it as being like a bath where the water runs out of the plug-hole faster than it comes in from the tap. The level of the bath water goes down, and so does the number of people in these areas.

Figure 3 *A deserted village near Fornazzo in Sicily*

48

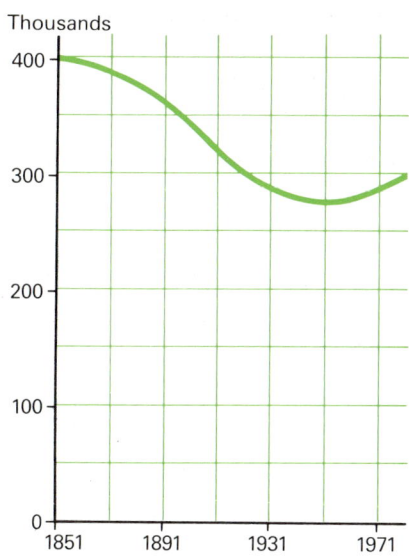

Thousands
400
300
200
100
0
1851 1891 1931 1971

Figure 4   A graph to show population change in the Scottish highlands

Homework ideas

Migration means moving from one place to another. Most people migrate within their own country, but some move to another country. Find out the meaning of the words *emigration* and *immigration*. What special problems would there be for a family which migrated from one country to another in the EEC?

Things to do

1 Write out this paragraph, choosing words from the list at the end to fill the spaces. There are more words than you need.

    In the north of Europe several areas including Ireland, _____, and rural areas of northern _____ have had a decrease in their population. These _____ areas have become emptier. The only other countries in Europe that have large areas where the population is decreasing are _____ and _____. In Italy, the islands _____ and _____ in particular have lost population. Many of these areas are hilly or mountainous, like the _____ hills in Scotland, but some are not. For instance the area around _____ has decreased its population, perhaps because people are tired of crowded city life. Also, old industrial areas like _____ France have lost population, as some of their industries have closed.

Words to choose from.

    Paris, empty, Denmark, Italy, England, Grampian, Scotland, France, Sardinia, crowded, Sicily, northern

2 Choose one of the photographs (Figures 1, 2 or 3) and imagine that you live in that area. Say which area you have chosen, then explain why you think it would be difficult for many people to live there. Think about how people could make a living, and why young people might decide to leave the area. You will get some ideas from the cartoon.

3 Why do some people find areas like those in the photographs attractive?

4 Why do you think the cartoon shows a **young** person being pushed away from the countryside, and not an older one?

5 What kind of area do you think these people are moving to?

6 The graph of population change in the Highlands (Figure 4) shows a steady decrease of population until 1971. Why do you think there has been a slight increase since then? Remember, the Highlands area includes the Orkney and Shetland Isles and we now drill an important fuel from the North Sea.

    The cartoon in Figure 6 illustrates some of the things which might 'push' a young person out of the countryside. How many different things does the cartoon show? Can you think of some more reasons why people might choose to leave rural areas like the Highlands of Scotland?

Figure 6

21 Crowded areas of Europe

Figure 1

In the last unit you saw the young migrant being 'pushed' out of the countryside. You have probably already realised that he or she is 'pulled' towards towns and industrial areas. The biggest pull on him is probably the hope of getting a job, but the cartoon also suggests some of the other attractions of cities. The photographs of London (Figures 2, 3 and 4) also show these attractions, such as large shops and cinemas, and jobs in offices, industries or government. So people have moved into densely populated areas and made them even more crowded.

Some of these crowded areas are on the coalfields of Europe. When the older industries like iron and steel were started in the nineteenth century, they had to be built on coalfields because coal was their main fuel. Workers in these industries needed somewhere to live so towns were built for the workers, and these areas became densely populated. The photograph of Corby (Figure 5) shows housing built for an industry. As more people moved to the towns, more of the population became urban instead of rural. This change can be seen in the graph showing the population of Britain (Figure 6), but it has happened in all the countries of the EEC.

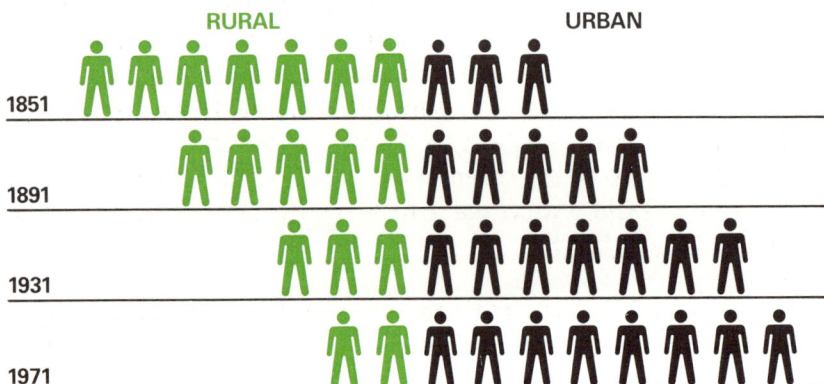

Figure 6   The urban and rural population of Britain since 1851

Figure 2   A shopping street in London, with offices above the shops

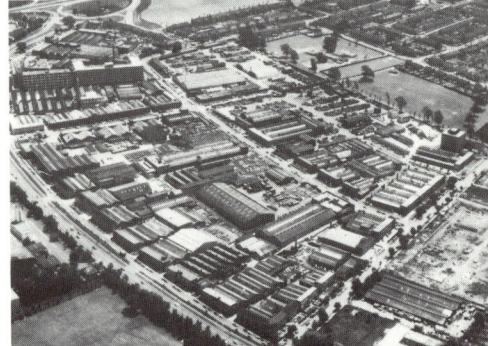

Figure 3   A trading estate at Elstree on the outskirts of London

Figure 4   The Houses of Parliament in London

50

Figure 5   Council housing in Corby. After the steelworks closed many people lost their jobs and moved out of the houses near the works

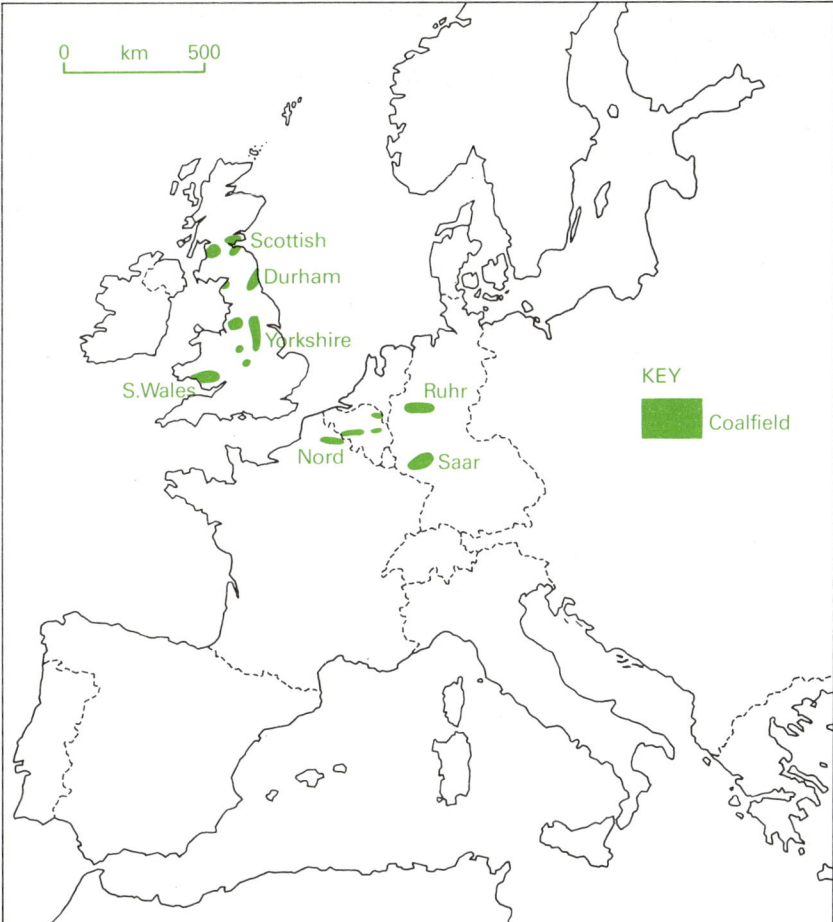

Figure 7   Major coalfields in Western Europe

Homework ideas

Imagine that you have left your home in the Highlands of Scotland, to start a job in Edinburgh. Write a letter to a friend of your own age who has stayed behind in the village and encourage him or her to come and join you in Edinburgh.

Table 1   *Urban population as a percentage of the total population*

Country	% population living in towns
Belgium	87
Denmark	82
France	71
W Germany	83
Greece	57
Ireland	55
Italy	54
Netherlands	77
UK	76

Things to do

1 Make a careful tracing of the map of European coalfields (Figure 7), and lay it over the map of population density in unit 19 (Figure 1). Write down the names of the coalfields which are in areas with a population density of over 250 people per km².

2 Do you think most of the crowded areas of Europe are on, or near to, coalfields?

3 Which crowded areas are a long way from coalfields? Can you explain why a lot of people live in these areas?

4 You already know that large cities have shops, offices, entertainments and industries. What other special buildings, which would provide extra jobs, would you expect to find in a capital city like Paris or London?

5 Look at Table 1 which shows the percentage of people in the other EEC countries who live in urban areas. Draw a bar graph to show these urban populations, starting with the country with the largest amount and going down to the one with the smallest. Use a scale of 1 cm to 5%, and give the graph a title. Look back to unit 9 if you have forgotten how to draw a bar graph.

6 In what ways do you think life in a big city might be so unpleasant now that people would want to leave it? The photographs of London may help you.

The cities of Europe are now so crowded that some people have decided to move out of them to live in a nearby town or village. These people may *commute* to work each day. This is another type of migration which we will look at in unit 22.

22 Commuters

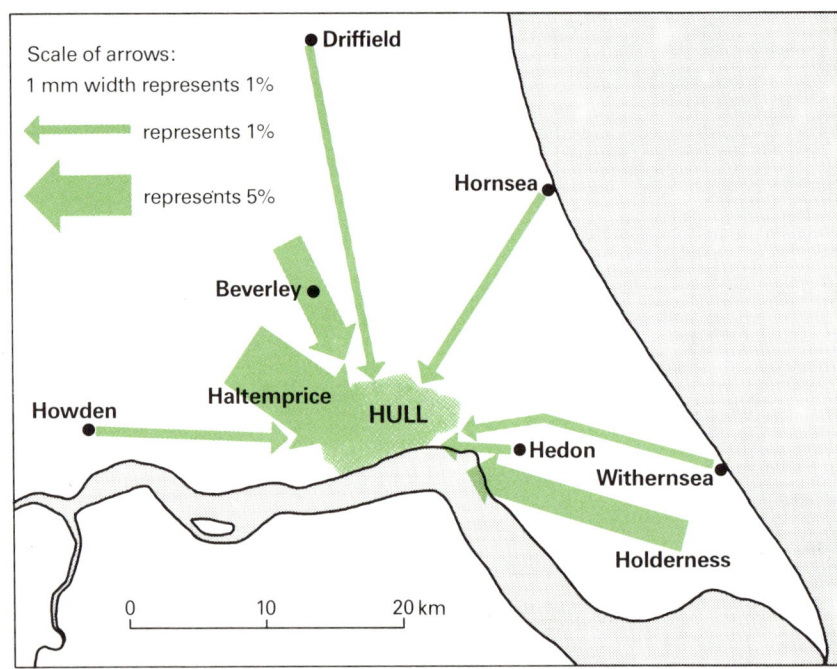

Figure 1   A flow map to show the movement of commuters into Hull

Scale of arrows:
1 mm width represents 1%

represents 1%

represents 5%

Driffield

Hornsea

Beverley

Haltemprice

HULL

Howden

Hedon

Withernsea

Holderness

0   10   20 km

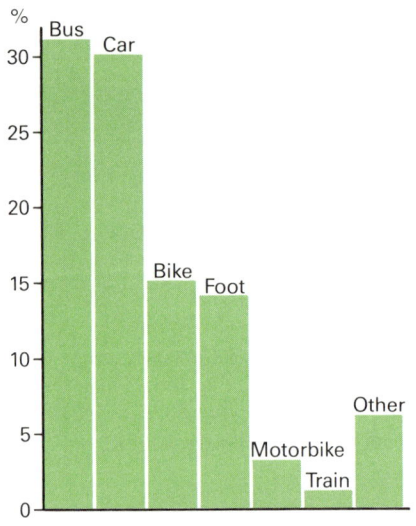

Figure 2   A bar graph to show how Hull's commuters travel to work each day

%
Bus
Car
Bike
Foot
Motorbike
Train
Other

We have seen how some people move from one country to live in another. There are other people who travel much shorter distances every day, to work. These temporary migrants are called *commuters*. A commuter is a person who lives in one area and goes to work in another area each day. The flow map (Figure 1) shows where the commuters who travel to Hull each day come from. The width of the arrow pointing towards Hull tells you how many people come from each place. For example, 4% of Hull's commuters come from the Beverley area, so the arrow is 4 mm wide. The bar graph (Figure 2) shows you what percentage of Hull's commuters travel to work by different transport methods. Over half of the commuters travel by bus and car. All these cars have to be parked in the city. Hull has enough room for these car parks. Some bigger cities, like London, cannot provide enough space for car parking, so far more people commute by train or bus. Most people start work between 8 and 9 am and finish between 5 and 6 pm. At those times the roads are very crowded, and traffic jams may happen, as the newspaper headlines show (Figure 3).

Figure 4   Car parking in the city centre

Figure 3   Some typical newspaper headlines about traffic jams

DRIVERS FUME IN 3 HOUR JAM

SHARE YOUR CAR:
– save petrol
– reduce traffic

Roadworks cause long tail-backs

Park-and-Ride scheme 'Great success'

BUS LANES INTRODUCED TO TRY TO STOP RUSH HOUR JAMS

Ambulance 'delayed by heavy traffic'

CAMPAIGN TO SWITCH COMMUTERS FROM CARS TO BUSES

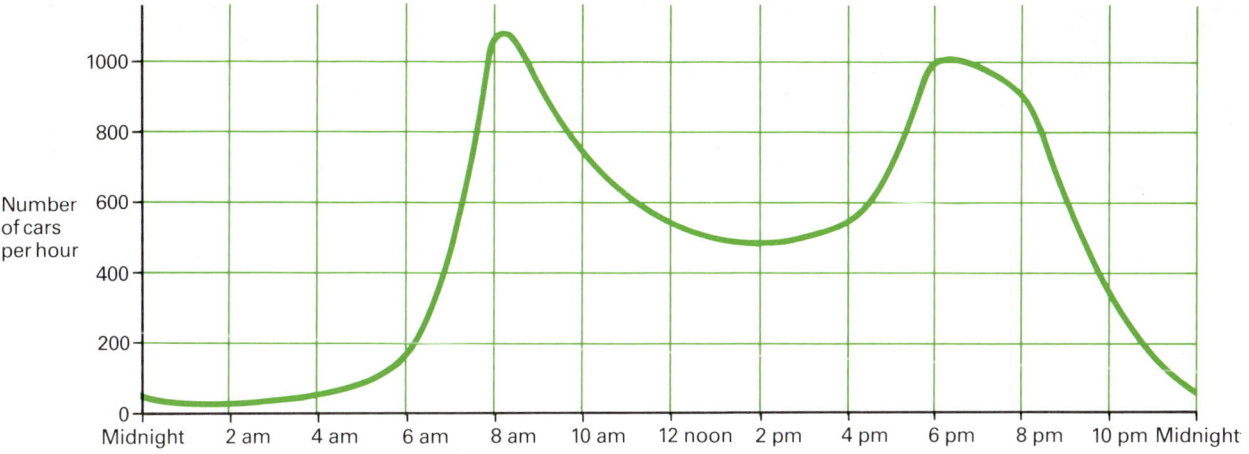

Figure 5   A line graph showing the number of cars travelling along a main road on the outskirts of Hull, in one day

Things to do

1 Look at the flow map showing commuters into Hull (Figure 1) and use it to answer these questions
  (a) What percentage of Hull's commuters come from Haltemprice?
  (b) There are five places which each supply about 1% of Hull's commuters. What are their names?
  (c) Do most people travel more or less than 10 miles to Hull each day?
  (d) The number of commuters travelling to Hull each day is about 30 000, but about 100 000 people work in Hull. Where do you think the other 70 000 people live?

2 The line graph (Figure 5) shows the number of cars travelling along one of the roads into Hull from Haltemprice. Describe what the graph shows. (Here are some hints: When are there most cars? Why is it busy at this time? When are there few cars and why? What differences are there between day and night-time traffic?)

3 Why are the times between 8 and 9 am, and between 5 and 6 pm called the 'rush hours'?

4 You have been asked by Humberside County Council to write a report. You need to explain how far most people travel to work, where most of Hull's commuters live, and how they travel to work. You should also mention the sort of problems there might be in Hull each morning and evening during the rush hour. Look at all the illustrations in this unit.

Homework ideas

Make a survey of your class at school. Find out where the members of your friends' families commute to. You might be able to find out how most people travel to work, how long the journey takes and what problems they notice in the rush hour. Make a poster to show the results of your survey. You could draw maps or graphs and perhaps find some newspaper cuttings about traffic jams.

Figure 6   (below left)   A traffic jam – a typical result of the rush hour

Figure 7   The quiet suburbs where commuters prefer to live

23 Guestworkers

There are some people who travel quite long distances for work, and who stay there for several months or even a few years, before returning home again. You will see in the next unit that more than a third of the people who emigrated from Italy in 1980 went to West Germany. In fact, many of the workers in West German industries are migrants from European counries. These people are called 'Gasterbeiter' which means 'guestworkers'.

Since 1945, when World War II ended, West Germany has rebuilt its war-damaged industries. But there were not enough German workers for the new industries. Instead migrant workers were recruited from nearby countries, like Turkey and Yugoslavia. The idea was for the guestworkers to spend a number of years working for a firm in Germany, and then return to their homes. So, most of these migrant workers were temporary. However some migrants took their families with them to West Germany and have now decided that they would like to live there permanently.

Figure 3   A Turkish 'Gasterbeiter' working in a West German factory

Table 1   The countries migrant workers in Germany come from

Yugoslavia	31%
Italy	23%
Turkey	18%
Greece	9%
Spain	6%
Austria	3%
Portugal	2%
Others	8%

Things to do

1 Trace the map, Figure 1. Now using Table 1, draw a flow map with arrows showing where migrants to West Germany come from. Use a scale of 1 mm to represent 1%. You can work out how wide the arrow must be by using this scale. Each arrow should point towards West Germany. Look back at Figure 1 in unit 22 to see how this sort of map is drawn.

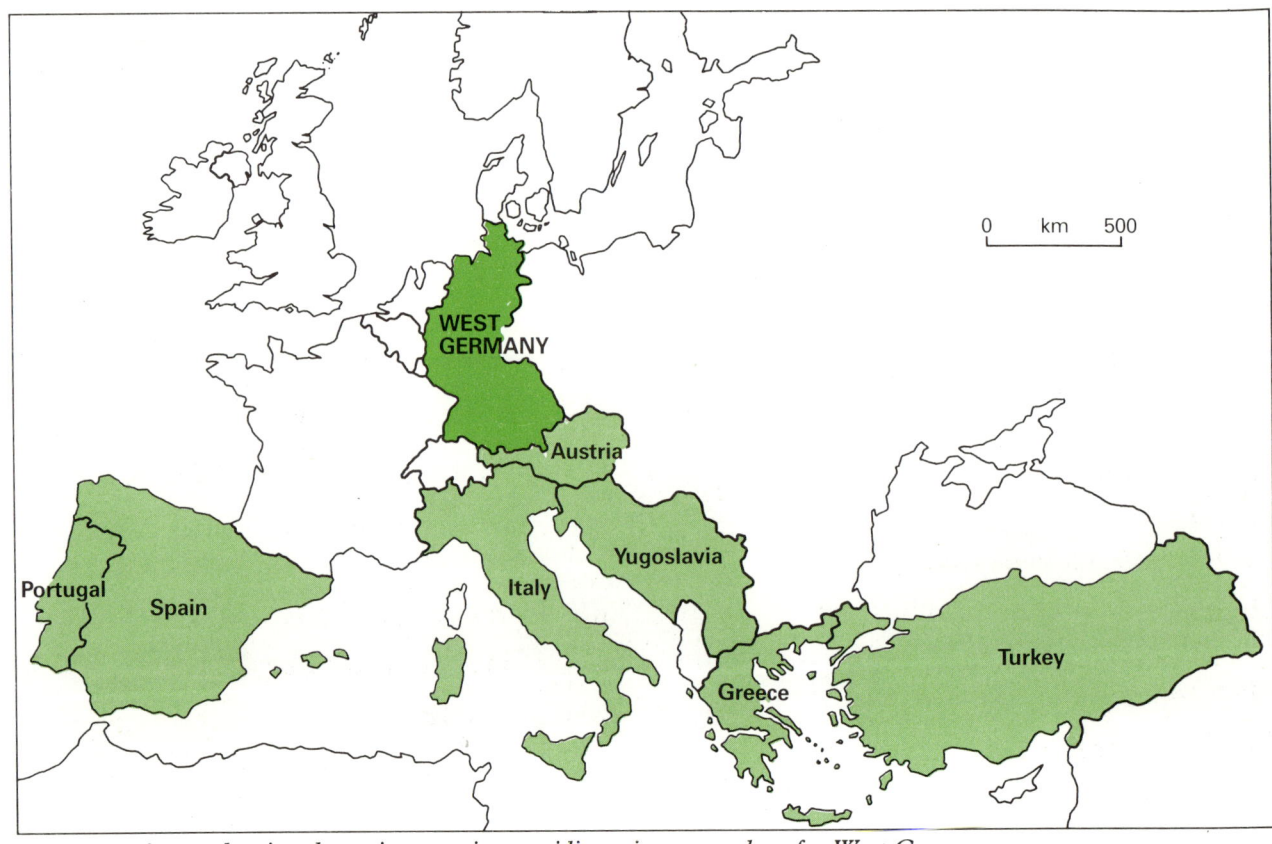

Figure 1   A map showing the main countries providing migrant workers for West Germany

54

2 Read the section on German guestworkers again and look at Figure 1 and Table 1. Decide which of the following statements are true and write out only the true statements.

Guestworkers in West Germany mainly come from areas to the east of it.

Most of West Germany's migrant workers come from countries which are not in the EEC. (Figure 1 in unit 19 shows the countries of the EEC.)

The nearer a country is to West Germany, the more migrants leave it to go to West Germany.

Migrant workers were needed to build up industries in the First World War.

Migrant workers are supposed to spend only a few years in West Germany before returning home to their own countries.

3 Imagine that you are a Turkish migrant worker going to West Germany, but you can't speak German. What problems will you have because of this?

4 The migrant workers usually spend only a year or two in West Germany. They leave their families behind. Do you think they spend all their money in Germany? Why might they send some money back home?

5 Today West Germany is starting to have its own unemployment problems. How do you think this will affect guestworkers?

Homework ideas

Imagine that your family is thinking about emigrating to Australia. Draw a diagram like Figure 2. Include questions you would ask yourselves before deciding to go.

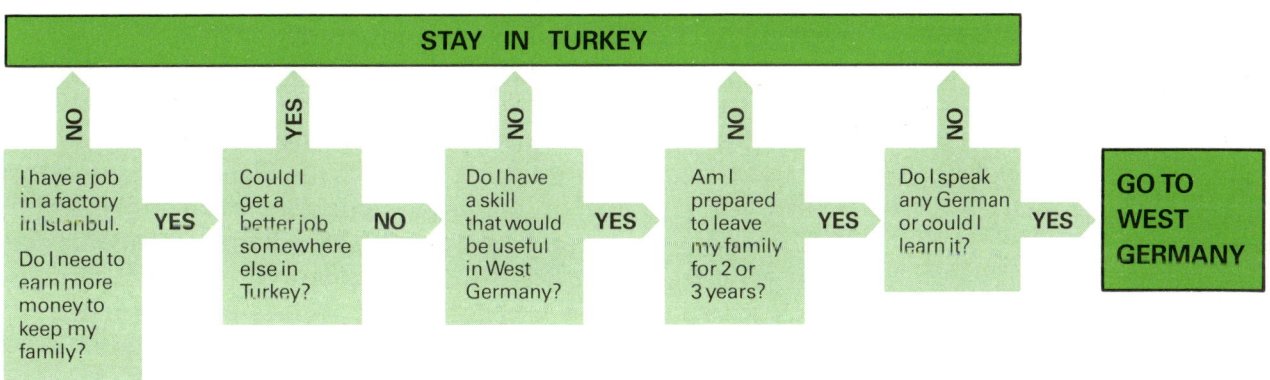

Figure 2   A flow diagram which shows some of the questions a migrant worker might ask himself before deciding to leave his home country

Summary

As a summary of the work on people in Europe you can test yourself by trying to match up the following 'heads' and 'tails' to make complete sentences.

Heads	*Tails*
1 The population density in Europe is highest	in some isolated rural areas of Europe.
2 The population is decreasing	is to increase the percentage of people living in urban areas
3 The main reason for migration in European countries	who moves to a different country for work.
4 A commuter is a person	in the industrial areas like the Ruhr.
5 A migrant is a person	is to find work.
6 The main effect of migration within countries	who travels elsewhere to work each day.

Immigration and emigration

Definitions

A *colony* is a territory overseas that is governed by another nation. For example, St Helena and Bermuda are colonies of Britain. Many countries which used to be colonies of Britain are now independent, eg, Ghana. *The Commonwealth* is an association of independent nations which used to be part of the British Empire. Ghana is a member of the Commonwealth, and the other countries range in size from Canada to Barbados.

Homework ideas

Would you like to emigrate to another country? If so, which one would you choose, and why? If not, explain why you would prefer to stay in Britain.

We have already seen that some people move from one part of their own country to another. There are also many people who move from their own country to a different country. The reason for moving, however, is often the same—to look for a better job.

An *emigrant* is a person who leaves his country; a person who settles in a new country is an *immigrant*. The pie charts (Figures 1 and 2) show numbers of migrants to and from Britain in 1981. You can see that most emigrants from Britain go to Australia, New Zealand and Canada. These three countries used to be colonies of Britain but now are part of the Commonwealth. For years people have gone there from Britain to farm the land and set up, or work in, new industries. Although these countries are large, they now have more unemployment than they used to have. This means that they cannot accept as many immigrants today as they used to accept. The EEC countries also receive many emigrants from Britain, especially since we joined the EEC in 1973.

Most of the migrants coming to Britain also come from Commonwealth countries. Because these countries used to be colonies of Britain, English is the language spoken in many of them. This makes it easier for immigrants to Britain. You can imagine that if you have to learn a new language as well as new customs and a new way of life when you emigrate, it makes it very difficult to settle quickly into your new country.

People have been entering and leaving Britain like this for many years. Some of the first emigrants were the Pilgrim Fathers who sailed for America in 1620. Their descendants are now Americans, not British. Many coloured people in Britain today were born here and are British, because their parents or grandparents came to live in Britain 30 or 40 years ago.

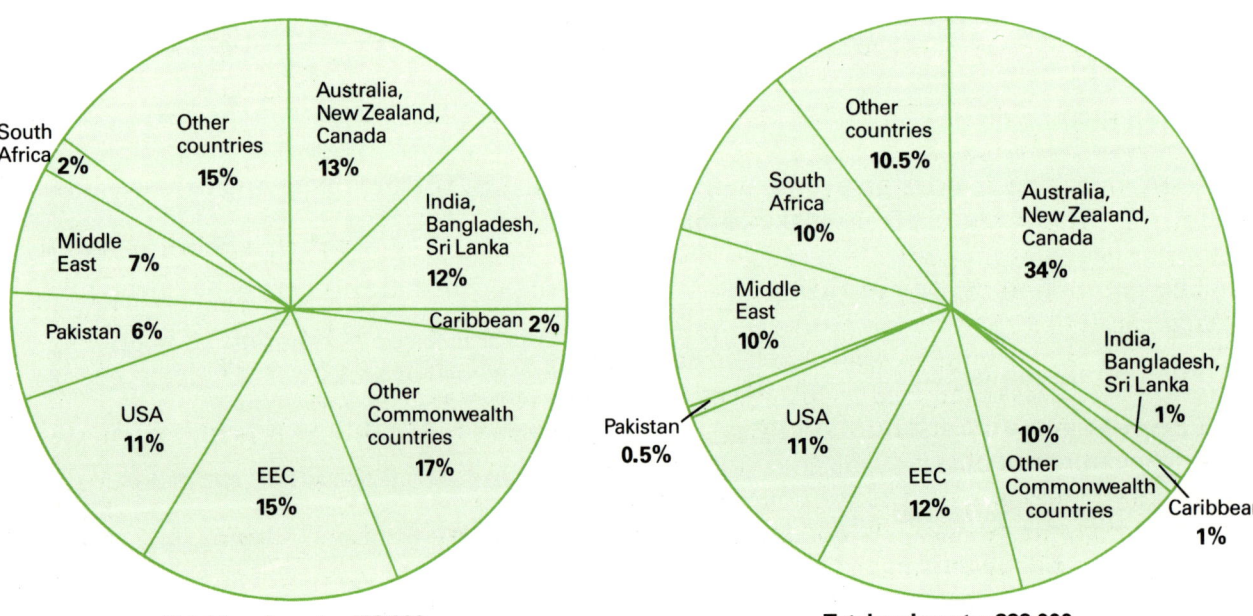

Total immigrants: 153 000

Figure 1 The origin of immigrants to Britain in 1981

Total emigrants: 233 000

Figure 2 The destination of emigrants from Britain in 1981

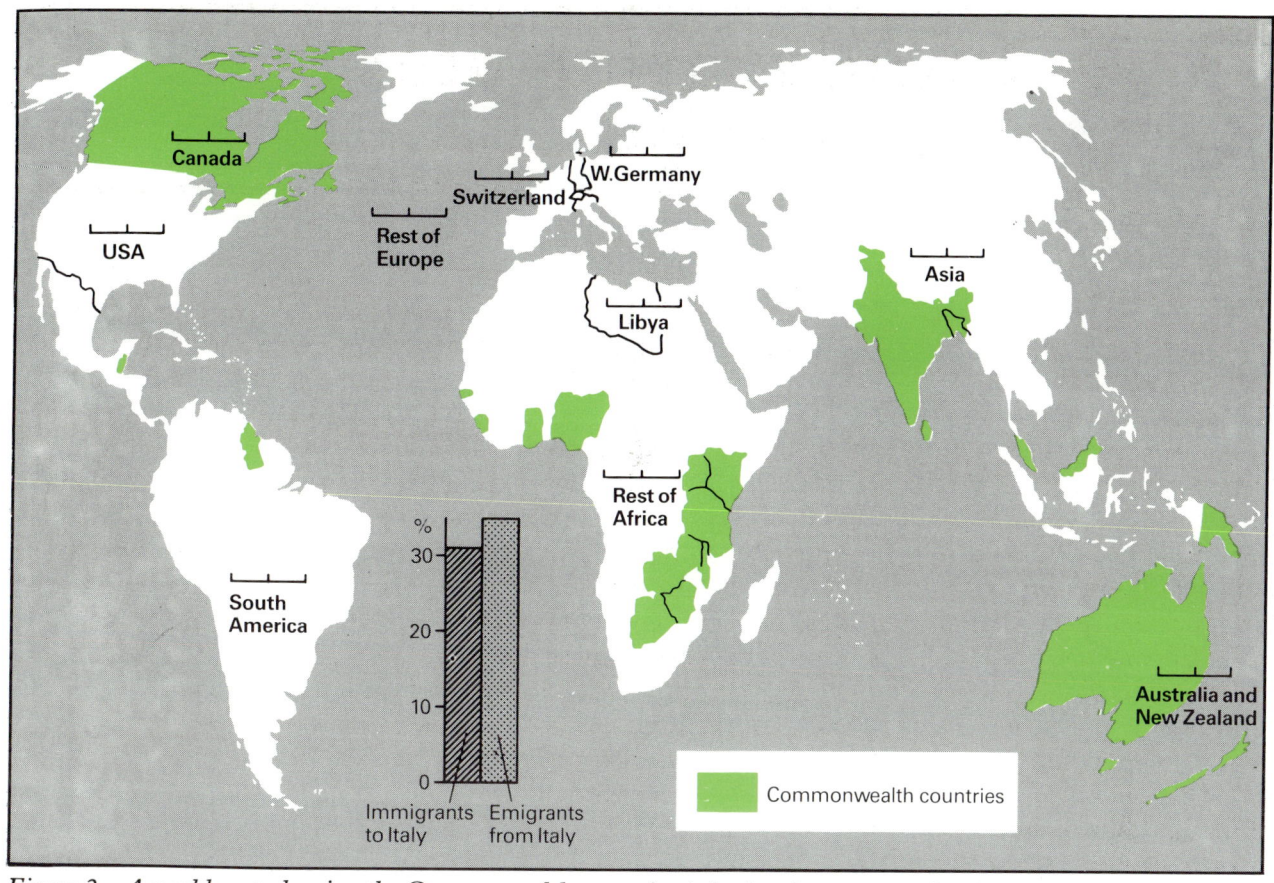

Figure 3   A world map showing the Commonwealth countries (also immigrants to and emigrants from Italy)

Things to do

1 (a) Use the world map (Figure 3) and an atlas to write down the names of the six largest Commonwealth countries.

(b) Find out from the pie chart (Figure 1) what percentage of the immigrants to Britain came from Commonwealth countries. Add them up to get the total percentage of immigrants from the Commonwealth.

(c) Then do the same for the percentages of emigrants going to Commonwealth countries.

(d) What do your results tell you about the links between Britain and the Commonwealth?

2 Do more people enter or leave Britain each year? Give a number in your answer.

3 What differences do you notice between the pie charts showing immigrants and emigrants? Look at the number of people who come from and go to each area. Are the numbers similar on both charts? For which areas are there the biggest differences?

4 Suggest why Australia and Canada are now strictly limiting the number of immigrants they will allow in.

5 Make a copy of the world map, Figure 3. Ignore the shading of the Commonwealth countries. Use Table 1 to draw proportional bars showing numbers of immigrants to and emigrants from Italy. Use a scale of 1 cm to 10% and draw each bar $\frac{1}{2}$ cm wide. The bars for West Germany have been drawn for you, as an example.

6 What do you notice about the positions of the countries that send most immigrants to Italy? Is the same true for the countries receiving most Italian immigrants?

7 Would a map of migrants to and from Britain also show that most migration is with countries close to us?
Suggest reasons for your answer.

Table 1
Emigrants from Italy went to

West Germany	35%
Switzerland	26%
Rest of Europe	15%
Libya	2%
Rest of Africa	5%
Canada	3%
USA	5%
South America	4%
Asia	3%
Australia and New Zealand	2%

Immigrants to Italy came from

West Germany	31%
Switzerland	27%
Rest of Europe	15%
Libya	2%
Rest of Africa	5%
Canada	3%
USA	6%
South America	6%
Asia	3%
Australia and New Zealand	2%

57

25 What is a village?

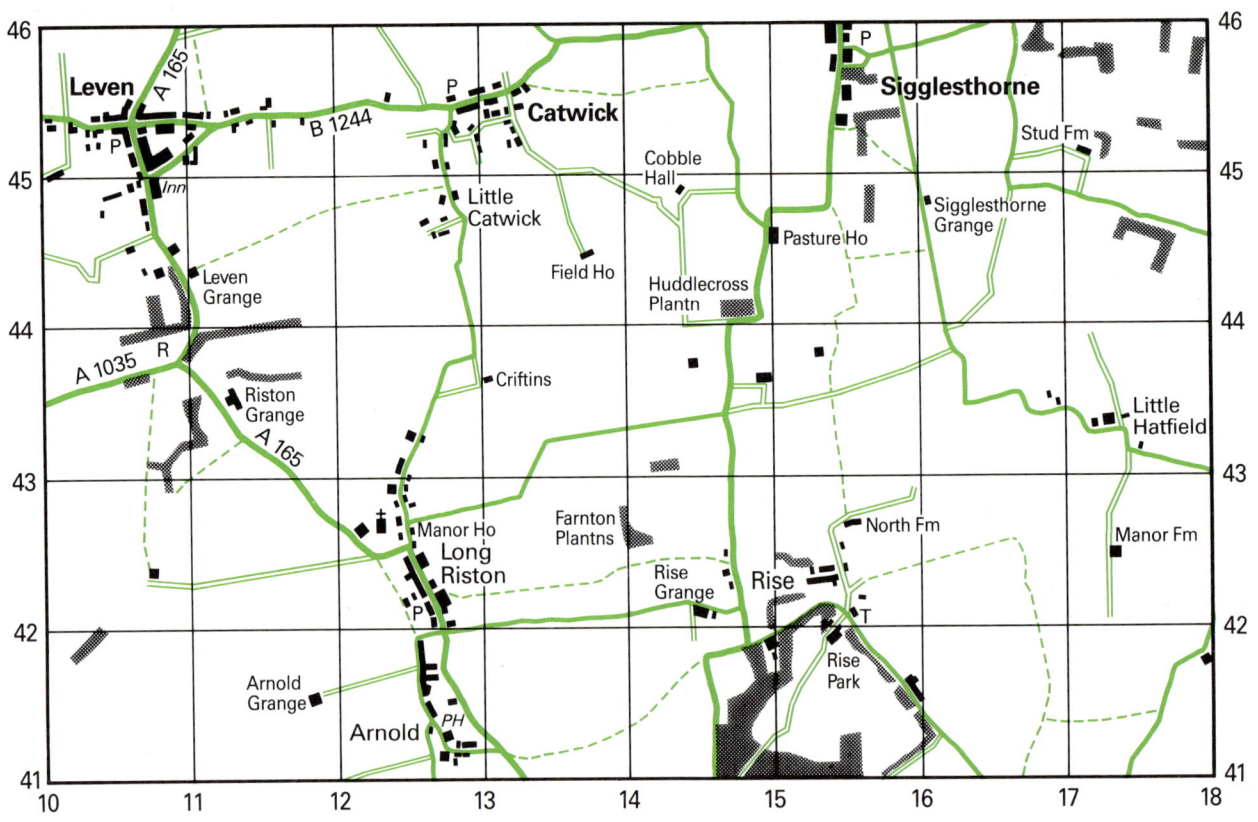

Figure 1 A sketch map extract showing part of East Yorkshire

KEY

▬▬ Main road	■■ Buildings
── Minor road	
══ Track	▓ Woodland
--- Footpath	
P Post Office	PH Public House
✝ Church	T Telephone box

0   1   2 km

Two hundred years ago most people in Britain lived in the countryside, mostly in villages. Today less than 10% of our population live in villages, and many villages are either much smaller than they used to be, or have completely disappeared. The map extract (Figure 1) shows part of Humberside which is an important farming area. There are a number of villages on the map; find Leven, Catwick, Sigglesthorne and Long Riston. These villages provide services or facilities like post offices, churches, public houses and shops for the people living nearby. Look at each village on the map and notice the size of the area of housing and the services each village has. The map cannot show all the services in the village, but Figures 2 and 3 give you some

Figure 2 The village stores in Sigglesthorne

Figure 3 The main street in Leven

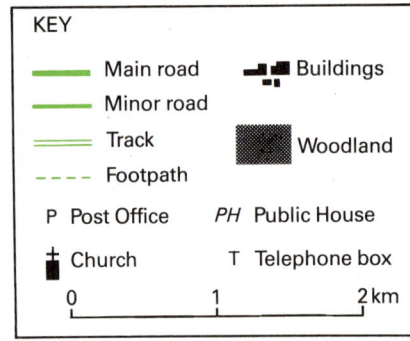

extra information. Can you identify the shops in the main streets of Leven and Sigglesthorne from our photographs?

To find places accurately on the map you will need to use six figure grid references, which were mentioned in unit 2. First give the number of the grid line to the west of the place. Look at Figure 4; here it is 13. Then imagine the grid square is divided into 10 equal spaces. Our place is one tenth from grid line 13. Our first three numbers therefore are 131. Now look at the grid line south of the place, which is number 43. It looks about seven tenths of the way up the grid square to our dot. So the whole grid reference is 131437. Look at Figure 1 and see what you can find at 131437.

Now we can use the map extract to show the difference between a village, a hamlet and an isolated farm. For example, if you look at 173425 you can see Manor Farm standing alone, isolated. The small group of houses at Little Catwick (128447) is a hamlet, and you can see that there are no services or facilities shown on the map there. The population of a hamlet may be only 15–20 people, but as you can see from Table 1, the village of Leven has 360 people living in it.

Things to do

1 Give grid references for two isolated farms and one hamlet.
2 Look carefully at the villages of Catwick, Leven, Sigglesthorne and Long Riston on the map. Copy out Table 1 and put a tick against the services which you can tell *from the map* that each village has:

Table 1 Village services

Service	Catwick	Leven	Sigglesthorne	Long Riston
Post Office				
Church				
Public house				
Telephone box				

3 Are there any other services you think a village might offer to its inhabitants?
4 Work out the average population of the 6 villages listed in Table 2. To work out an average, add the populations and divide by the number of villages there are.
5 Decide where the centre of each village is. Now measure the distance from the centre of each village to the centre of the village nearest to it. For instance the village nearest to Leven is Catwick, so find out the distance between these two villages. Remember the scale of the map is 2 cm to 1 km. Write your results in a copy of Table 3.
6 Villages in the Highlands of Scotland are not as close together as these villages are. Can you see why from looking at Figure 1 in unit 20?

You should now have a clear idea of what a village in eastern England is like. It consists of a small group of about 100–200 houses clustered together, with a few basic services. You will see later on that in other countries villages might be much larger than this.

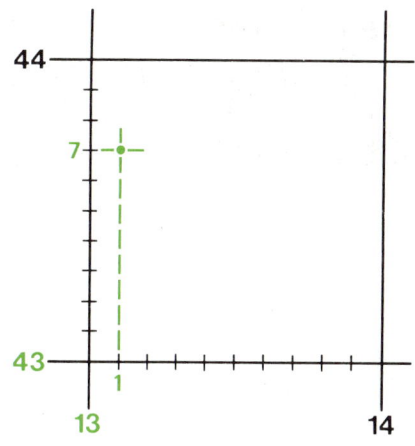

Figure 4 Diagram to show how to give six-figure grid references

Table 2 Village populations

	population
Leven	360
Catwick	200
Sigglesthorne	310
Long Riston	470
Little Hatfield	80
Rise	120

Table 3 Distances between villages

Village	Nearest Village	Distance
Leven	Catwick	

Homework ideas

Visit a village near where you live and find out the services it offers to the local people. If you cannot go to a village, you may be able to find out about the shops, public houses etc by looking in the Yellow Pages of a local telephone directory, or at the advertisements in one of the local newspapers.

59

26 The site of a settlement

A defensive site

A castle or church may be built on the hilltop.
The houses group together close to it.

A dry site

A small hill provides dry
ground in a marshy area.

A bridge site

This is the lowest point on
the river where a bridge
can be built.
Several roads meet at the
bridge to cross the river.
A market might begin here.

Figure 1   Some examples of settlement sites

When people first chose a place to build a village, they needed to look for certain things. Water was probably the most important of these, because it is vital for life. But it would be no good if the area was flooded frequently.

It might be necessary to find a place like a hill-top, which would be easy to defend against enemies. A place where a bridge could be built across a river would be useful for people wanting to trade with others or to transport goods by water.

The piece of land that was chosen for the first houses is called the *site* of a settlement. The sketches in Figure 1 show some examples of settlement sites. Look carefully at each one and see if you can work out why it was chosen.

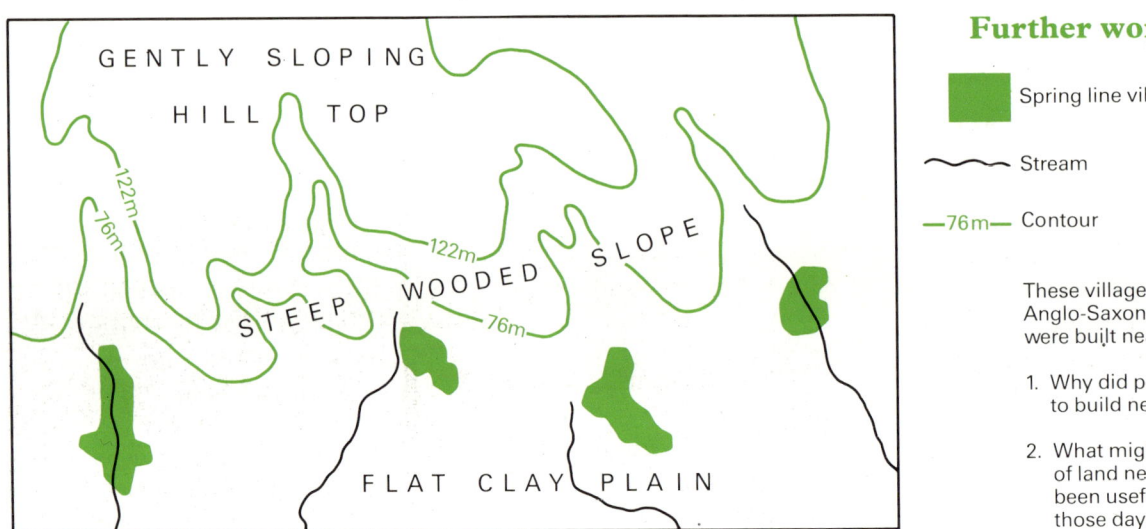

Further work

▮ Spring line villages

〜〜〜 Stream

—76m— Contour

These villages date from Anglo-Saxon times, and were built near springs.

1. Why did people chose to build near springs?

2. What might each type of land nearby have been useful for in those days?

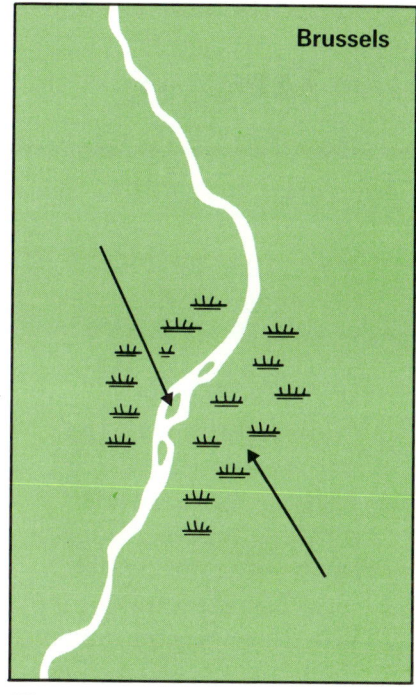

Figure 2 Brussels

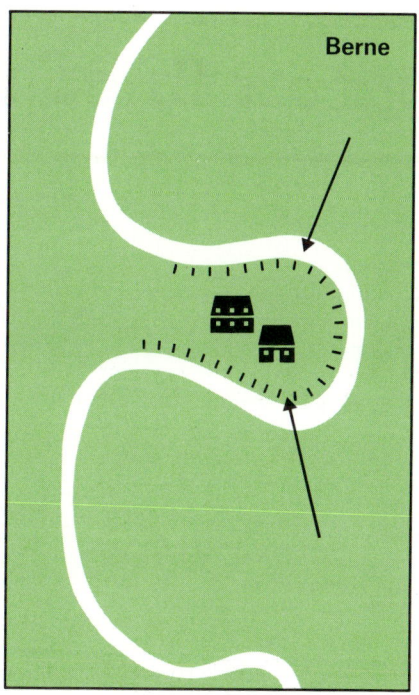

Figure 3 Berne

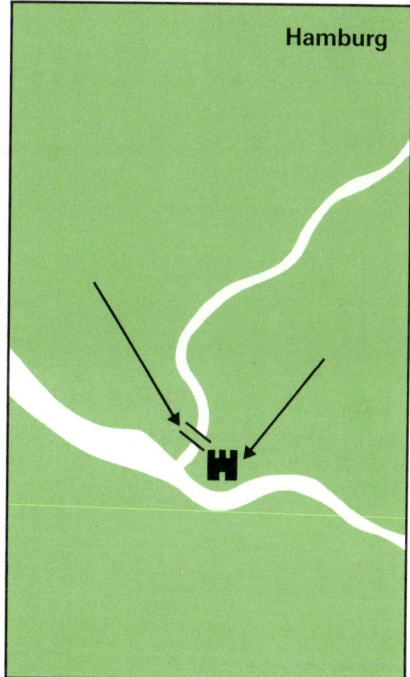

Figure 4 Hamburg

Things to do

1 The sketch maps (Figures 2, 3, 4 and 5) show the sites of four European cities. Copy Figures 2, 3 and 4 into your book and add the correct labels to the end of each arrow. The labels have been muddled up so that they are in the wrong order.

    River forms a natural moat on three sides of the site
    Bridge built at the point where ships must unload
    Island provided a dry site among the marshes
    Steep sides of meander bend give protection
    Marshland beside River Senne often flooded
    Castle built on a rocky spur between two rivers

2 Look at the map and photograph (Figure 6) of Orvieto. Either copy the map and make up some labels of your own about the site, or make a sketch from the photograph and put labels on to that instead.

3 Which of the four sites would have been easy to defend? Try to give a reason in each case.

4 Which of the sites would be likely to become a port?

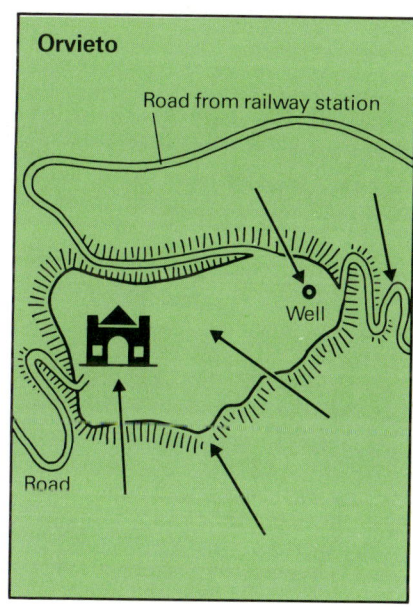

Figure 5 Orvieto

Figure 6 The hill-top town of Orvieto

Homework ideas

1 Find out which country each of these five cities is in. You might also be able to find out what each city is famous for today.

2 Try to find out what sort of site your home town is built on. You might be able to find out about the original site of London too.

27 The growth of towns

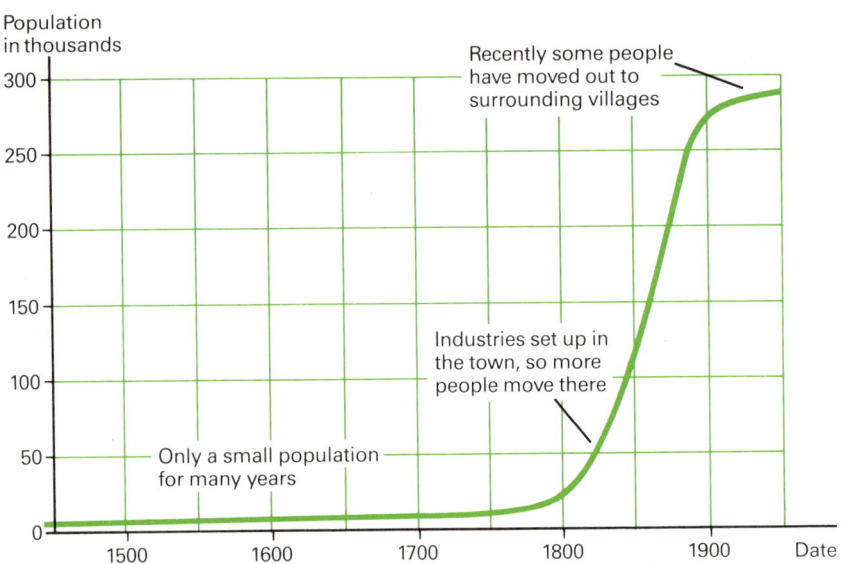

Population in thousands

Recently some people have moved out to surrounding villages

Industries set up in the town, so more people move there

Only a small population for many years

Figure 1   A line graph showing the change in the population of Bradford

Look at the line graph showing the population of Bradford (Figure 1). Until 1800, it was just a small town, with a few thousand people. At that time, there were many other towns in Britain that were about the same size as Bradford. Suddenly from about 1800, towns started to grow very rapidly—just as Bradford did. This was partly caused by the following changes (Figure 2).

Homework ideas

1 See if you can find out how many people lived in your town, or in a nearby one, 100 years ago. You may be able to draw a graph with the information you obtain.

2 Figures 3 and 4 show pictures representing the birth rate and the death rate. Draw pictures to illustrate the equations in Figures 5 and 6. Try not to use many words in your diagrams.

Figure 2   Changes that affect the birth and death rates

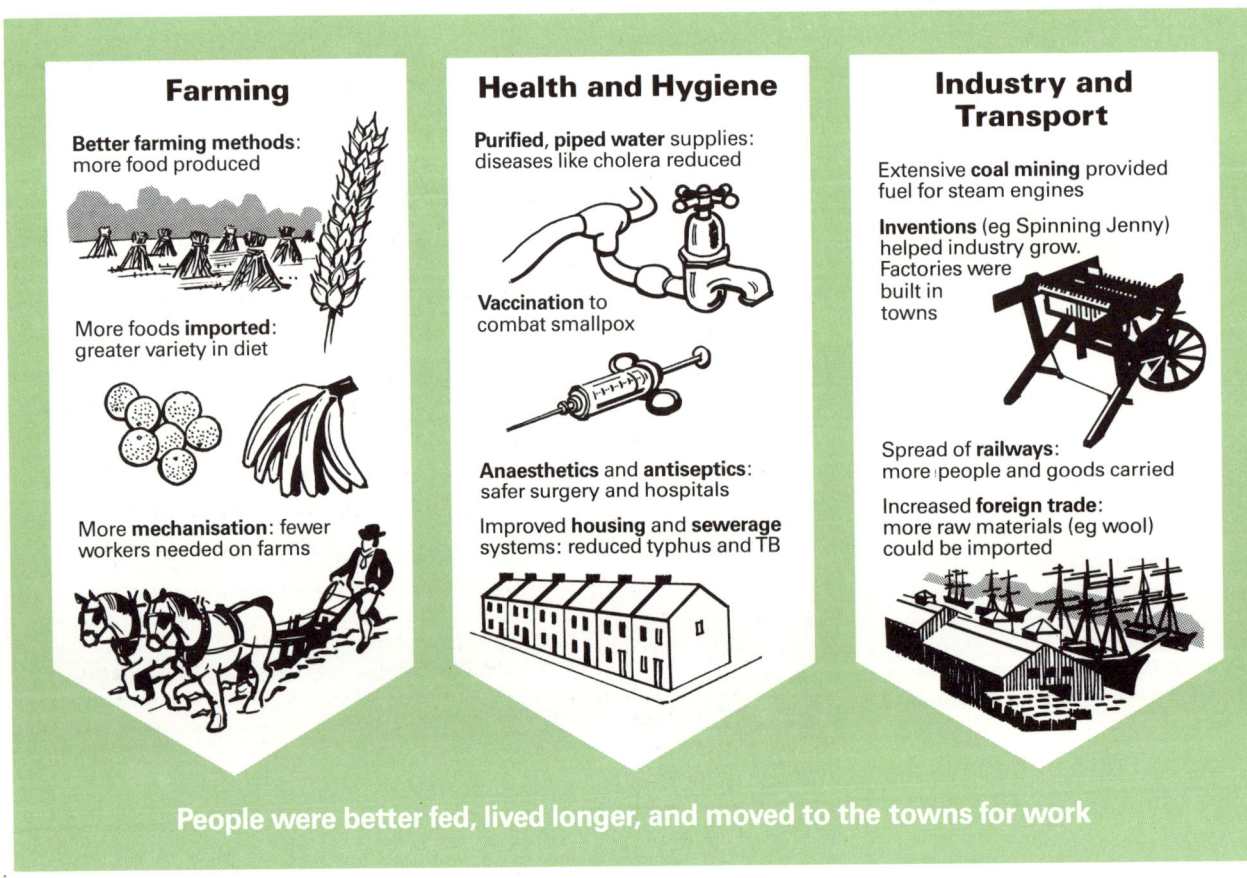

Farming

Better farming methods: more food produced

More foods imported: greater variety in diet

More mechanisation: fewer workers needed on farms

Health and Hygiene

Purified, piped water supplies: diseases like cholera reduced

Vaccination to combat smallpox

Anaesthetics and **antiseptics:** safer surgery and hospitals

Improved **housing** and **sewerage** systems: reduced typhus and TB

Industry and Transport

Extensive **coal mining** provided fuel for steam engines

Inventions (eg Spinning Jenny) helped industry grow. Factories were built in towns

Spread of **railways:** more people and goods carried

Increased **foreign trade:** more raw materials (eg wool) could be imported

People were better fed, lived longer, and moved to the towns for work

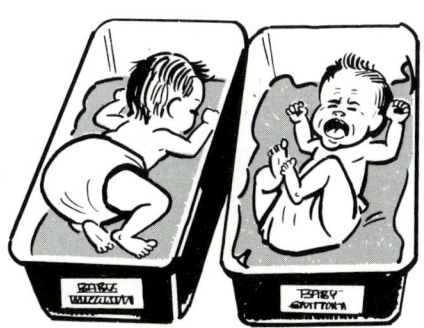

Birth rate means the number of babies born for every 1000 people in the town

Figure 3   The birth rate

Death rate means the number of deaths out of every 1000 people in the town

Figure 4   The death rate

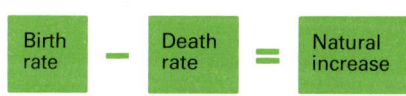

Figure 5   Natural increase

Figure 6   Total population increase

All these things together meant that there were more and more people living in towns like Bradford. As the graphs show, the number of people in Britain as a whole went up as well.

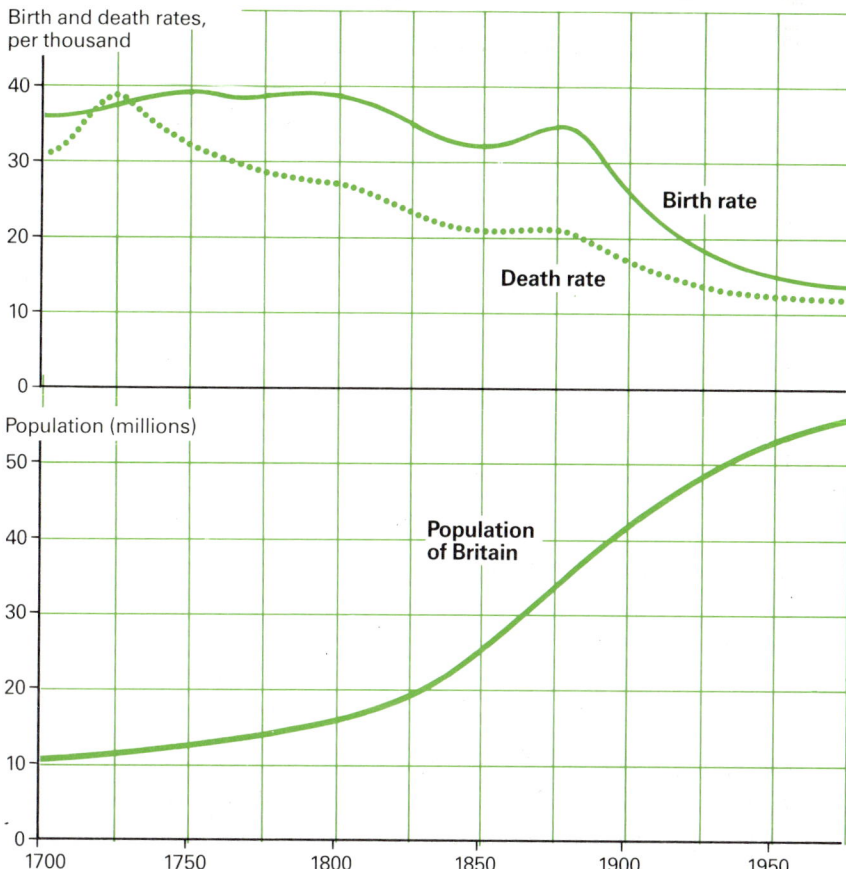

Figure 7   The birth rate, the death rate and the total population in Britain

Things to do

1   Look at Figure 2. Use the ideas there and some of your own to draw a diagram yourself. Then write a few sentences explaining why towns like Bradford grew rapidly in the 1800s.

2   Practise reading information from Figure 7 by answering these questions.
   (a) What was the population of Britain in 1800?
   (b) What was the date when the birth rate in Britain was highest?
   (c) What has happened to the death rate in Britain since 1830?
   (d) When did Britain's population start to rise rapidly?
   (e) Is Britain's population still rising as fast as it did then?

3   Draw a line graph to show the population of France from 1800 to 1975. Use the information in Table 1, and the same scales as Figure 7. You could add lines to show the birth and death rates.

4   Colour in the space between the death rate line and the birth rate line on your graph. Can you work out what this area represents? Look back to the diagram you drew to illustrate Figure 5.

Table 1   The population of France

Date	Population	Birth rate per '000 population	Death rate per '000 population
1800	27 million	33	27
1850	36 million	26	23
1900	38 million	22	21
1950	42 million	19	13
1975	53 million	14	11

28 The purpose of a place

We have seen what the site of a settlement may be like, now we will look at the purpose of the place or the reason why it exists there. This is usually called its *function*. Its function is what the place was built for, or what it is now important for. It might also suggest what jobs are done by the people who live there. Small places might only have one function, such as being a market town. Large cities usually have lots of functions. If we look at Manchester as an example, we see that it is a port, it is a service centre providing shops for the surrounding area, it has a university and it is an industrial centre (Figure 1). These are just a few of its functions.

Figure 1   Manchester: the main shopping centre, the industrial area and the university

Things to do

1 Look at the sketch map of Europe (Figure 2). Read the descriptions of the functions of the five places marked. The letters of the place names on the map have been muddled up. Use an atlas to find out the proper names. In your exericse book write the name of each place and the description which you think goes with it.

2 Use the atlas to find the names needed to complete these sentences. When you write out each sentence, write the correct place name instead of 'place A' etc.
   (a) Place A is found in a range of mountains called _____ _____.
   (b) *Place B* stands on the west coast of the _____ peninsula.
   (c) *Place C* is in the middle of an important farming area in the north of _____.
   (d) *Place D* is on the _____ coalfield in West Germany.
   (e) The country in which *place E* is found is _____.
   (f) *Place F* is on the coast of the _____ Sea.

3 Now use your atlas, this textbook and your general knowledge to write a list of about five ports, five capitals and five resorts in Europe.

Homework ideas
Write down the name of the place you live in, or a nearby town or city. Then list all its functions—or purposes. If you can, give the actual types of industry.

A *market town* began as a place where farmers from the surrounding area brought their produce to sell.
Sometimes there still is a cattle market, or perhaps a more general market selling many different things, once or twice a week. In Britain, **Bury St Edmunds** is a good example of a market town.

A *fishing port*, like **Grimsby**, usually grew up where there was a sheltered harbour for boats to dock in. It would also need to be near good fishing grounds like those in the North Sea.

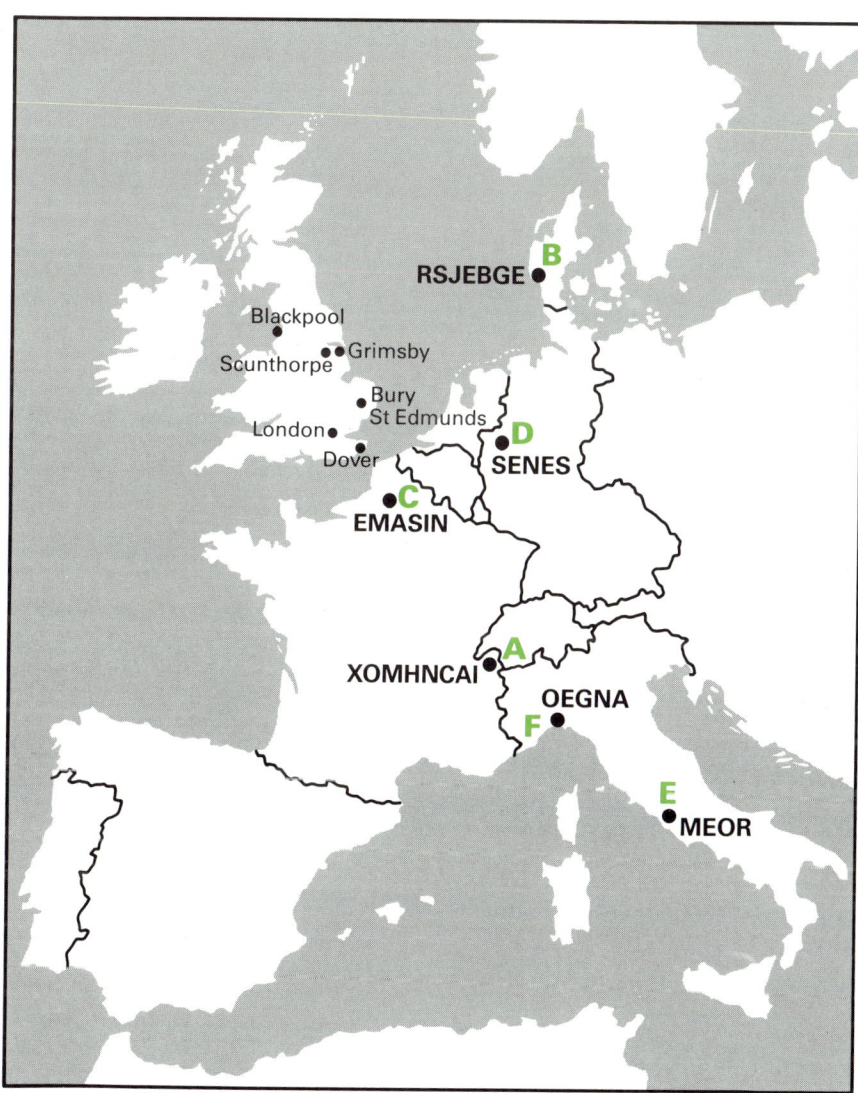

Figure 2   Sketch map of Europe showing different types of places

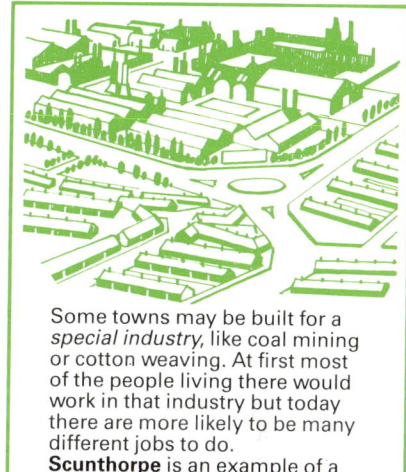

Some towns may be built for a *special industry*, like coal mining or cotton weaving. At first most of the people living there would work in that industry but today there are more likely to be many different jobs to do.
Scunthorpe is an example of a town built for a steel works.

Resorts are places that people go to for holidays. A lot of these are on the coast, like **Blackpool**, but they can also be inland, as ski resorts are.

Can you match the place and the description?

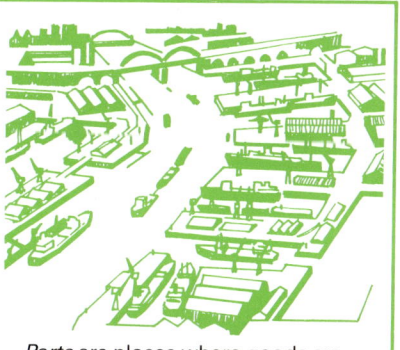

Ports are places where goods are loaded in and out of ships. They are either on the coast or on a major river or canal. They need a harbour which is sheltered and where docks can be built. **Dover** is a good example of a port in Britain.

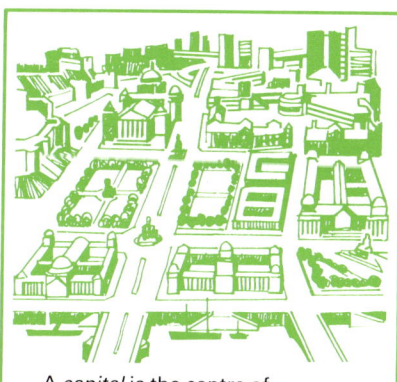

A *capital* is the centre of government in a country. It is the place that the country is ruled from. The Prime Minister or President lives there. Our capital is **London**.

29 New settlements

```
W X C G S E N Y E K E P E
A X R U L E A S T G E L E
S E A X M E X E A T A H L
H F W X X B N N E D L A R
I F L X X I E R S N E R E
N I E X V V B R O X M L T
G L Y R E O E D N T E O E
T C I T R M L Y X A H W P
O Y S O L I W X X X U E X
N A U E S L Y B R O C L S
X G K A E H A T F I E L D
H S B W H C T I D D E R X
```

New towns word search
The names of the new towns have been written backwards, forwards, upside down and diagonally in this box. The letter X has been written in the spaces which are not part of a word.

Figure 1   New towns in the UK

Homework ideas

Try to think of some more reasons why a completely new settlement might have to be built. Make a list in your book. (Hint: think about new sorts of industry, discoveries of mineral resources, natural disasters and man-made disasters.)

Some towns have a long history, like those we have been looking at. Others are purpose-built and less than fifty years old. These are called *new towns*. There are a number of new towns in Britain as Figure 1 shows. Later on you can try to find the names of the unlabelled towns in the word search.

The first new towns in Birtain were built to provide better

housing and new job opportunities for people living in overcrowded conditions in London. Later, more new towns were built closer to other cities, such as Birmingham, Newcastle and Manchester, to accommodate their extra population. Some new towns, like Peterlee, have been built almost completely from scratch. Others, like Basildon, have been built round an existing village, and some were already towns which have been deliberately expanded, for example, Peterborough.

There are other reasons for building new settlements in Europe. Can you think of any? You might perhaps have been to a ski resort which has been built specially for skiing holidays. Flaine in France is an example of a purpose-built ski resort. The photograph (Figure 2) shows the modern apartment blocks and hotels built near to the ski slopes.

Italians have a different reason for building new villages. In the south of Italy, much farmland has been taken from the rich landowners and reorganised. New villages have been built for the farmers who have each been given small areas of farmland to look after. The villages have been built close to the farmers' land.

New settlements have also been built in the Netherlands, because new land has been created. This land has been *reclaimed* from the sea. First walls are built around the area, then the sea water is pumped out. This polder land has been reclaimed for farming, so villages and towns have been built to provide services for the farmers. Figure 3 shows an area of new settlements in the Nordoostpolder, Netherlands.

Figure 2 Flaine a ski resort in France

NORDOOSTPOLDER, NETHERLANDS

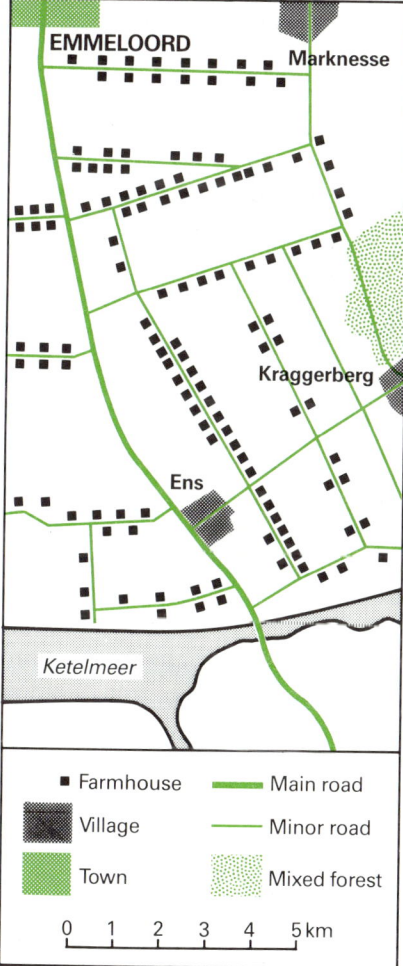

Figure 3 New settlements in Nordoostpolder, the Netherlands

Things to do

1 Carefully copy the map of Britain (Figure 1). Use the word search to find all the missing names, and write them on your map. To help you, the first letters of each name have been put on the map.
2 Count the number of new towns which are close to each of the cities in Table 1 and fill in the number in a copy of this table.

Table 1 Cities and their associated new towns in Britain

City	Population	Number of new towns
London	6 765 000	
Birmingham	1 017 000	
Glasgow	761 000	
Liverpool	510 000	
Manchester	458 000	
Edinburgh	445 000	
Newcastle	285 000	

3 What does Table 1 tell you about where new towns have been built? Can you explain your answer?
4 In which season of the year will the resort of Flaine be busiest?
5 Can you suggest why people might go to a ski resort in summer? Look at the scenery in Figure 2.
6 Write a short description of Figure 3. How are the farmhouses distributed? Are they scattered anywhere or spread out evenly? Why? How far apart are the villages? Why have the villages been built?

30 The layout of new towns

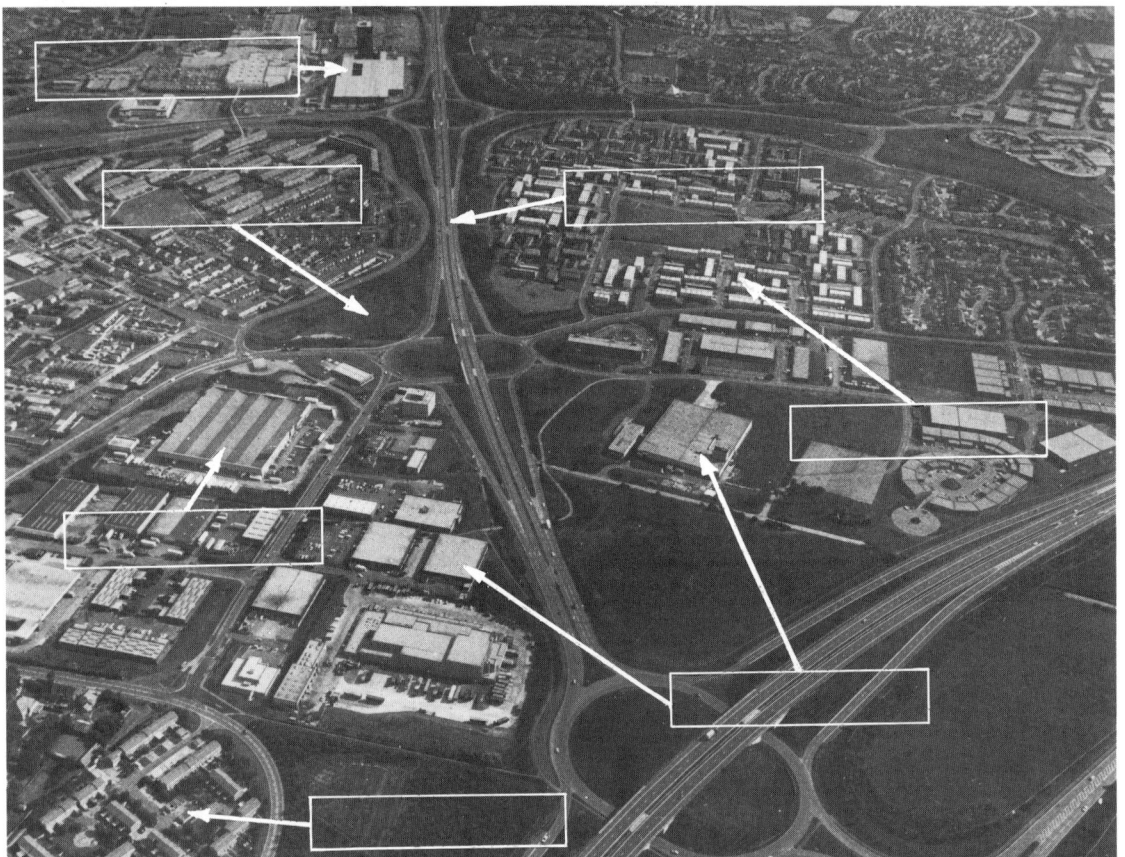

Figure 1   A view of Washington new town, looking south down Washington Way

Figure 2   A housing area in Washington new town

In the previous unit, we have seen why new settlements are built. Now we are going to look at how they are laid out. Since new towns are built from scratch they can be planned very carefully to suit the needs of the people who will live there. The photographs (Figures 1, 2, 3 and 4) show some detailed views of the new town of Washington. This town was built near Newcastle in the 1960s and 1970s. It now has a population of about 60 000 people.

Things to do

1 Look at the photographs of Washington. Make a simple copy or a tracing of Figure 1. Several features are arrowed. Choose a label from the list below to write at the end of each arrow.

    The factories are clean, attractive, low buildings.

    The houses are built in neighbourhoods or 'villages' with no *through* roads.

    A wide main road has been built through the town, on open land.

    Factories are built at the edge of the town, near the main roads.

    A large amount of open space has been left in the town.

    The houses all have gardens and garages.

    The town centre has shops under cover, tall office blocks and plenty of car parks.

Figure 3   Washington town centre

A1(M)

Washington Wildfowl Refuge

River Wear

0   2km

Figure 5   Washington new town plan

Figure 6

2 Look carefully at the town plan of Washington (Figure 5). Use the headings in Figure 6 to write a description of the plan. The questions in each section should help you.

Figure 4   One of the areas of open space in Washington

Homework ideas

Now that you have some ideas about why new towns are built and how they are planned, you could try to plan one yourself. What do you think a new town of the future will look like?

31 Europe's cities

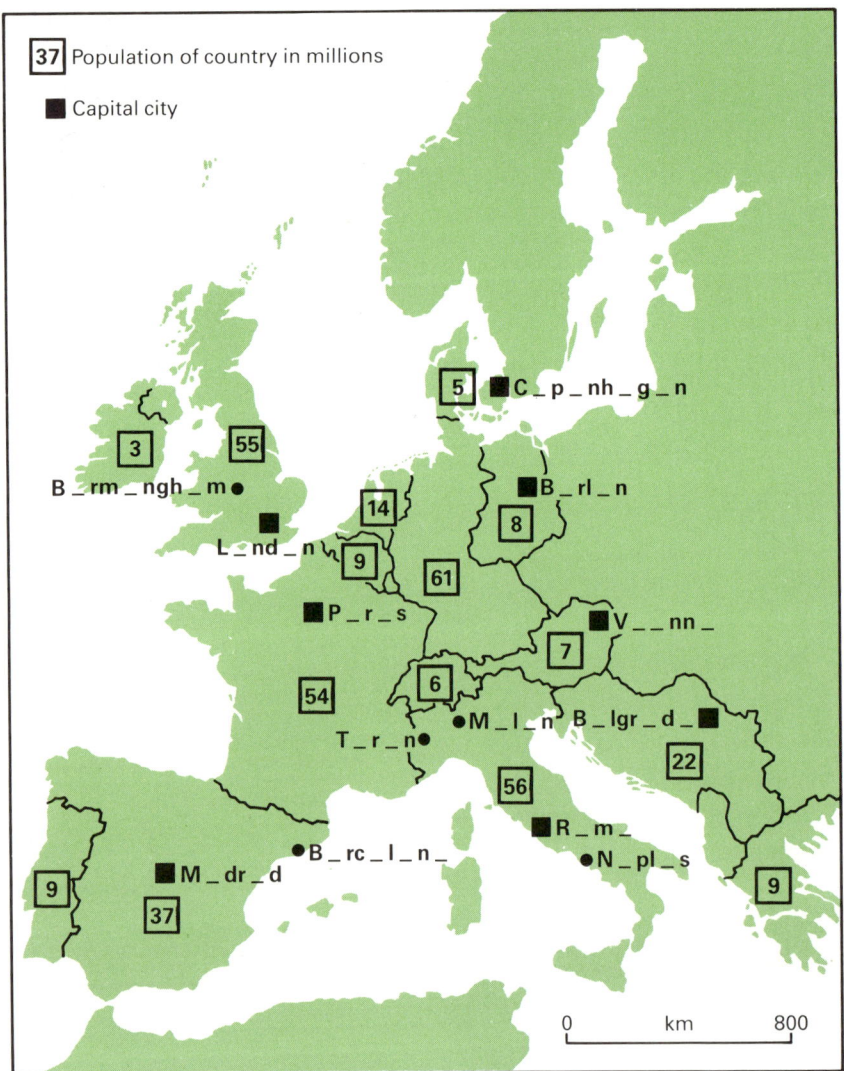

Figure 1   *Europe's millionaire cities*

Map legend:
- **37** Population of country in millions
- ■ Capital city

Map labels:
- 5 ■ C_p_nh_g_n
- 3
- 55
- B_rm_ngh_m●
- ■ B_rl_n
- 14
- 8
- L_nd_n●
- 9
- 61
- ■ P_r_s
- ■ V__nn_
- 7
- 54
- 6
- ●M_l_n   B_lgr_d_● ■
- T_r_n●
- 22
- 56
- ■ R_m_
- ●B_rc_l_n_
- ●N_pl_s
- 9
- ■ M_dr_d
- 37
- 9
- 0   km   800

Figure 2   *The Pompidou Centre, Paris*

Figure 3   *The CBD of Paris taken from Notre Dame Cathedral*

Some towns grow into cities as more people move there, and more jobs are provided. We call the very biggest cities *millionaire cities* because over one million people live in each of them. Some millionaire cities are also capital cities. We have already seen that a capital city is a centre of government and that our government meets in the Houses of Parliament, in London.

Cities are special in other ways too. They are places where there are many services, such as cinemas, ice-skating rinks and museums. They usually have a cathedral and often a university. As so many people live in a city, there are always enough customers to keep these places open. If a cinema seats 200 people, for example, there has to be a lot of people living nearby to fill it every night of the week.

Things to do

1 In Figure 1 all the vowels (a, e, i, o, u) have been left out of the names of the millionaire cities. Use an atlas to write out a list of the complete names. Remember to give your list a title.

Homework ideas

1 Ask four or five adults (your parents, friends or neighbours) the following questions.
   (a) Where do you usually buy bread?
   (b) Where do you usually go to the bank?
   (c) Where would you go to buy large electrical goods, like a fridge?
   (d) Where do you go to the cinema?
2 Put all the results together, and draw some graphs to show what your class found out. Do people in your area travel further for more expensive goods?

2 Look at the map of millionaire cities in Europe and notice the boxes showing the number of people living in each country. Can you name the country (or countries) described in each of these statements?

There are more millionaire cities here than in any other country in Europe.

This country has the highest population, but no millionaire cities.

There are four countries where the only millionaire city is also the capital.

This country has two millionaire cities, one is the capital, the other is a port.

3 Look at the photographs of Paris (Figures 2, 3 and 4). Write a list of the services Paris offers which you can see in the photographs. Can you add some more things to your list which you think there are in cities, but not in towns or villages?

Figure 4   The National Assembly Building, Paris

Summary

Read this interview with Mrs X from Walkington and look at the map of the area where she lives (Figure 5).

Interviewer: 'Where do you go to buy a loaf of bread?'
Mrs X: 'I just pop round to the local shop in the village. It's so convenient because it's only a five minute walk from here, and they have groceries there as well as a post office counter.'
Interviewer: 'Can you buy fresh meat and fish there?'
Mrs X: 'No. I have to go into Beverley for that. I only go there once a week as I have to catch the bus.'
Interviewer: 'Where do you go if you want to buy something more expensive, like a carpet?'
Mrs X: 'Well we have to go to York or Hull to get the best choice. We don't go there very often, perhaps once a month on a Saturday. When we do go, we take the car and make a day of it.'

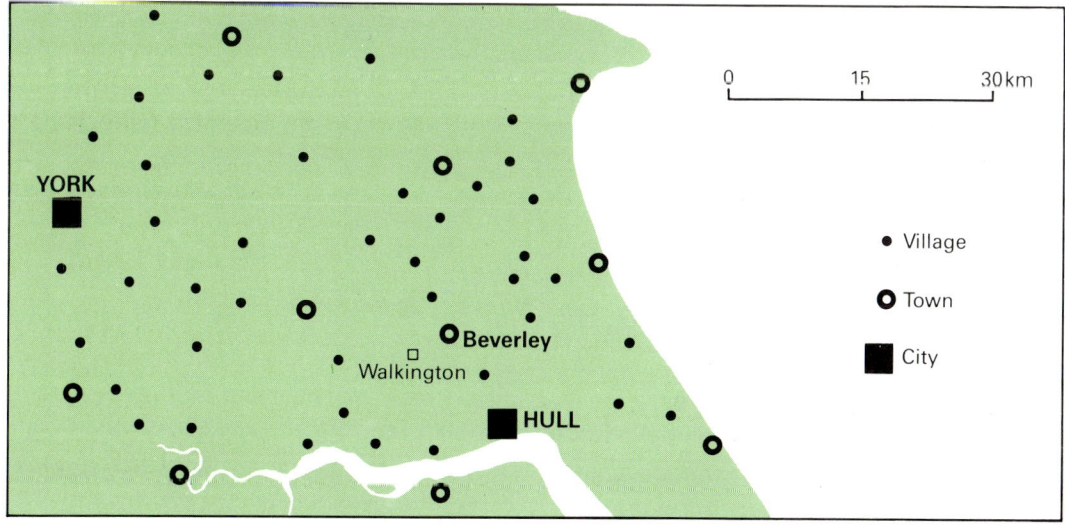

Figure 5   Settlements in East Yorkshire

If you have understood the work on villages, towns and cities you should be able to answer these questions now.

1 What sort of services does a village offer?
2 Why are there many villages in the area shown in Figure 5?
3 What sort of things does a town provide which a village doesn't?
4 Why is Mrs X happy to travel a long way to a city?
5 Why are cities further apart than either towns or villages?

32

The population of a city

Cities have a very mixed population. There are people of all ages and of different races. Some people are rich, others are poor, and between them they do many different jobs. The city of Leeds shows some of this variety. Figure 1 shows richer and poorer areas of the city. In the richer areas, most people own a car and their own home. The houses are usually large. In the poorer areas, fewer people own cars, the houses are smaller and people are more likely to rent them. As you can see large areas of Leeds are in between these two extremes.

Figure 2 shows where most immigrants in Leeds live. These are people who have moved to Britain to find work. You will see that they mainly live in a few wards of Leeds, mostly near the centre of the town.

Figure 3   An inner city shopping street

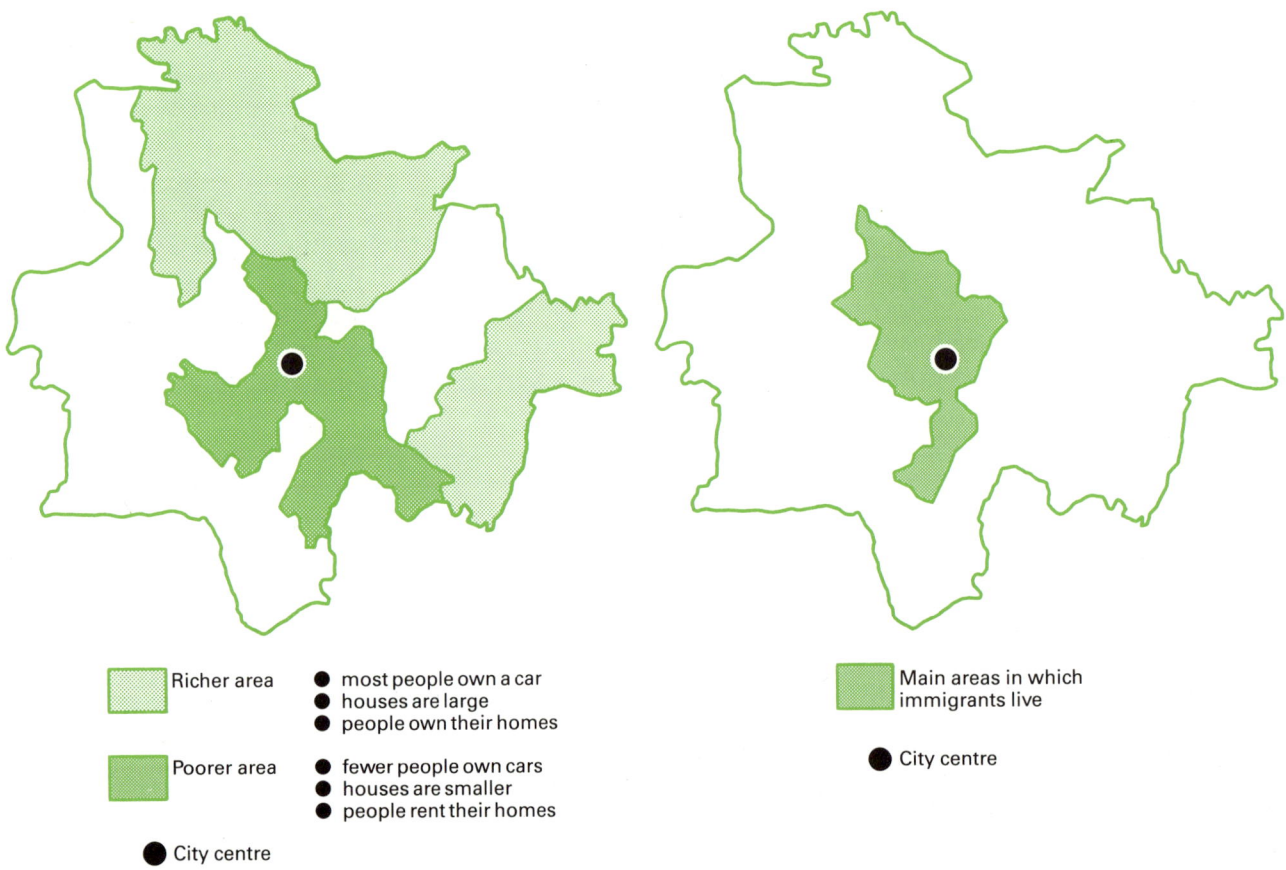

| | Richer area | ● most people own a car
● houses are large
● people own their homes |

| | Poorer area | ● fewer people own cars
● houses are smaller
● people rent their homes |

● City centre

| | Main areas in which immigrants live |

● City centre

Figure 1   A map to show differences in wealth in Leeds

Figure 2   A map to show the areas of Leeds in which most immigrants live

Things to do

1 Draw a map showing the age of the people in Leeds. Table 1 tells you the age of people in each ward. Make a careful tracing of the map of Leeds' wards (Figure 4). Colour in each ward using the key given. For example ward number 1 has people of all ages living in it so it is in Group B. You should colour it orange.

2 Are there more old people near the centre of Leeds or on the edge of the city?

3 In what parts of Leeds are there many young children?
4 Read the descriptions of families living in Leeds (Figure 5). On the map there are four places labelled A, B, C and D. Decide which place each family might live in. Write down your suggestion and give a reason for it.

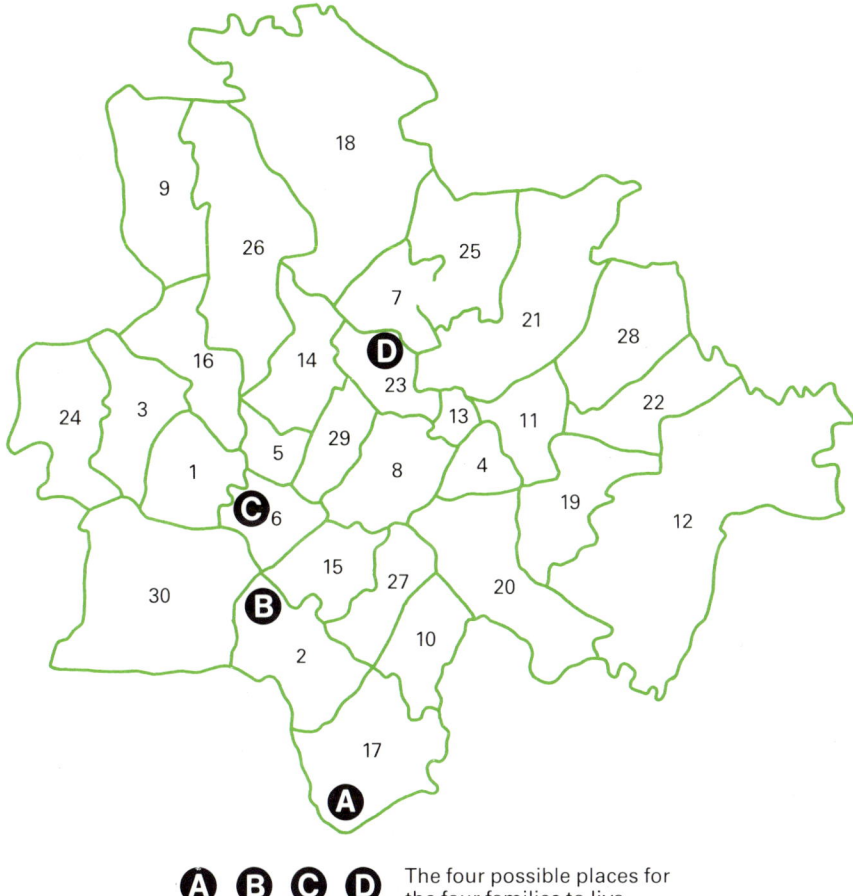

A B C D   The four possible places for the four families to live

Figure 4   *A map to show the wards of Leeds*

Definition

What is a ward? Cities are divided into wards so that local elections can take place. There are several candidates in each ward, and the people living there choose which candidate to vote for. So a ward is simply a small area of the town or city.

Family 1
A family of four who have recently arrived from Uganda in Africa. The parents work in clothing factories near the city centre, and they do not own a car. As the family spent most of their savings coming to Britain, they cannot afford a very large house.

Family 2
A couple in their twenties who used to live near the city centre. They have saved up to buy a larger house for when they have children. They have a car, and want somewhere pleasant and open for their children to grow up in.

Family 3
A young couple, one a nurse and the other a student teacher. They are both training in the city centre. They rely on public transport and often go to the cinema and concerts in the city centre.

Family 4
An elderly, retired couple who have only a small income, and no car. They need to be near shops, but want to live in as quiet an area as possible.

Figure 5

Homework ideas

Write a list of some things that might help you to tell if an area of a city is rich or poor. For example, you could see if the gardens are large or small, or how many cars are parked in the area. Try to think of some other things to look for, and write them in your book.

33 Land use in a city

In this unit we are going to see if you can plan the layout of a city using the base map given here (Figure 1). There are seven different types of land use which have been suggested (Figure 2). Read each description carefully. Each type of land use needs a different size area of land and has a different amount of money to spend. You have to decide where to build each particular land use.

Things to do

1 (a) You will need a tracing of the base map and seven different colours, one for each land use. When you have decided where to build each land use, colour in the squares on your tracing. Make sure your finished map has a title and a key.

(b) When you have done this you might have some space left in the city. What could it be used for? Colour it with an eighth colour and add it to the key.

(c) When you have finished, compare your map with others in the class. Do you see any similarities between them?

Homework ideas

1 Visit a shopping centre near you, either the local shops or part of the town or city centre. Make a list of the shops you find there, noting down each type of shop. Compare lists with the rest of the class.

2 Can you find any differences between the shops found in small shopping centres and those found in the town centre?

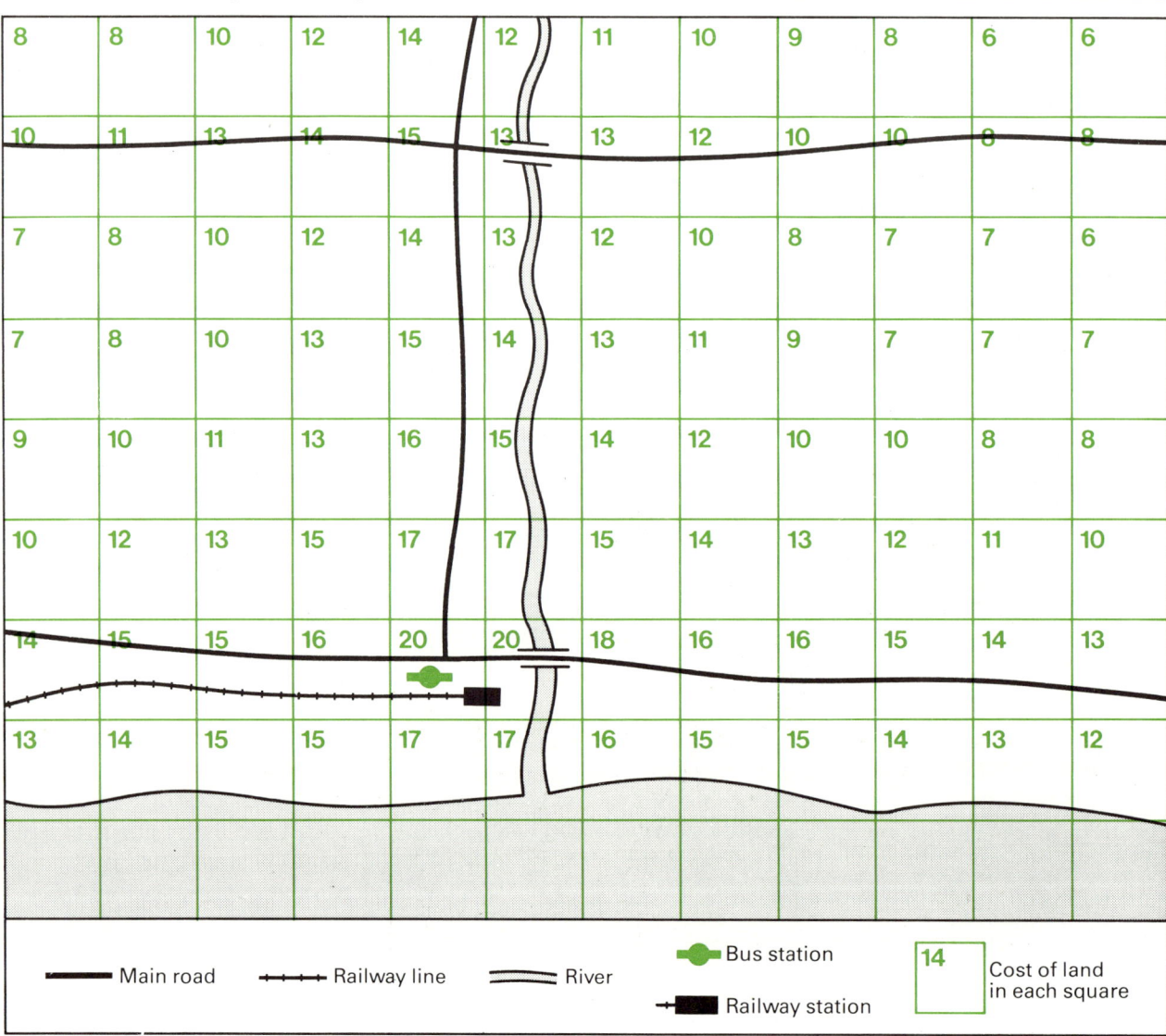

| Main road | Railway line | River | Bus station | 14 Cost of land in each square |
| Railway station | | | | |

Figure 1 Base map to use when planning the land use in a city

74

Department stores and large shops

These need to be central and easy to reach so that as many people as possible will be able to travel to them. Their profits are large, so they can afford a high rent.
Build 3 squares, costing up to 60 units altogether.

Offices

Offices also have to be central so that workers can reach them easily. They also like to be close to one another and to banks. They can afford land costing about 18 units.
Building 5 squares, costing up to 90 units altogether.

Industry

Industry needs to be close to roads, railways and perhaps a river. It needs large areas of land and can afford a reasonable price, about 17 units per square.
Build 12 squares, costing up to 200 units altogether.

Warehouses, large superstores and do-it-yourself stores

All of these use large areas of land, especially for car-parking, so they cannot afford the most expensive land. They also need to be near main roads so that people can reach them easily.
Build 3 squares, costing up to 40 units altogether, about 13 units per square.

Small shops

These need to be easy to reach and close to the people who use them everyday. Some will be built near the city centre.
Build 10 squares, costing up to 140 units altogether.

Flats

Some housing is built for people to live near the city centre in tall blocks of flats. These can be built on quite expensive land because a lot of people can live in a small area.
Build 3 squares, costing up to 45 units altogether.

Houses

Houses will cover most of the city. They have to be built on the cheapest land because they use up such a lot of space.
Build 40 squares, costing up to 400 units altogether.

Figure 2   Seven types of land use to be located in the city. It is a good idea to read through these descriptions before you begin question 1.

2 Now look at the land use plan for the city of Paris (Figure 3). Write out these sentences, filling in the blanks.
   (a) _____ covers most of the land in the city.
   (b) Much of the industry has been built beside the _____ _____.
   (c) Government offices and the _____ buildings are near the centre of the city.
   (d) Some _____ and _____ areas have been left for recreation in the city.

3 Why are offices near to the city centre of Paris?

4 Why are the industries only found in certain places in cities, such as besides rivers or railway lines.

5 Why is it a good idea to leave some open space in a city?

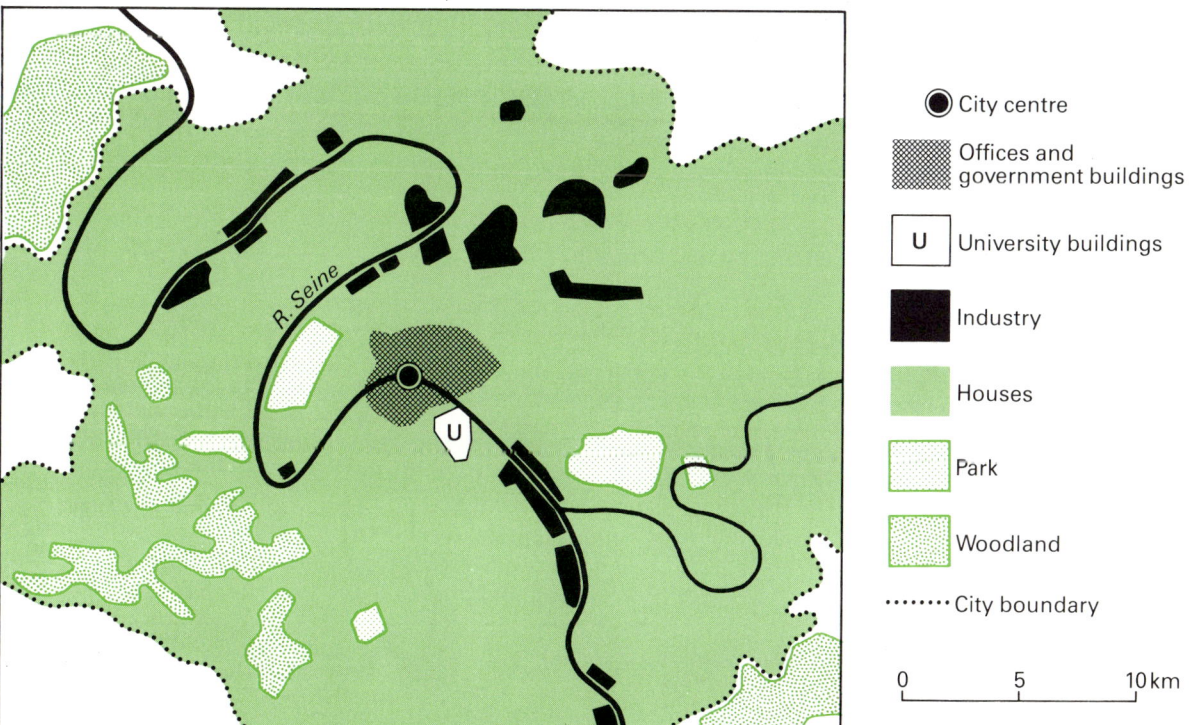

● City centre

▨ Offices and government buildings

U University buildings

■ Industry

 Houses

 Park

 Woodland

······ City boundary

0   5   10 km

Figure 3   A map to show the land use in the city of Paris

34 The CBD

The Central Business District (or CBD) is the busiest part of a town or city. The name of the district tells you that it is in the *centre* of the town, and that it is where most businesses are found. Figure 1 shows the CBD of an English city. The three small maps (Figures 2, 3 and 4) show detailed plans of parts of the CBD, and name the actual buildings found in each street. By working through these exercises you will be able to find out what is special about the Central Business District.

Figure 1   Part of the Central Business District of a British city

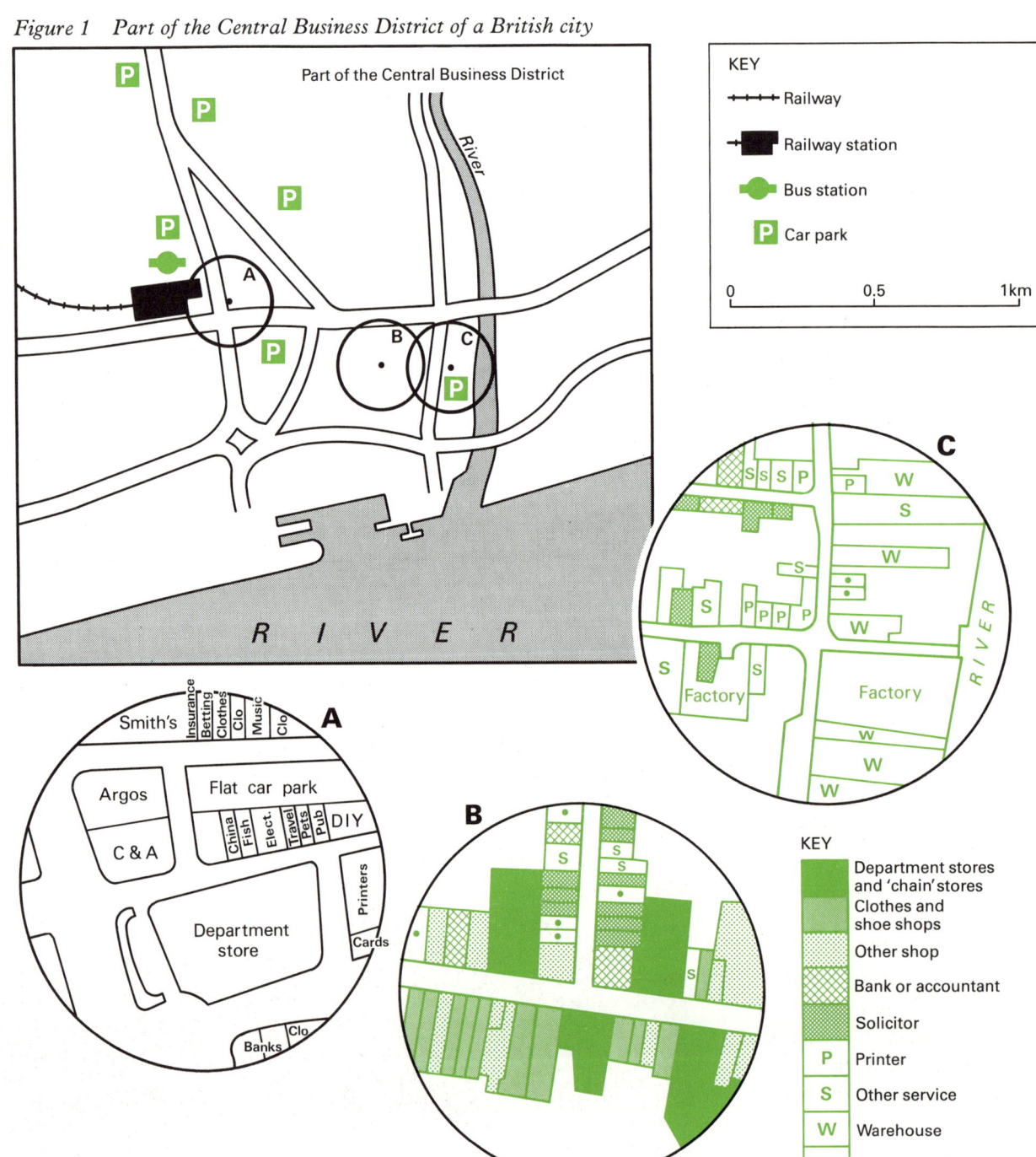

KEY

	Railway
	Railway station
	Bus station
P	Car park

0   0.5   1km

KEY

	Department stores and 'chain' stores
	Clothes and shoe shops
	Other shop
	Bank or accountant
	Solicitor
P	Printer
S	Other service
W	Warehouse
•	Empty building

Figures 2, 3 and 4 (maps A, B and C) Detailed land use plans of three parts of the CBD

Figure 5 *Wide pavements are a feature of the main shopping streets of the CBD*

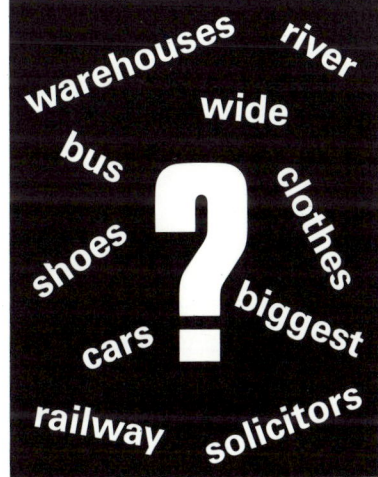

Figure 6 *Words you will need to answer question 6*

Homework ideas

1 Look up in the Yellow Pages of the local telephone directory the addresses of the solicitors in your town or city. Write down the street names, and count how many solicitors are found in each street.

2 Then do the same thing for shoeshops and for banks. Are these businesses found in certain streets in the centre? Which of the three businesses is found in the busiest part of the town? You might be able to visit the streets you have listed to see how busy they are.

Things to do

1 Trace Figure 2 and colour in the shop types using the key given. (To answer questions 2 and 3, you need to look at Figure 1. Look carefully at the scale of the map before you start.)

2 Measure the distance in kilometres from the centre of each circular area to the bus station.

3 How many car parks are there less than 0.5 km from the centre of each circular area?

4 Count the number of different shops or buildings inside Figures 2, 3 and 4.

5 Copy out Table 1, and put your answers to the above questions in the spaces.

Table 1

	Area A	Area B	Area C
Distance from bus station			
Number of car parks within 0.5 km			
Number of buildings			
Roads	Wide	Pedestrianised	Narrow
Size of buildings	Mainly large	Medium	Small

6 Write out this paragraph, filling in the spaces. Use all the information in the maps, photographs and Figure 6 to help you.

The busiest part of the CBD is where the _____ shops are found. It is close to the _____ and _____ stations, and has several car-parks nearby. Here the roads and pavements are _____ to cope with all the people. Part of the CBD has been pedestrianised, which means it is closed to _____. Here the shops are smaller and they sell a variety of goods including _____ and _____. Off the main street is an older side-street in which many _____ offices are found. They do not need to attract passing customers as the other shops do. In the oldest part of the CBD, near the _____, there are more empty and run-down buildings. There is also some industry, such as printing, mixed with _____ and offices.

7 Where in the CBD do you think the land is most expensive?

8 Do you think the buildings would be the same height all over the CBD? If not, where would they be tallest?

Figure 7 *A pedestrian precinct*

35 Housing areas in a city

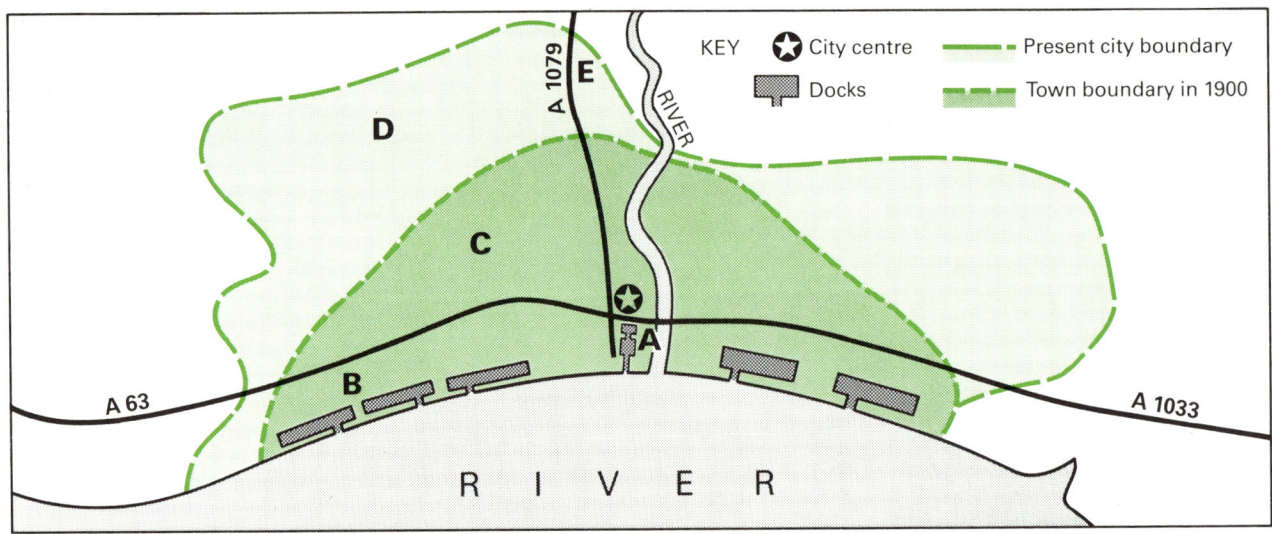

Figure 1   Sketch map showing the layout of the city and the position of the five areas identified

Things to do

All the information in this unit is about a British city which is also a port. It has several different sorts of housing areas as you can see. You need to study the maps (Figures 1 and 2), the photographs (Figure 3), and the written descriptions (Figure 4) very carefully. The aim is to match the information for each area. Then you can copy and fill in a large table (like Table 1) in your book.

Homework ideas

Find some different types of houses near where you live or near your school. Sketch three or four different types of houses and label your drawings. Try to find out how old each house is. You could draw your own house too.

Table 1

Location	Street plan	Photograph	Description
A			
B			
C			
D			
E			

Figure 2   Street plans of the five areas of the city

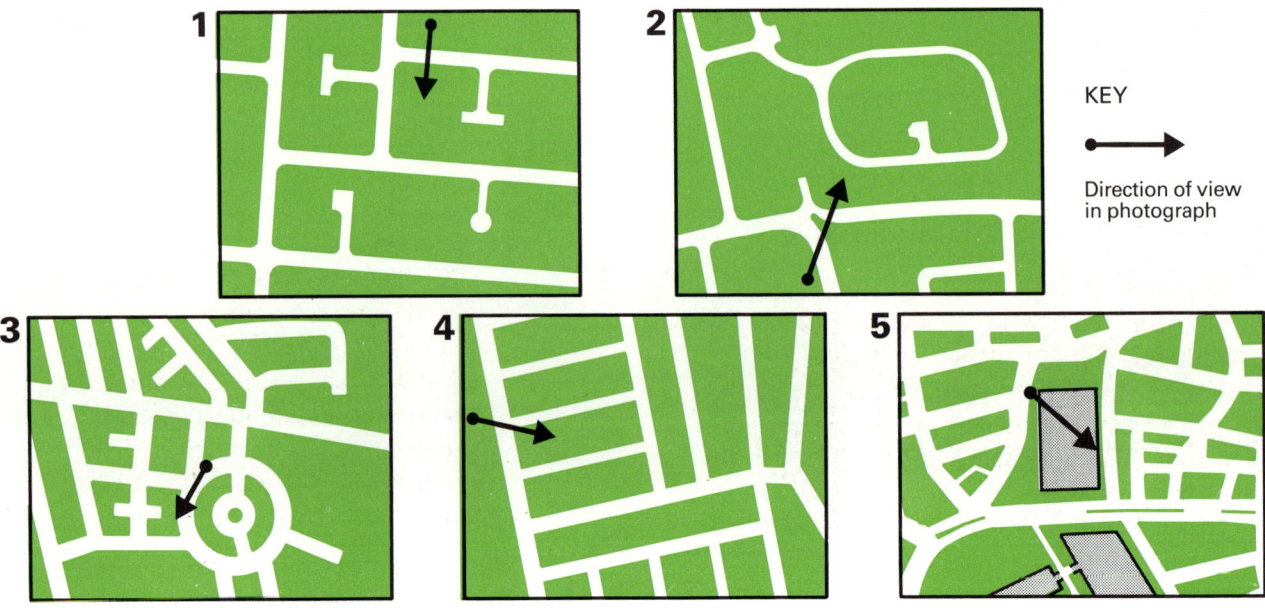

KEY

Direction of view in photograph

I

V Recently city centre areas have been redeveloped and modern housing is often found replacing old industries or waste land. This housing is often tightly packed as the cost of the land is high, and few houses have gardens.

II

W In the 1930s, council estates were built near to the outskirts of the town. These were planned carefully to give each house a garden, and a more interesting street pattern. People probably moved here from crowded conditions nearer to the city centre.

III

X These houses were built in the late nineteenth century, at what was then the edge of the town. The avenues were laid out carefully with wide pavements and fountains at some of the crossroads. As the houses were built by different people, there is a variety of styles.

IV

Y Most recent housing has been built at the edge of the city where there is still some open space. Houses are often built on estates where there is one entry road leading into the estate, and a number of closes or cul-de-sacs leading off it.

V

Z Closely-packed terraced housing was built in the 1800s for workers in the factories and docks. No gardens were laid out as they would take up too much room, and there were no garages because people didn't have cars. The streets and pavements were narrow, again to leave more room for houses.

Figure 3   Photographs of the housing in the five areas

Figure 4   A description of the housing in each of the five areas

36 Changes in the city

Figure 1   Two British stamps issued in 1984 with the theme 'urban renewal'

The centres of cites have been changing rapidly in recent years. A good reminder of this is a set of stamps issued in 1984 with the title 'Urban renewal' (Figure 1). *Urban renewal* means replacement and improvement of city centre areas. As you already know, many inner parts of cities are derelict. Planners have sometimes tried to improve the existing buildings, for instance by adding bathrooms to houses that were built without one. In other cases, whole areas of old housing have been demolished and new buildings put in their place. This has happened in the area shown on the two plans (Figures 2 and 3). Figure 2 shows the original houses and Figure 3 shows the newly-built replacements. You can recognise some names which are the same on both maps, but even the street layout has changed. The photographs of 'before' and 'after' will help you to imagine the differences more clearly (Figures 4 and 5).

Figures 2, 3, 4 and 5   An inner city area before and after redevelopment

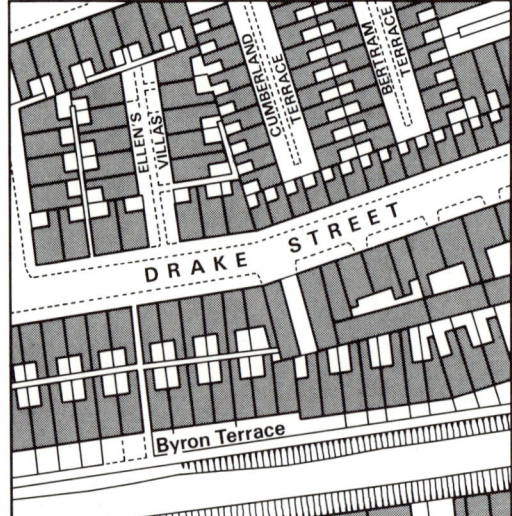

Figure 2

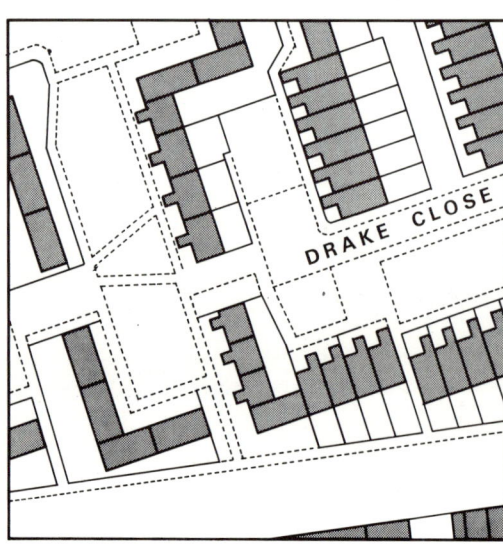

Figure 3

Figure 4

Figure 5

Some cities have put the existing buildings to new uses. Bristol's dockland is a good example. The old docks are in the city centre, but are hardly used for the shipping trade today. Ships are now too large to get into the old docks. Instead the docks are used for sailing and windsurfing, and the warehouses and buildings nearby are used for an art gallery, a museum, and various shops. These are only a few of the uses of the old buildings. New houses have also been built and some of them are behind the front wall of an old warehouse. These changes have made the city centre a much more attractive place. This may also mean that people will take better care of it.

Things to do

1 Look carefully at the two street plans. Count the number of houses you can see on each plan. Which plan has most houses?
2 Write two headings in your book—**Before** and **After**. Find as many differences as you can between the two plans and list them in your table. For example, you could count the number of houses, look at the size of the gardens and gauge the width of the roads and pavements. The photographs will help to give you some more differences.
3 Sometimes high-rise blocks of flats are built when old houses are demolished. Why might high-rise flats be better than the new houses you have been looking at. Are there any problems with living in high-rise flats?

Homework ideas

Imagine that you are an older person who has lived for many years in a street of old houses near the city centre. You have just found out that your street is to be demolished and you will have to move to a new flat. Write a letter to the local paper telling them what you think of this idea. You may be pleased with the idea or you may be unhappy about it. Try to give as many reasons as possible for your opinion.

Summary

In the last few units you have looked in detail at the way cities are organised. Now this is your chance to plan the redevelopment of an inner city area. Figure 6 shows part of a city where there are old houses, some derelict factory and warehouse buildings and quite a lot of empty land. A new dual-carriageway ring road is to be built across the area. Decide what new building you would do, and what changes you would make to the land use. Lay a piece of tracing paper over Figure 6 and trace off the line of the new road. You should also trace the river, the railway, and existing main roads, because these things can't be moved. Then draw and label the new buildings and land uses that you decide on. Some suggestions for new land uses have been made in this unit, but you can try to think of some others on your own or working with a partner.

Figure 6   Base map to use when planning inner city redevelopment

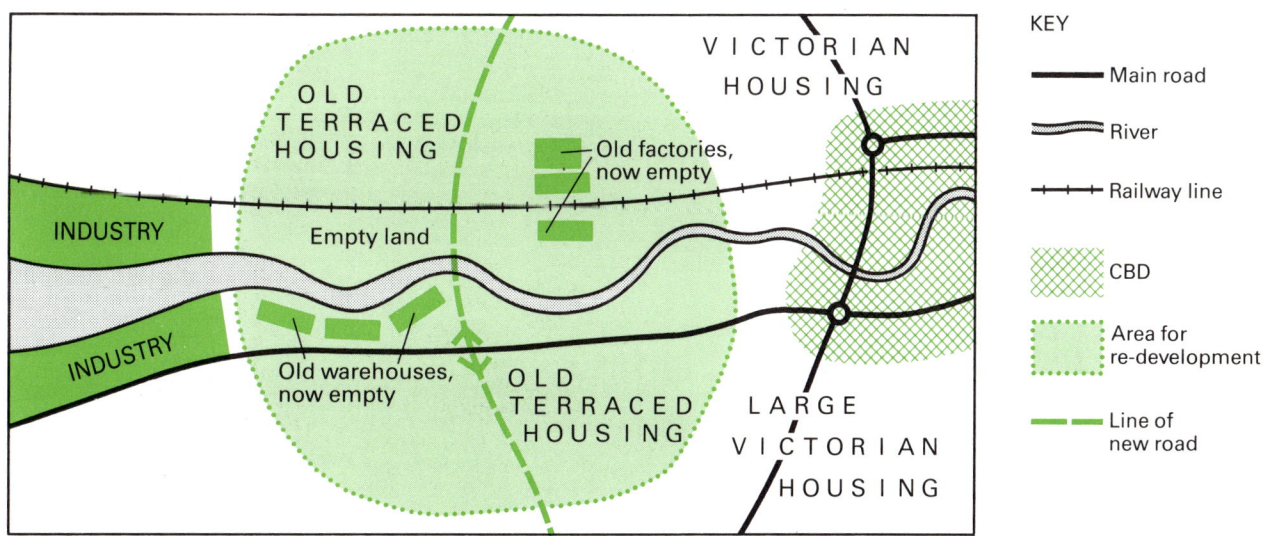

81

37 What is industry?

What does the word *industry* really mean? If we were asked to explain its meaning we would probably think of factories or places where things are made. In fact, *industry* can be used to describe any sort of work which is done in order to make a profit. So, if we made a list of people involved in industry, we could include anyone who works for a living, for example, bus drivers, factory workers, teachers, farm labourers or bank clerks (Figure 1).

In the next few units we shall be looking at the sort of industry in which the workers put together various materials to make something, a process or operation we call *manufacturing*.

It is easy to understand what is meant by manufacturing industry if we look at a simple example. Figure 2 shows the stages in the making or manufacturing of a T-shirt. You can see that certain basic things are required to make the shirt. Materials (fabric and thread) and equipment (scissors and measuring tape) will certainly be needed. Electricity may be used to provide power for a sewing machine. It may be necessary to pay for these things. A person must be able to spend time sewing the shirt. We call all these things *inputs* because they are put into making the shirt.

The next stage is the combination of the inputs to produce the *finished product*—in this case the T-shirt. The fabric is cut out and sewn-up and any pieces of waste material thrown away. We call the completed T-shirt and waste material the *outputs*, ie, those things which come out at the end of the process.

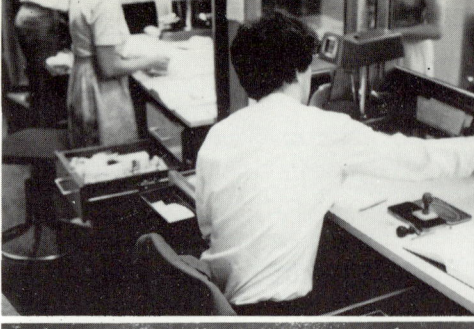

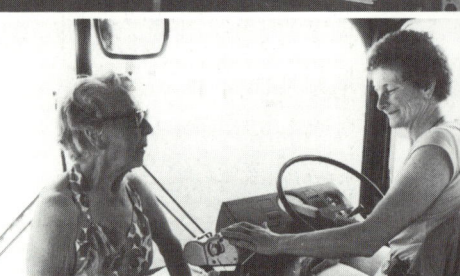

Figure 1   People employed in different jobs

Figure 2   The stages in the manufacturing of a T-shirt

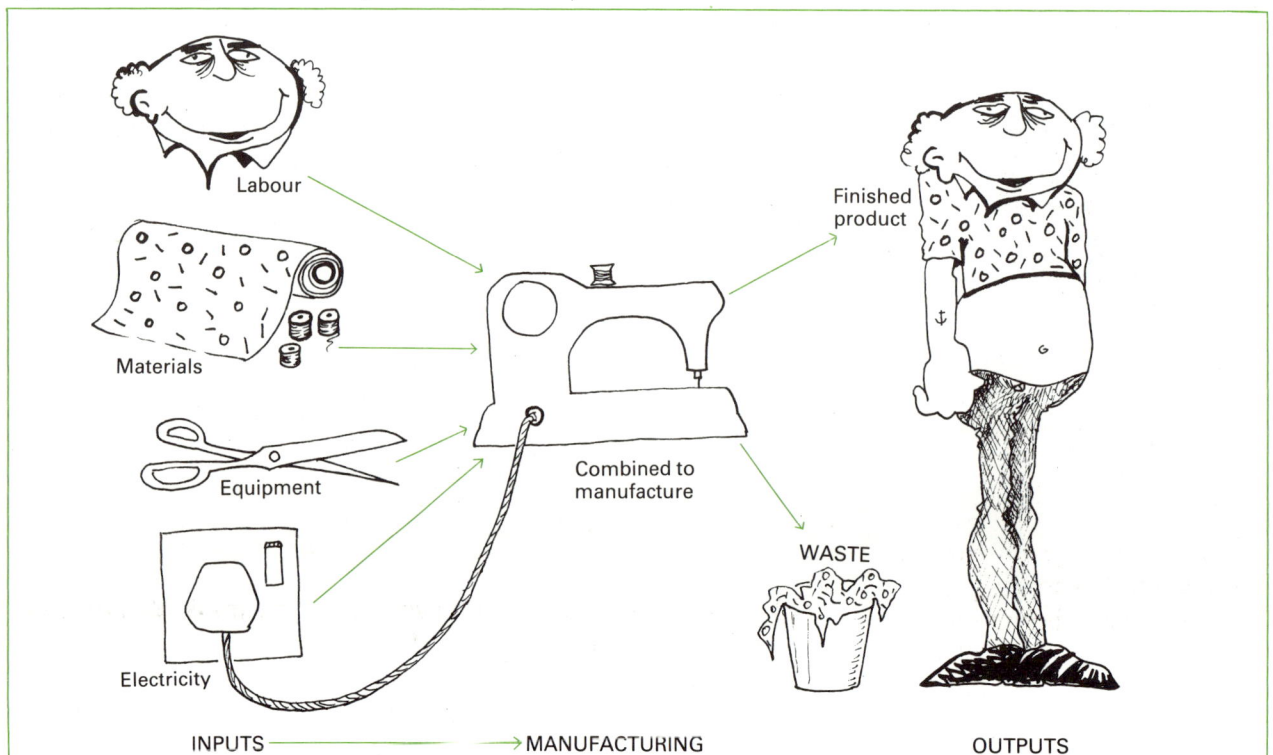

Labour

Materials

Equipment

Electricity

Combined to manufacture

Finished product

WASTE

INPUTS ⟶ MANUFACTURING   OUTPUTS

82

We can now carry the idea of inputs and outputs a step further and see how it can be applied to a real factory. Look at Figure 3 which shows the process of manufacturing at the Wedgwood Factory in Stoke-on-Trent which makes plates, jugs, dishes etc.

INPUTS

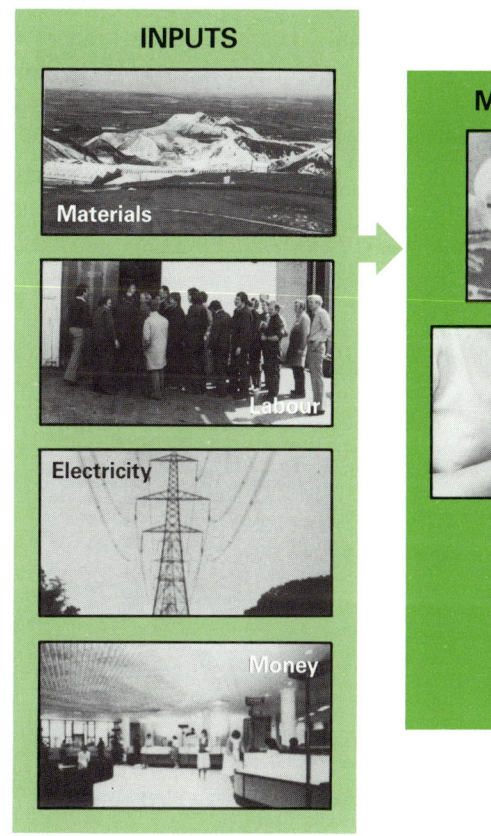

MANUFACTURING PROCESS

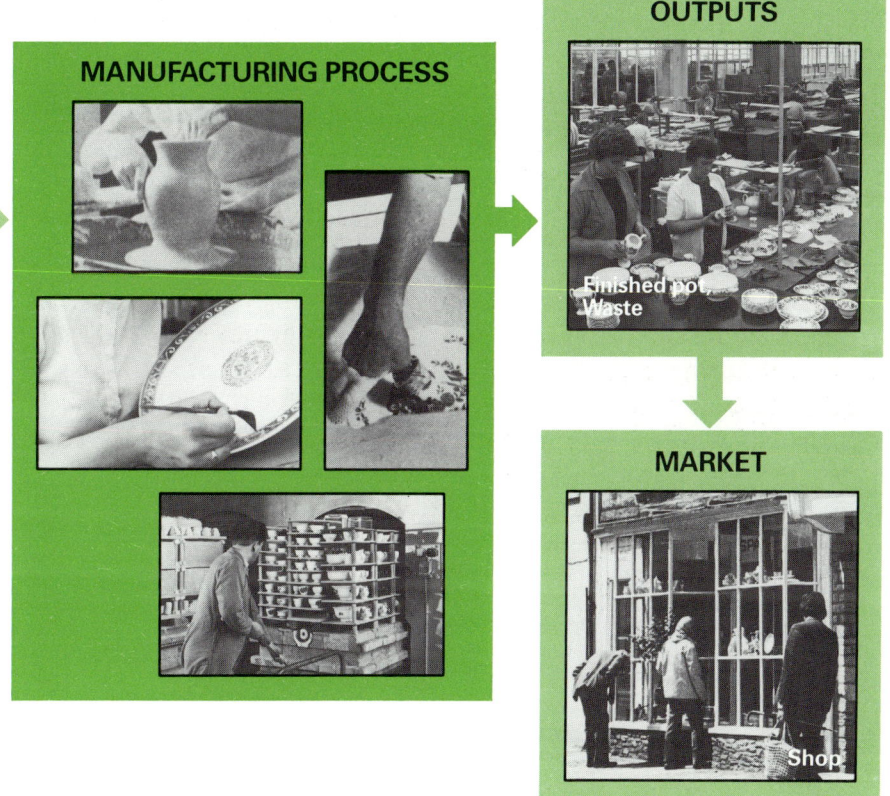

OUTPUTS

MARKET

Figure 3   The process of manufacturing at the Wedgwood factory

Things to do

1 Use Figure 3 to explain in your own words all the steps or stages involved in manufacturing a plate.

2 Mr Ivor Lotocash has decided to set up a factory in Hometown to manufacture cakes. He has bought the building that will house the business but is not sure what else he will need before he can manufacture the product. The materials required to make cakes are eggs, butter, and flour and Mr Lotocash can sell all of his finished products in Hometown.

(a) Make a copy of the Lotocash factory shown in Figure 4.

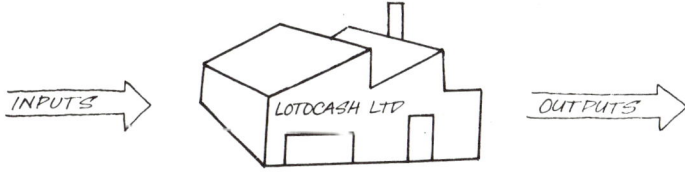

Figure 4   The Lotocash factory

(b) Label your diagram with everything you think Mr Lotocash will need as inputs into his factory.
(c) Show the outputs he will produce.
(d) Draw a road leading to the factory so that he can transport his materials and finished products away.

Homework ideas

Produce a diagram similar to Figure 1, showing the inputs, manufacturing and outputs for an item of your choice, for example, a chair, a shoe or a bag.

38 Manufacturing cars

One very important type of manufacturing industry is car production. The making of cars takes place on an *assembly line* where large numbers of parts, which have been manufactured in other factories, are put together or assembled to make a car. These parts are called *components*. One example is the windscreen. Each component is manufactured from raw materials at another factory; the material used to make windscreens is glass.

Figure 3   *The Metro factory at Longbridge, Birmingham*

Figure 1

Figure 4   *The Metro production line*

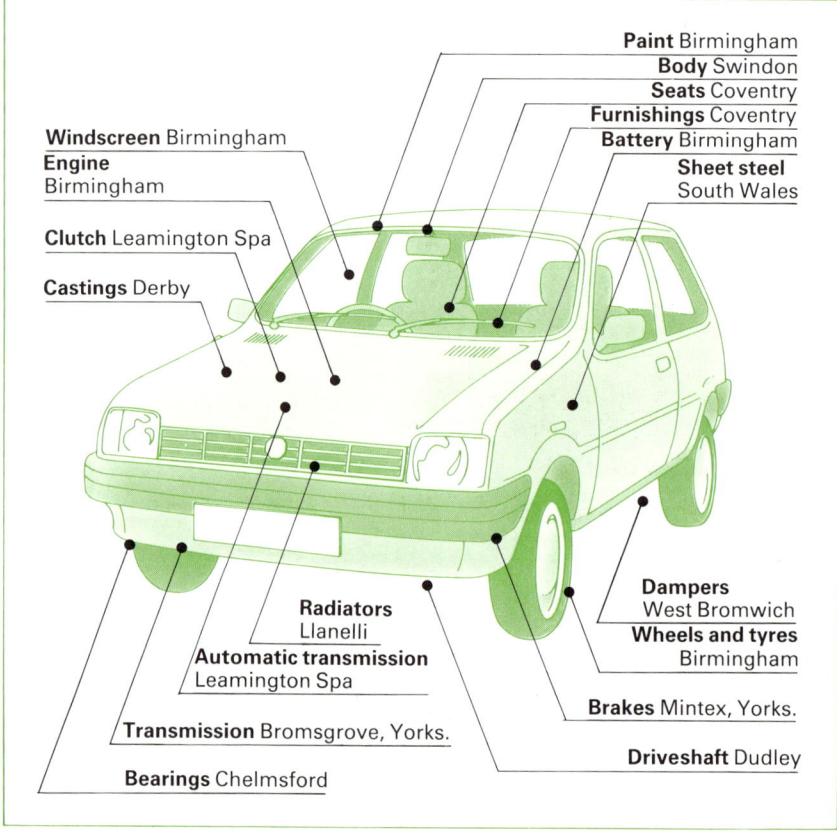

Figure 2   *Places where components for the Metro car are made*

Things to do

1 On an outline map of the British Isles like Figure 1, label all the places where components for the Metro car are made, as shown in Figure 2.

2 Look at the completed map. What area of the country do you think would be the best place for a car assembly plant to be sited? Why?

3 Metros are manufactured in Birmingham. Mark this place on your map.
   (a) Which component is the furthest away from Birmingham?
   (b) How far does it have to travel to get to the Metro assembly plant?

All manufacturing industry needs to make a profit. Profit is the money left over from the sale of the finished product after all the costs or bills have been paid.

Homework ideas

Imagine you work on an assembly line. What do you think you might not like about the job? Draw a cartoon explaining how you feel about your work.

Figure 7 *Transporting goods on a motorway*

Homework ideas

See if you can find out information about a factory in your area using what you have learnt in the last two units.

4 Look at Figure 5. Describe what happens on a car assembly line.

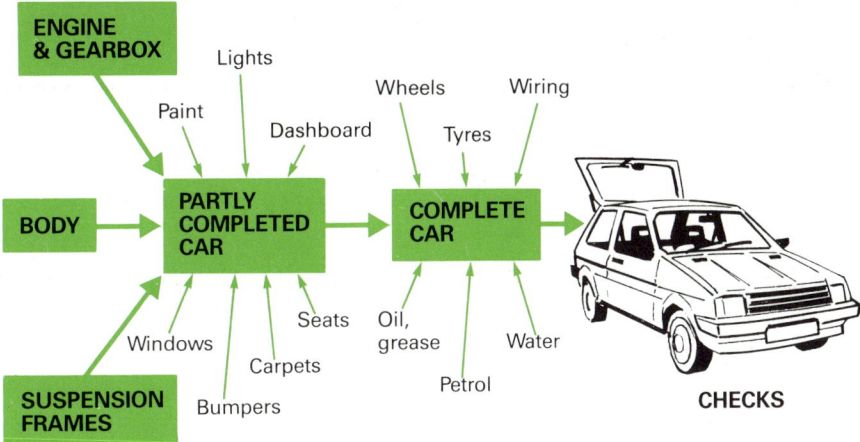

Figure 5 *Manufacturing on an assembly line*

5 Look at Figure 6. Copy the diagram and put the correct word from the following list next to its symbols.

Materials, gas, machinery, electricty, management, water and labour.

Figure 6 *The costs of manufacturing*

All the things that you have labelled on your diagram must be paid for by the owner of the factory. They can be called the *processing costs* because they are the bills that must be paid in order to make the product.

There are two other bills to pay when manufacturing. It costs money to transport materials or components to the factory and also to transport the finished product to where it will be sold—the *market*.

Look at Figure 6, what do we call these two costs?

Things to do

6 Imagine you own a factory that manufactures pencils. What are the raw materials you use?

7 The processing costs will probably be the same wherever you decide to build your factory. How will the other costs vary?

8 Suggest two ways that you could increase your profit by reducing your costs.

9 Draw a diagram showing the inputs and outputs of your factory. Show also the transport you use to collect your raw materials and to distribute your finished products.

39 Where is industry?

When the owners of a business decide to build a new factory, there are a number of things they must think about before deciding where the factory will be. Look at Figure 1.

A We know that the factory will make most profit if it keeps its costs, or bills, as small as possible. To do this, the owners must work out the collection costs, that is to say, the cost of bringing the raw materials to the factory. They will also need to make sure that the factory can be reached easily by road, or perhaps by railway, and to find out how much it would cost to transport the finished product to the market—the distribution costs.

If it costs more money to bring the raw materials to the factory than to carry the finished product to the market, it would make sense for the factory owners to buy land as near as possible to the raw materials.

B A *labour force* living nearby may be important if people with special skills are needed in the factory.

C A *power supply* may be important for certain types of factory. In the making of aluminium, for example, large amounts of electricity are needed, so an aluminium factory will need to be built near its source of power to keep its costs as low as possible.

D The owners will also need to make sure that the area they plan to buy for building on, the *site*, is large and flat enough for the factory.

Homework ideas

Kelly's Directory is a useful book that lists industries in each town.

Try and find out what factories there are in your area and what products they make. You might be able to find out why they chose their location.

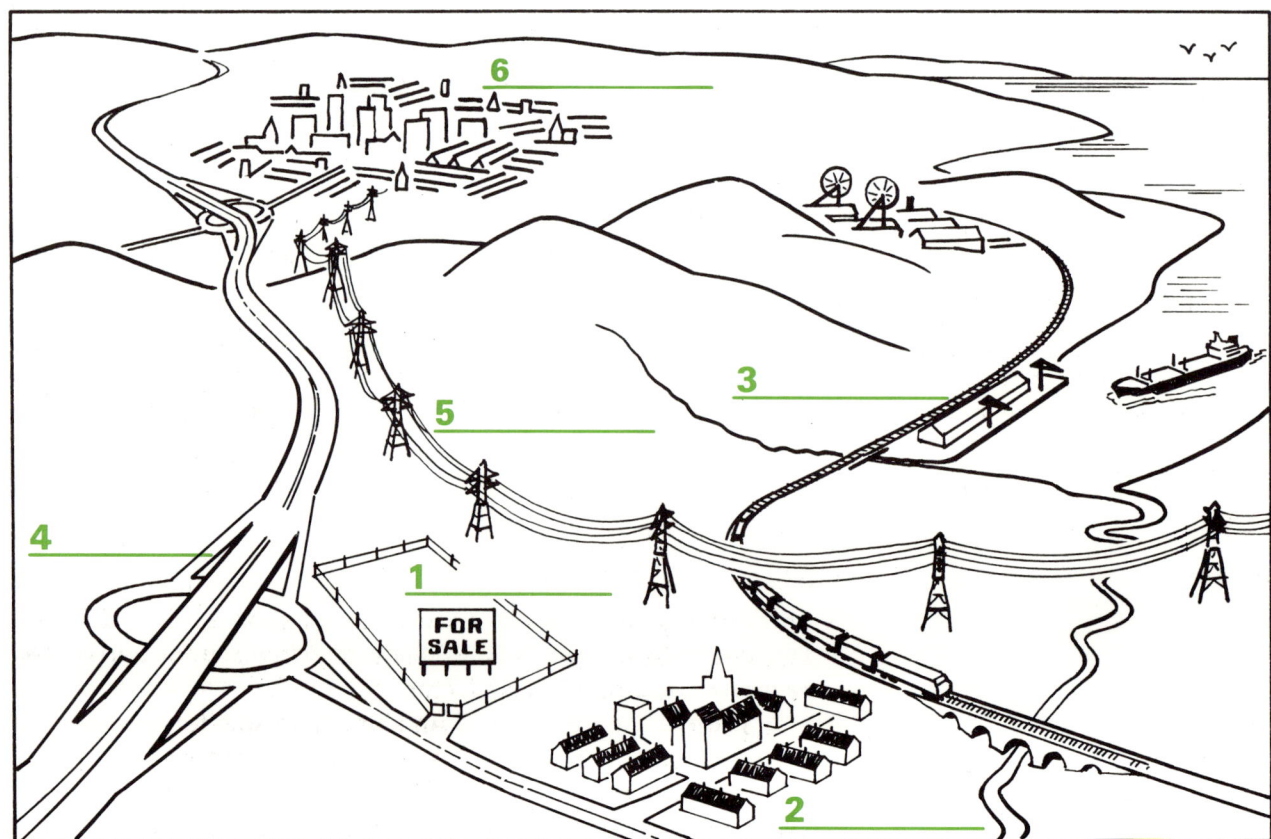

Figure 1   The important things to consider when deciding where to build a new factory

86

Figure 3   Hops: one of the main raw materials used to make beer

Things to do

1 Look at Figure 1 which shows all the different things that are important in deciding where to build a new factory.
   (a) Trace the outline.
   (b) Fill in the missing labels from the list below.
       site, fuel/power, transport for raw materials, market, labour force, transport for finished products

The place that the owners finally decide to build the factory is called its *location*. Sometimes, one or two things will be much more important than the others in deciding where a factory should be located. Raw materials and market are often very important. Look at Figure 2.

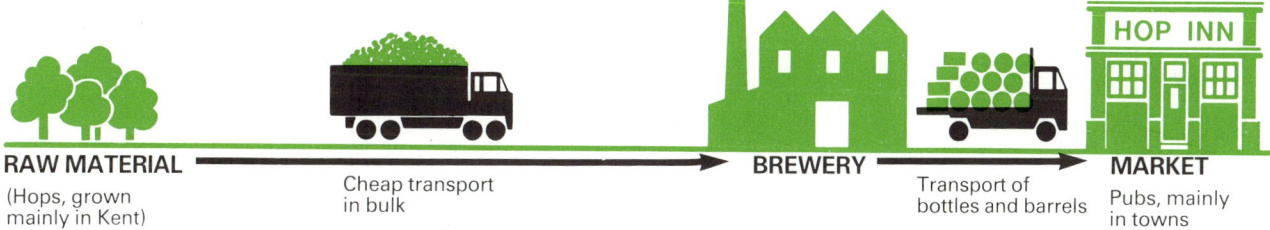

RAW MATERIAL
(Hops, grown mainly in Kent)

Cheap transport in bulk

BREWERY

Transport of bottles and barrels

MARKET
Pubs, mainly in towns

Figure 2   Factors influencing the location of a brewery

The basic raw materials for the brewing industry are hops and water. Since water can be supplied almost anywhere it is not an important factor in deciding where to build a brewery. Beer is much heavier than the hops that are used to make it because water is added in the processing. So, to keep costs as low as possible, brewing takes place near its market, that is to say, in towns.

2 Write down which of the things discussed earlier would be most important if you were choosing a location for the factories in Figure 4. The hints in brackets should help you.

A bakery (A loaf of bread is much bulkier than the flour used to make it. Bread goes stale quickly.)

An iron and steel works (The raw materials are heavy, bulky and usually imported. It is cheaper to transport the lighter finished product.)

A car factory (Large numbers of components are transported from far afield and finished cars are distributed widely so a central location is important.)

An aluminium smelter (Great heat and much power is required to smelt the bulky ore called bauxite which is often imported.)

A woollen cloth factory (Cloth making is a skilled job and it costs about the same amount to transport the raw materials and the finished cloth.)

Figure 4

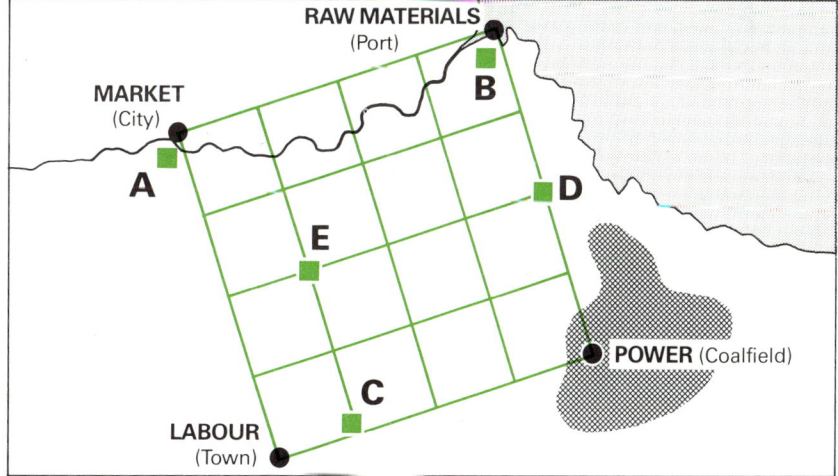

Figure 5   The location of five different factories

3 Look at Figure 5 which shows the location of five different factories labelled, A, B, C, D, and E. Which letter shows the probable location of these factories?
   A bakery   An aluminium smelter
   An iron and steel works   A woollen cloth factory
   A car factory

4 What other things can you think of that may affect the location of a factory?

40 Changing sites for industry

We can now understand what things affect the location of different industries today. However, sometimes the raw materials themselves, or where they can be found, change over a long period of time. This means that the industry using the raw materials may also have to change. A good example of this change in location is that of the iron and steel industry.

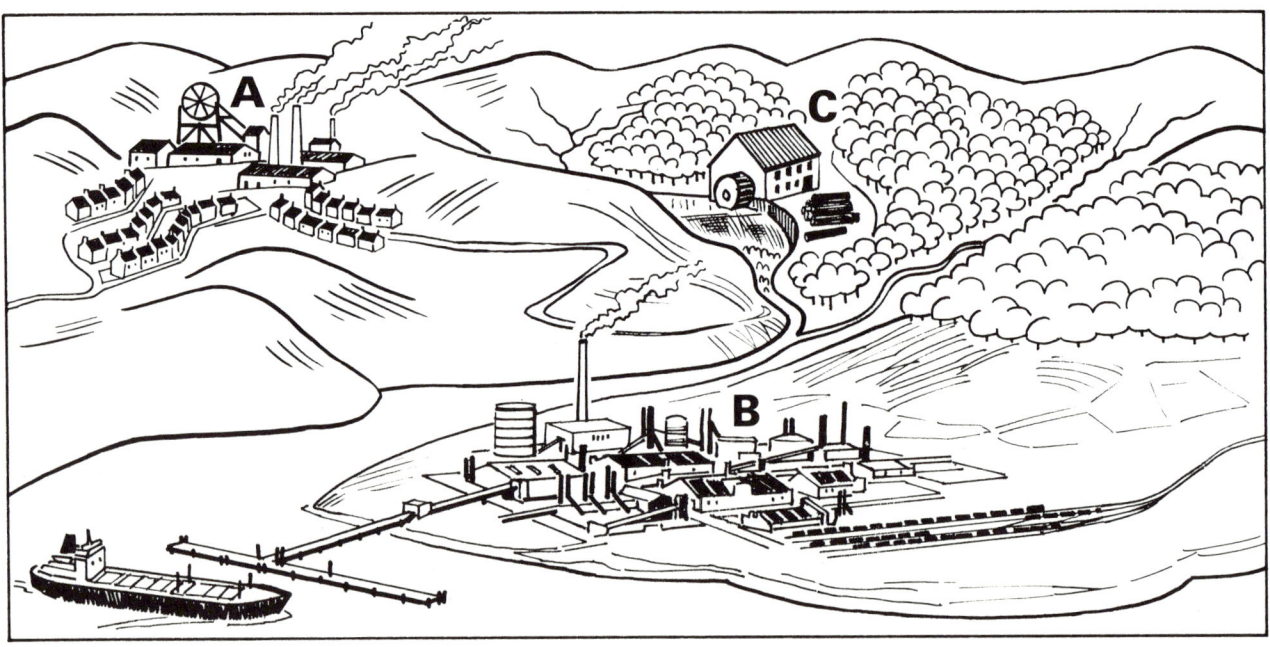

Figure 1   The changing location of the iron and steel industry

Things to do

1 Look at Figure 1 which shows three different locations which the iron and steel industry has chosen over the last 200 years.
2 Now read the following extracts (Figure 2) and decide which location each describes.

Figure 2   Early iron works; iron and steel works in the 1800's; present day steel works at Sheerness

1 Before 1750 the raw materials for producing iron were iron ore and limestone (to remove impurities). Wood was used to make charcoal, which was burnt to produce the heat necessary to smelt the iron ore. Running water was used as the source of power to drive the machinery in the iron works. So, places where iron ore and limestone were found together, with woodland and fast flowing streams nearby, were the ideal locations for the industry at this time. The Forest of Dean is a good example of such an area.

2 By the early part of the nineteenth century, wood was replaced by coal which was turned into coke as a source of power to heat the furnaces. The coalfields became the ideal location for the new iron works. One place where iron ore, limestone and coal were found together was in South Wales.

3 When steel became more important than iron, the local ore was found to be unsuitable and in any case Britain's stocks had almost been exhausted. So, by the twentieth century iron ore had to be imported from abroad. In a modern steel works the iron is processed into sheets of steel in huge factories which require very large areas of flat land. Both of these things mean that the best location for a new steel plant today is on flat land near the coast.

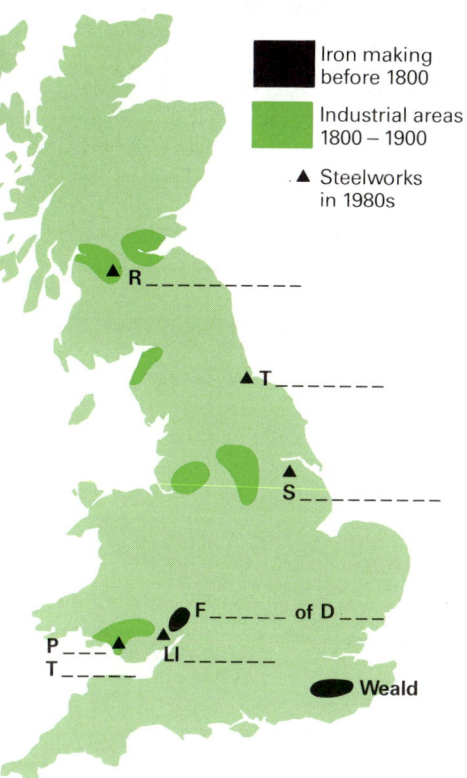

Legend:
- Iron making before 1800
- Industrial areas 1800 – 1900
- ▲ Steelworks in 1980s

▲ R _ _ _ _ _ _ _ _
▲ T _ _ _ _ _ _
▲ S _ _ _ _ _ _ _ _
● F _ _ _ _ _ _ of D _ _ _ _
P _ _ _ _ ▲ ▲ LI _ _ _ _ _ _
T _ _ _ _ _
● Weald

Figure 3   The changing location of the iron and steel industry in the UK

3 Now explain in your own words how the location of the iron and steel industry has changed in the last hundred years.
4 Look at Figure 3 which shows the changing location of the iron and steel industry in the UK. Some of the sites are only labelled with the initials of the place name. Can you find out their full names from an atlas?

Figure 4   Inside a steelworks

Places like Ebbw Vale in South Wales are no longer a good location for the iron and steel industry. However it costs a great deal of money to rebuild factories at a new site and many of the workers who live in the area do not wish to move away. This means that industries remain in the area long after the original reasons for their location there have changed.

5 Imagine that you are the director of a company in Ebbw Vale who is thinking about moving to a new location, perhaps on the coast near Cardiff. Write down why you think it may be better to stay. Use the cartoon (Figure 5) to help you.

CARDIFF HAS BETTER SHOPS, SPORTS AND ENTERTAINMENT FACILITIES

HOUSES COST MORE IN CARDIFF

OUR LABOUR FORCE IN EBBW VALE IS HARD WORKING AND RELIABLE

AT CARDIFF WE WOULD HAVE TO ATTRACT WORKERS FROM OTHER AREAS, WHERE WOULD THEY LIVE?

IT WOULD BE NICE TO MOVE INTO A MODERN LARGER FACTORY

IF WE MOVE, WHAT ABOUT THE FIRMS IN EBBW VALE THAT RELY ON US?

IT WOULD COST A LOT OF MONEY TO BUILD A NEW FACTORY

WE COULD PROBABLY GET MONEY FROM THE GOVERNMENT TO EXPAND AND MODERNISE THE OLD FACTORY

WE HAVE FRIENDS HERE. OUR CHILDREN WOULD HAVE TO CHANGE SCHOOL

Figure 5   Move or stay? A difficult choice

Homework ideas

Make a list of all the things you can think of that are made of steel. Try and find out where they were made.

41 Industry in towns

Figure 1   A heavy engineering plant

Heavy industries are industries that need large areas of land and use large amounts of raw materials and fuel to produce a heavy or bulky finished product. Examples of heavy industries are iron and steel making, cement works, oil refineries, gas works and brick making (Figure 1).

Factories that use small sites and less raw materials to produce smaller, less bulky finished products, are called *light industries*. Examples of light industries are clothing factories, printing works, jewellery making, furniture manufacturing, food processing and factories making electrical goods (Figure 2).

Things to do

1 Write down three examples of heavy industries and three examples of light industries.
2 Look at Figure 3 which shows different industrial areas in a typical British city. Using the photographs to help you, write down the advantages that each area has for industry.

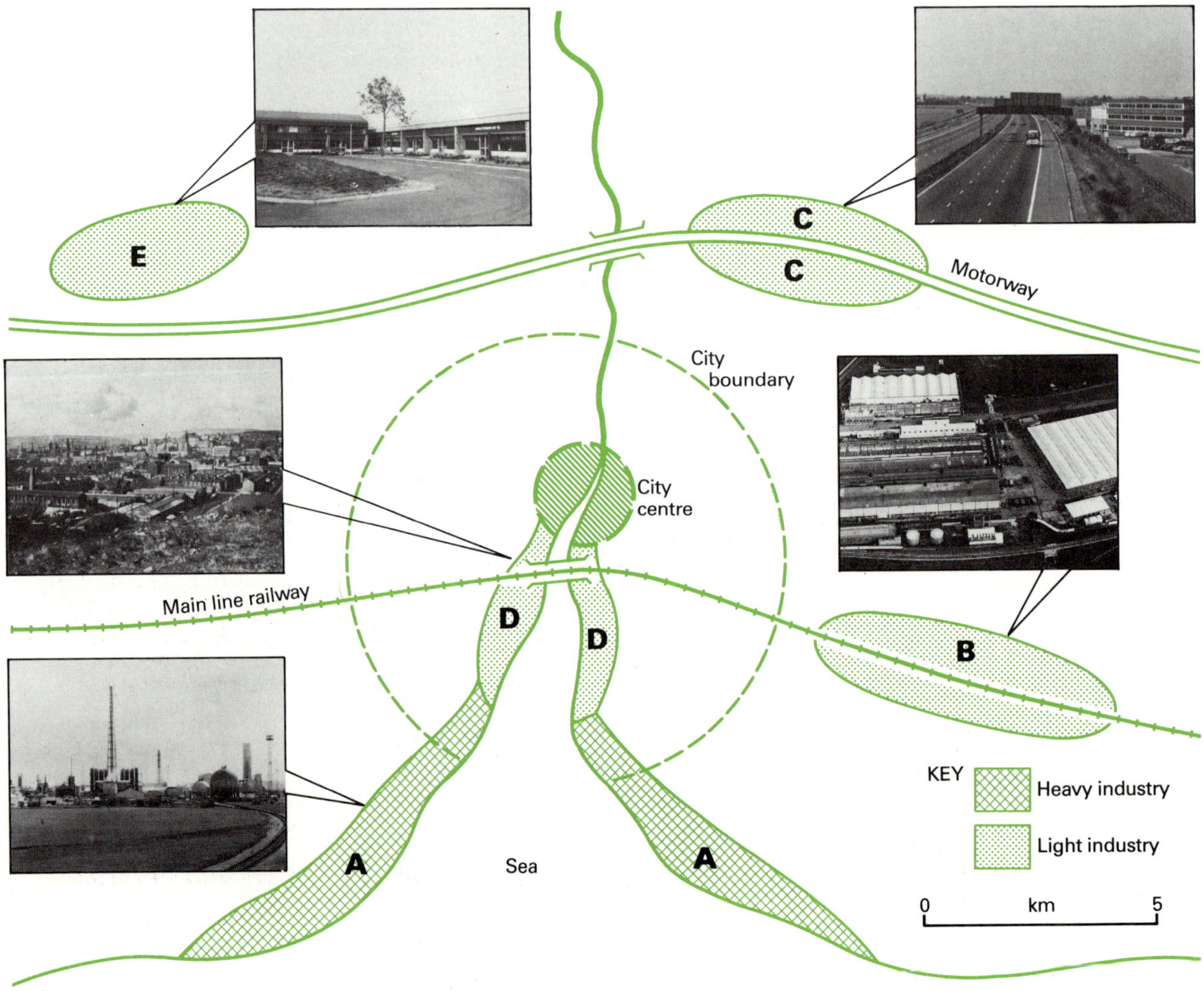

Figure 2   Cadbury's Bournville factory – a light industry

Figure 3   Five different industrial areas in a typical British city

1 Industrial estates are areas made up of factories and warehouses which have been planned and laid out to suit many different industrial uses. They are usually sited on cheap land outside a city and close to good roads.

2 The first place that industries were located in towns was near the centre. Today these areas are often old and run down, with little space for new building or traffic.

3 Large, heavy industries need plenty of flat, cheap land and often use large amounts of raw materials which arrive by train and ship. They first grew up near the city's docks and now have spread out along the coast.

4 Alongside motorways is often an ideal site for new light industries because they provide good transport links with other parts of the country. The land is quite cheap as it is not usually wanted for houses as people prefer quieter, more attractive sites to live.

5 Many light industries site along railway lines, partly because land is cheap there, and also because the transport links are good.

Figure 4

3 In place of the photographs in Figure 3, include the correct label from the five choices in Figure 4.

4 Now on a copy of Figure 3, label each area A to E with examples of factories you might expect to find there. For example, an oil refinery in area A.

5 If you have an industrial estate close to your school, go and collect information about the area. Put the results in a table like Table 1.

Table 1

Name of industrial estate . . .

Name of company	Activity (eg warehouse)
1	
2	
3	
4	
5	
6	
7	
8	
9	
10	

6 Draw a graph (like Figure 5) of the results to show how many companies on the estate are involved in similar activities.

Manufacturing e.g. bicycle factory **Storage and distribution** e.g. fruit warehouse **Retailers** e.g. car showroom **Services** e.g. fire station

Figure 5   Bar graph to show the number of companies of different types on the .... industrial estate

Homework ideas

Collect information from local newspapers and libraries about industry in your area.

With other members of the class, produce a map to show where industry is located in your local area.

42 Types of industry

Figure 1

Figure 2

Figure 3

So far we have really only talked about one sort of industry, the type that takes raw materials or components and changes them or combines them to produce something new and more useful—a finished product. We call this sort of industry manufacturing or *secondary* industry.

If we think about industry being something that involves people working for a living, we can see that there are two other sorts of industry.

People working in *primary* industry are involved in getting natural, unchanged products from the earth. So, a miner, a farmer, a fisherman or an oil-rig worker would all be working in primary industry.

Jobs in *tertiary* industry are those which involve people providing a service for other people. A bus driver, a teacher, a doctor, a waiter, a policeman or policewoman are all working in tertiary industry. In fact, all those jobs which don't actually make or manufacture something or get natural things from the world around us are in tertiary or *service* industry.

Things to do

1 Look at the photographs (Figures 1, 2 and 3). Write down what you think each one shows and to which type of industry it belongs.
2 Table 1 shows a list of 30 industrial jobs. Write each one down under its correct heading.
   Primary/extractive industry,
   Secondary/Manufacturing industry,
   Tertiary/Service industry.

Table 1

hotel manager	dustman	oil rig worker
pilot	grocer	brick layer
car worker	dentist	accountant
steel worker	quarryman	carpenter
solicitor	train driver	pop singer
van driver	chef	photographer
social worker	miner	nurse
shepherd	trawlerman	weaver
shop assistant	panel beater	tailor
lumberjack	welder	dairy worker

3 Primary, secondary and tertiary industries may often be linked together. Look at Figure 4. Now look at the nine photographs in Figure 5. They show three different sets of linked industries. Separate them and put them in the correct order: primary, secondary, and tertiary.

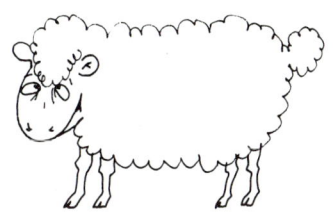

PRIMARY – rearing sheep for wool

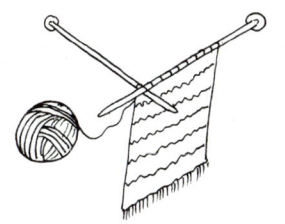

SECONDARY – making a scarf from wool

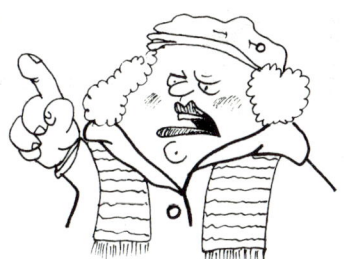

TERTIARY – selling the scarf to the public

Figure 4 How different types of industry may be linked

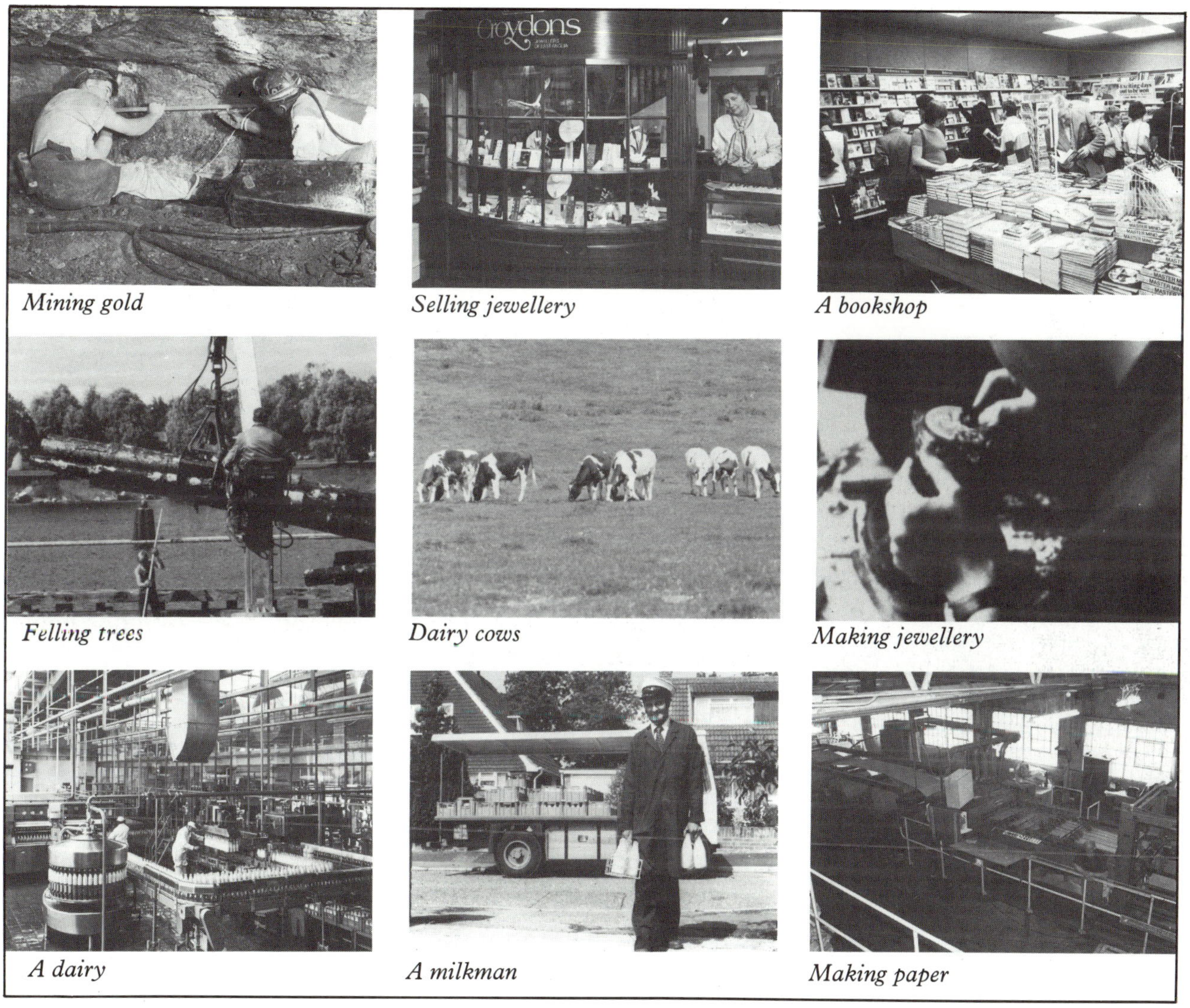

Mining gold | *Selling jewellery* | *A bookshop*

Felling trees | *Dairy cows* | *Making jewellery*

A dairy | *A milkman* | *Making paper*

Figure 5

Homework ideas

1 Open a local telephone directory at any page and look at the entries in **heavy** or **bold** print.
2 Write down the first ten you find and divide them into primary, secondary and tertiary industry.
3 Put all the class results together and work out the proportion of the different sorts of industry in your area.
4 Do you think the pattern you find is typical of the rest of the country?

43 Services

Tertiary industries are those that provide a service for other people, for example, a shop-keeper, a school-teacher, a bus driver, a nurse and a policeman.

Things to do

Table 1

	1961	1982
Primary	6%	3%
Secondary	46%	28%
Tertiary	48%	69%

1 Look at Table 1.
 (a) Which sector of industry has grown over the last twenty years in this country?
 (b) Which sector has declined most?
2 Look at Figure 1.
 (a) Make a list of the services found in the High Street.
 (b) How many other services can you add to the list?

Figure 1   Some of the services found in two high streets

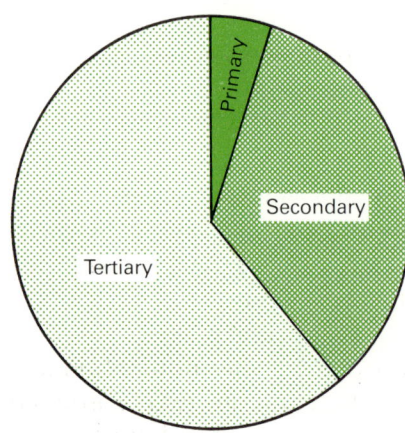

Figure 2   Pie diagram to show the numbers of people known to the class who work in the three sectors of industry

3 Now fill in the blanks in the following passage.
  In 1982 ___% of Britain's workforce was employed in primary industry. ___ times as many people were employed in secondary or _____ industry. Not all industries make their profits by selling finished products. A third type of industry provides us with a _____ or something we need done. Tertiary industry employs most people in this country, ___% of the workforce in 1982. The rest of Europe shows a similar pattern.
4 (a) For each of ten people you know who go out to work, write down the job they do and the sector of industry to which they belong.
 (b) Put your information together with the rest of the class's. Draw a pie chart similar to that shown in Figure 2 to show the results of your survey. Which sector of industry employs more people in your survey? If it is not service (tertiary) industry, can you suggest why not?

5 Look at Figure 3 which shows the percentage of the workforce employed in each sector of industry in three British towns. One is a mining town, one is a seaside resort and one is a manufacturing town. Which one is which and why?

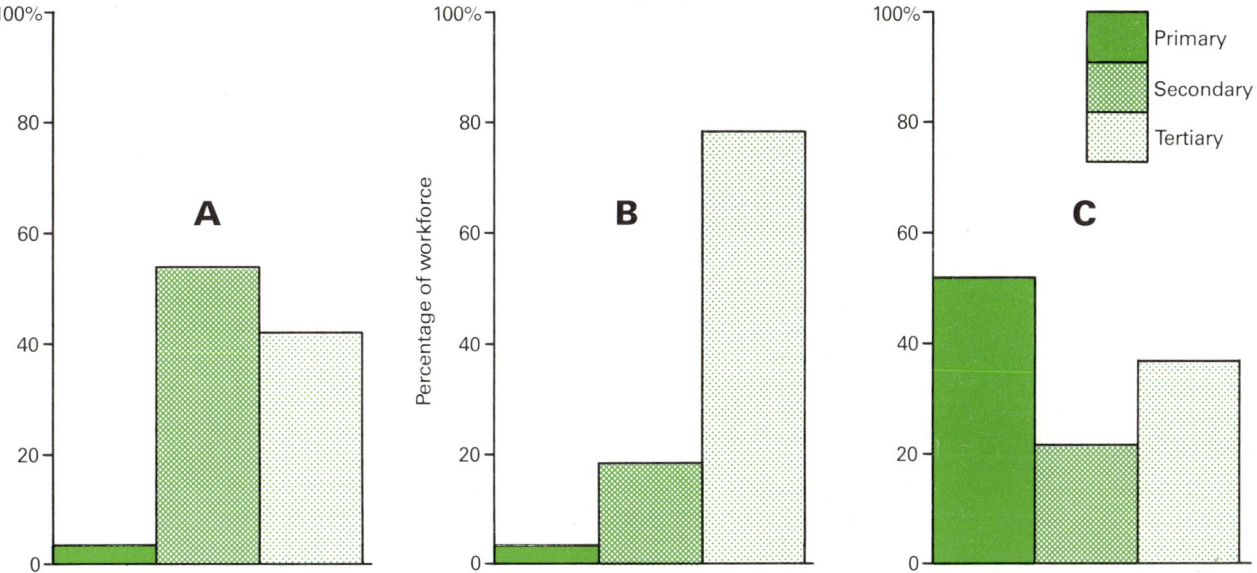

Figure 3   Bar graphs of employment in three British towns

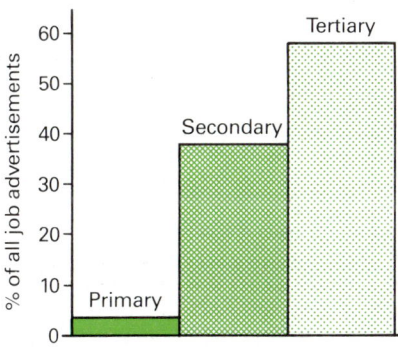

Figure 4   Bar graph of job advertisements in the local paper

Homework ideas

One way to compare towns is to use job advertisements in the local paper. You can then produce a graph like the one in Figure 4 by counting up the number of advertisements for each type of industry.

6 To which sectors of industry do the following descriptions apply?
    Providing natural, unchanged materials from the earth
    Dealing with people rather than things
    Providing a service for others
    Changing materials into things that are more useful to us
    Providing raw materials
    Working in a factory
    Transporting goods
    Growing food, fishing and mining
    Working in an office
    Making something that can then be sold
    A job that doesn't actually make anything
    Selling things

7 The proportion of people working in the three sectors of industry in a place can tell us a great deal about that place. Generally, areas with many people working in secondary or tertiary industry are the wealthy areas. Why do you think this is so?

8 Look at Figures 5 and 6 which show the proportions of people working in the three sectors of industry in two European countries. West Germany is a wealthier country than Italy. Look at the position of Italy and West Germany on a map of Europe. In what way does West Germany's position give it an advantage over Italy?

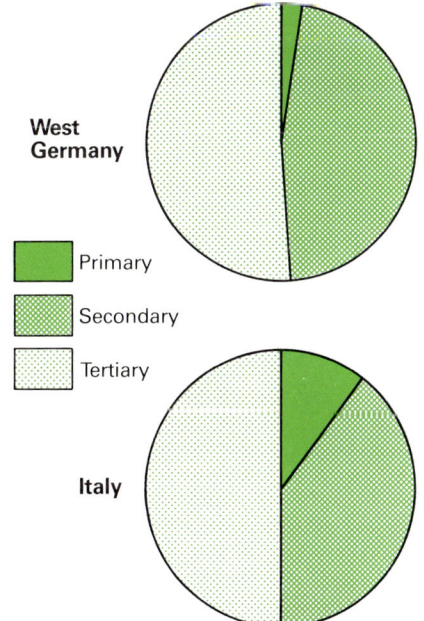

Figures 5 and 6   Pie diagrams showing the proportion of people working in the three sectors of industry in West Germany and Italy

44 How do we see places?

Figure 1

Figure 2

The owners of a factory will decide where to locate their business by considering the things mentioned in unit 39, such as, how easily the inputs (raw materials, labour, fuel and power) can be brought to the factory, how easily the finished products can be transported to the market and if the chosen site is large and flat enough. But, if there is more than one site to choose from, the owner may simply choose the area that he or she likes best. Different owners may well prefer different places.

Things to do

1 Look at the two photographs, Figures 1 and 2.
   (a) In which area would you prefer to live?
   (b) Write down the reasons you prefer the area you have chosen.
   (c) How many people in your class agree with you?
2 (a) Make a copy of Figure 3 and, using an atlas to help you, label all the towns marked on the map.
   (b) Now give each square on the map a score of 1, 2 or 3 according to how much you would like to live in that area. If you feel that the area would be very pleasant to live in, give it a score of 3. If you have no strong feelings about the area give it a score of 2. If you would not like to live there very much, give it a score of 1.
   (c) Colour in the squares according to the key in Figure 3. Those areas shaded darkest are the ones you think are the most attractive to live in the UK. Do you know why?
   (d) Put the results of the class together and produce a group map of preferred places to live in Britain.
   (e) Compare your map with Figure 4 which shows the views of hundreds of school leavers who did the same exercise.

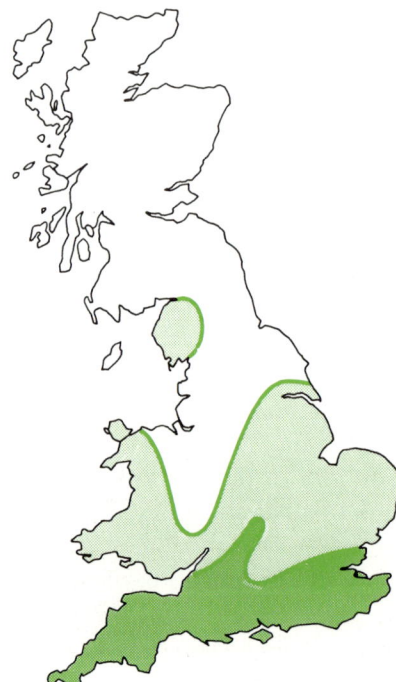

Figure 4 The areas in which people preferred to live in Britain

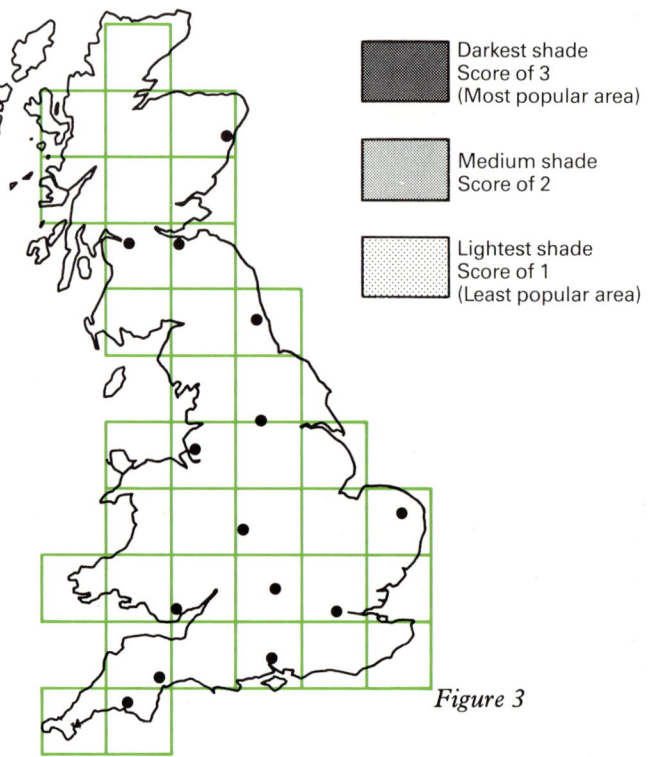

Darkest shade
Score of 3
(Most popular area)

Medium shade
Score of 2

Lightest shade
Score of 1
(Least popular area)

Figure 3

3 Look at Figures 5 and 6.
  (a) Why do you think some people remember some parts of an area better than others?
  (b) Can you suggest the sort of person who might have drawn each map?
  (c) Make a sketch map of your own area like those in Figures 5 and 6. Compare your map with the rest of the class.

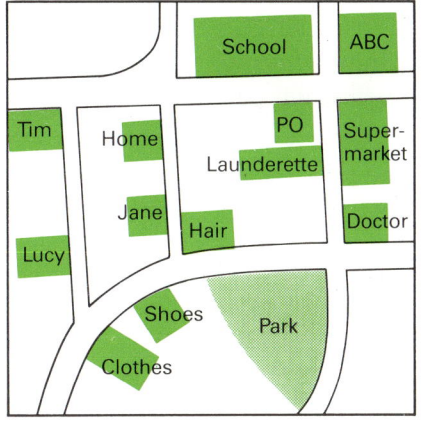

Figure 5

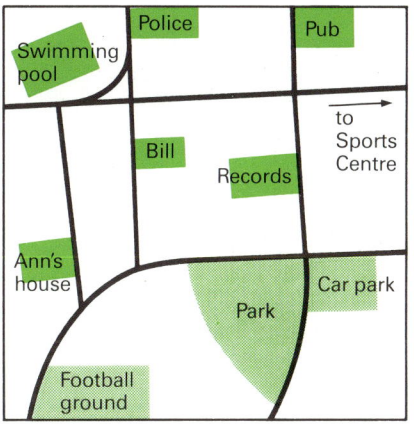

Figure 6

Two maps of the same area drawn by people with different viewpoints

4 Look at Figure 7 which shows how Londoners see the north of Britain. Compare it with your atlas map of Britain.
  (a) How do you think people from the north of Britain view the south?
  (b) Make a list of words people from the north might use to describe Londoners.
  (c) Compare your list with the rest of the class.
5 Many people prefer to live in areas towards the south of England and avoid other areas of the country.
  (a) How might that affect the location of industry?
  (b) What can be done to persuade workers and owners of businesses to locate in the less popular areas of the country?

Figure 7   How Londoners see the north

Homework ideas

1 Make a poster designed to persuade people from the south to live in the north. You might use pictures from holiday brochures or magazines to help you.
2 Figures 8 and 9 show two very different views that people in the south often have of the north. Explain why each of them is misleading.

Figure 8

Figure 9

45 Unemployment

Unemployment is a tragedy for the families who are out of work. Their standard of living gets lower and the unemployed person often feels they have failed or may never work again. Unemployment also costs the country a great deal in lost taxes and social security payments

Figure 1   A job centre

Figure 2

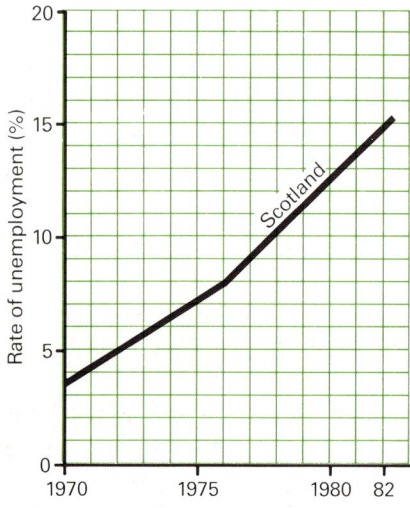

Figure 3   The percentage of people unemployed in Scotland

Table 1

Region	% unemployed		
	1970	1975	1982
Scotland	3.9	7.0	15.3
Northern England	4.3	7.2	16.7
North West	2.5	6.6	15.7
Yorkshire and Humberside	2.6	5.4	13.6
West Midlands	2.4	5.0	15.3
East Midlands	2.2	4.6	11.5
Wales	3.5	7.4	15.6
N. Ireland	4.9		20.3
East Anglia	2.2	4.9	10.4
South East	1.5	4.4	10.9
South West	2.4	6.6	9.3

Things to do

1 Look at Table 1 which shows the percentage of people out of work in the main regions of the United Kingdom.
  (a) On a copy of Figure 2 shade all the regions with *less* than 12% of people unemployed in a light colour, for example, yellow.
  (b) Shade the regions that have between 12% and 16% in a medium shade, for example, orange.
  (c) Finally shade those areas that have *more than* 16% of people out of work in a dark colour, for example, red.
2 (a) Name the four regions which had greatest unemployment in 1970. Write all the regions in *rank order*, that is, the region with the highest unemployment, first, and the region with second highest, second, and so on.
  (b) Which regions had the lowest unemployment in 1970?
  (c) Do the same for 1975 and 1982.
  (d) What do you notice?
3 (a) Complete the graph begun in Figure 3 for the South East, Wales and Yorkshire and Humberside regions.
  (b) In which region has the rate of unemployment increased quickest (it will be the region that has the steepest line on the graph).

Homework ideas

Imagine you are a director of a small company. Write a short speech either supporting the idea of moving your factory to a Development Area, or arguing against a move.

Present your arguments to the rest of the class as if you were in a board meeting.

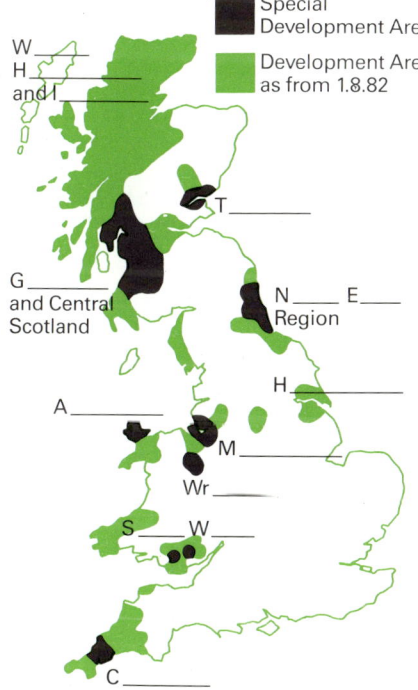

Figure 5 *Employment structure in Britain by regions*

Figure 6 *Development Areas in Britain*

Special
Development Area

Development Area
as from 1.8.82

W_____
H_____
and I_____

T_____

G_____
and Central
Scotland

N_____ E_____
Region

A_____

H_____

M_____

Wr_____

S_____ W_____

C_____

Primary
Secondary
Tertiary

Million employees
8
3
2
1
0

Scotland

Northern Ireland

Northern England

North West

Yorkshire and
Humberside

East Midlands

West Midlands

Wales

East Anglia

South West

South East

1 Building grants

2 Machinery and
   equipment grants

3 Money for
   moving costs

4 Factories for sale
   or cheap rental

5 Loans and
   tax allowances   £ $ £ £

6 Training for
   new jobs

Figure 7   *Government help*

Use the cartoons below (Figure 4) to help you explain why some regions with high unemployment find it difficult to encourage new employers to move to the area.

4 Look at Figure 5.
  (a) Which regions have half or more than half of their employees in (i) services (ii) manufacturing?
  (b) Which region has the highest proportion of its workers in primary industry?
  (c) Why do you think that unemployment is worst in Scotland, Northern Ireland and northern England?

A "There is so little space and the steep hills make this a difficult place to get to."

B "It's far too cold and wet."

C "It seems such a dull place with factories and shops closing down and long dole queues."

D "It seems so far from the centre of things. It would cost a great deal to transport the goods to where they are sold."

E "Everything looks so old and run down. The labour force want to live in modern houses in pleasant surroundings."

Figure 4   *Why some regions find it difficult to attract new employers*

5 The map, Figure 6 shows areas of the country that the government has called Development Areas. The areas with most difficulties are called Special Development Areas. Development Areas get special help like that shown in Figure 7 to attract firms to the area.
  (a) Use your atlas to name the areas shown on the map by their first letter.
  (b) How closely do the areas match the areas of highest unemployment shown on the copy of Figure 2 which you shaded in question 1?

6 Now look again at Figure 7 which show several ways that governments try to get firms to set up in the areas where unemployment is high. What do you think the advantages and disadvantages of starting a new business in these areas would be?

46 **Hi-tech industries**

Figure 1   School children using computers

The term *hi-tech* is short for high-technology and is used to describe those industries which manufacture or sell electronic goods, for example, computers and calculators. The hi-tech industries produce very up-to-date equipment. Many people are employed by these firms to think up new ideas which can then be made in the factories. People who are employed to think of new ideas work in a department called *research and development*. So, hi-tech industries may be divided into three main areas, (i) research and development, (ii) production and (iii) marketing. *Marketing* is selling the product to the public.

In California, in the USA, there is a valley which is so famous for its firms making hi-tech silicon chips for computers, it has become known as Silicon Valley. In the UK, a similar area lies along the M4 motorway in southern England and is called Silicon Strip (Figure 2).

Figure 2   Silicon Strip

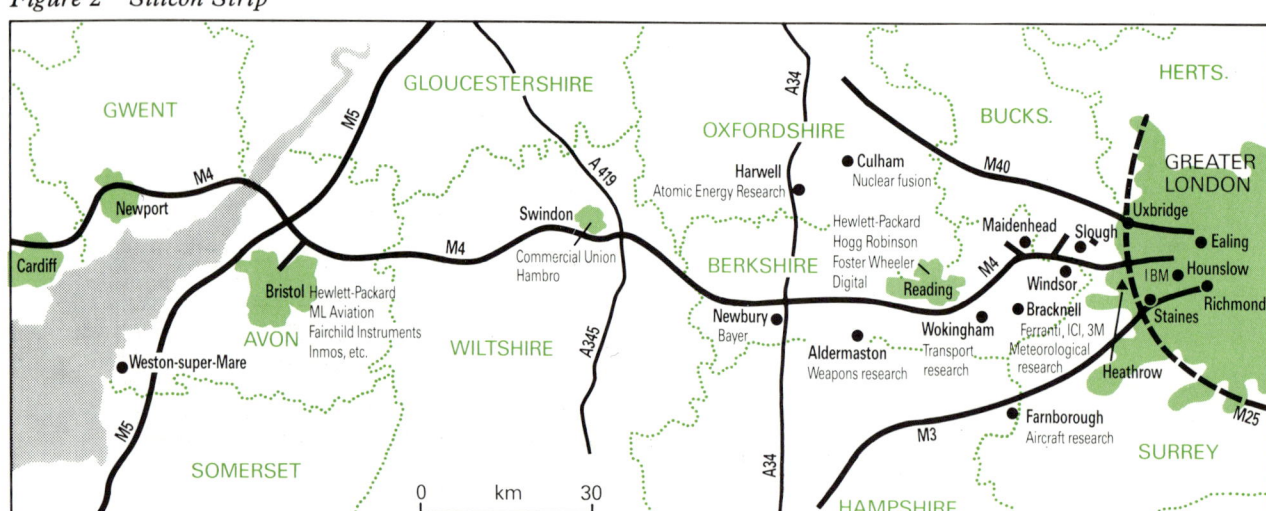

Figure 3   The site of a hi-tech factory

Figure 4   Working in a computer factory

Let us try and understand why hi-tech industry decided to locate near to the M4.

Things to do

1 Look at Figures 3 and 4. Now answer the following questions.
  (a) Does the computer industry need a great deal of power?
  (b) Does it use large amounts of heavy or bulky raw materials?
  (c) Does it produce a heavy, bulky finished product compared with steel works, for example?
  (d) How would the finished product be transported to the market?
  (e) What sort of labour force would the industry employ?
     (i) for research and development and (ii) for production.
     (Remember, much of the work is delicate and needs considerable care.)
  (f) How large a site would be required?

Your answers should show that hi-tech industry can locate almost anywhere. It is what we all a *footloose* industry.

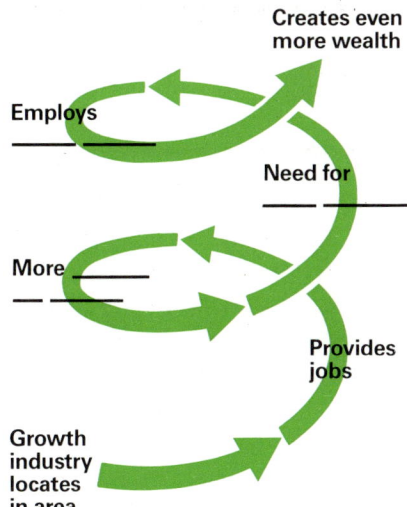

Figure 5   The wealth spiral

Figure 7   The location of Warrington–Runcorn

Table 1   Some hi-tech products

Televisions
Transistor radios
Clock radios
Headphones
Cassette recorders
Car radios/stereos
Hi-fi-systems
Video tape recorders
Electronic organs
Button telephones
Hearing aids
Refrigerators
Micro-wave owens
Gas and electric ovens
Toasters
Blenders
Water-heaters
Dish washers
Vacuum cleaners
Electronic calculators
Electric irons
Air Purifiers
Electric fans

One of the most important things new hi-tech firms consider when deciding where to locate, is how pleasant the area is to live in. They look for rural areas with a good climate and local facilities like theatres, golf clubs and schools and perhaps a University. Why do you think these things are so important to a computer company?

Industries that are taking on more employees and producing more goods are called *growth industries*. Areas with high unemployment are keen to attract growth industries to locate in that area because they will provide new jobs. This will mean that people have more money to spend which will increase the need for more services and goods, which will in turn employ even more people.

2 Complete the diagram in Figure 5 to show why areas are so keen to attract growth industries.

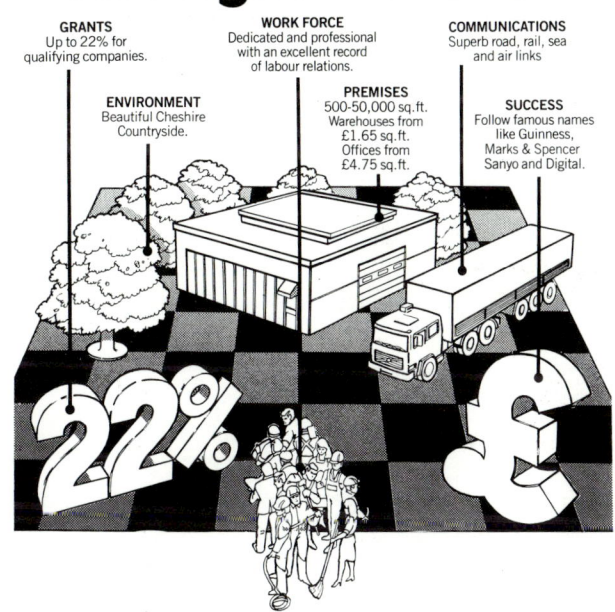

Figure 6

3 Look at the advertisement (Figure 6) which is designed to attract growth industries to Runcorn.
   (a) Explain why communications in the area are said to be 'superb'. (Look at Figure 7.)
   (b) What other advantages does Runcorn claim to offer new industries?
   (c) Explain why each of them is important.
4 Produce a newspaper advertisement designed to encourage growth industries to come to your area. You should include information about roads, rail, the countryside and entertainment; in fact all the best things about your area of the country which might persuade a company to set up industries there.
5 Can you add any more products to the list in Table 1?

Homework ideas

Use a telephone directory to find out how many firms in your area are involved in the hi-tech industry.

101

47 Problems of industry

So far we have looked at some of the different sorts of industries that we find in Europe and particularly in the UK. We have also considered the reasons for their locations and how they have developed. Europe is one of the richest areas in the world; for centuries we have been taking resources from the land and changing the world in which we live – our *environment*. Today many of the raw materials that have helped to make us rich are running out. Also we are beginning to realise that, as we try to have a higher and higher standard of living, we may damage the environment in which we live.

There are many different ways that industry can damage the environment. Mining and manufacturing take up space that could be used for farming and recreation, and destroy wildlife. Chemicals and waste products from industry pollute streams and rivers. Quarries and mines scar the landscape. Oil tankers pollute the sea and beaches. Smoke pollutes our atmosphere and damages wildlife. It even affects the health of people far from where the smoke was produced. Cars, trains and aircraft make noise and give-off fumes.

Things to do

1 Draw a diagram similar to Figure 2 and add labels to explain the ways that industry can destroy the environment.

Figure 1 Damaging the environment

Figure 2 How industry can destroy the environment

Homework ideas

1 Make a note of all the pollution you notice in your local area.
2 Produce a scrap book or wall display of the information you collect with the rest of the class.
3 Draw a cartoon which highlights the problem.

2 Choose one of the pollution risks mentioned and try and find out its effects in your own area.
3 Produce posters designed to convince people of the dangerous effects industry can have.
4 It can be very difficult to decide whether or not to build a factory in an area. Some of the factors that have to be taken into account are: taking care of or *conserving* the landscape,
     providing jobs,
     providing facilities for local people,
     needing raw materials,
     making more profit,
     protecting wildlife,
     earning more money for the country.

(a) Which of these things do you feel is most important? Why?
(b) Discuss any differences of opinion that exist between people in your class.

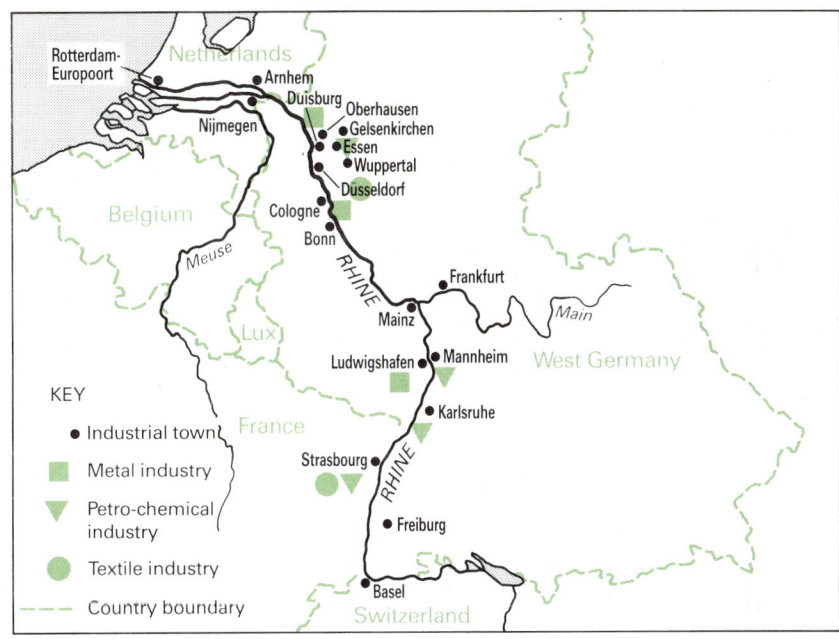

Figure 3   Industries along the Rhine

The River Rhine has been described as the 'lifeline of Europe'. Can you explain why? Look at Figure 3. It has also been described as 'Europe's Sewer' because factories pump their waste products into the river and ships leave oil in the water. At first, it is cheaper to dump waste into the river, but over a long period of time it can be an expensive mistake. The polluted water can destroy machines by breaking down the materials of which they are made. Fishing, swimming and boating become dangerous. Drinking water and water for industry has to be found somewhere else. All of these things cost money.

In Britain the Government has passed many laws controlling industry and making grants for improvements, to reduce the pollution by old established industries and ensure that new industries are placed where they will be least harmful. The following are some examples of government controls.

A Establishing smoke control zones in cities.
B Controlling the disposal of damaging waste liquids into rivers and canals.
C Providing controlled sites for dumping refuse and dangerous chemicals, which are buried.
D Refusing licences for dangerous chemical plants and noisy factories in residential areas.
E Levelling the ground and planting grass and trees on unsightly abandoned mine tips.
F Converting old water-filled quarries for recreational use such as sailing and fishing.
G Insisting on the infilling of new quarries and the replacement of topsoil so that the land can be returned to agricultural use.
H Placing electricity cables below ground in places of special natural beauty.

Figure 4   Government controls on industry

5 Study the map, Figure 3 and your atlas.
(a) Why do you think so many factories have been built along the banks of the River Rhine? (Try to include transport, raw materials and cooling in your answer.)
(b) How would you convince industries and governments to do something about the problem?
6 (a) Study the photographs in this unit. For each, describe the type of pollution it indicates.
(b) Now suggest which of the eight forms of government controls listed in Figure 4 is appropriate for each one.

48 What are recreation and leisure?

In the areas of the world like Europe, where people are generally wealthy, we have time and money to spend on enjoying ourselves—time for *recreation*. We can use this free time or *leisure time* in many different ways (Figure 1).

We shall look at some different kinds of leisure activities in the next few units and see how something which is fun for us may also provide jobs for other people. The time that we spend enjoying ourselves can be divided into the sorts of activities we do (i) every day in our free hours, (ii) only at weekends, or (iii) just once or twice a year.

Things to do

1 Look at Table 1 which shows a large number of leisure activities.
   (a) Divide the list into things you can do at home and activities that you can only do somewhere else.

Table 1

Watching TV	Sailing	Drawing/art	Sewing
Fishing	Ponytrekking	Car	Listening to
Reading	Pubs/drinking	Cookery	records
Gardening	Shopping	Knitting	Climbing
Cycling	Dancing	Tennis	Camping
Walking	Cinema	Swimming	Museums
Golf	Football	Bingo	Skateboarding
Gambling	Skiing	Youth Club	Seeing friends
			Ice skating

   (b) Underline those activities that need special facilities, for example, a tennis court or sports track of some kind. Write down how often you would expect to take part in each activity: D for daily; W for weekly; Y for once a year.
2 Some pastimes actively involve us, for others we are only spectators or onlookers. Write down three active pastimes and three spectator sports.
3 Copy Table 2 and fill in what each member of your family does in his or her free time. Compare your table with those of the rest of the class.
4 (a) Do you notice any differences between what your parents do for recreation and what you and your friends do?
   (b) What differences are there between the pastimes of the boys and the girls?

Table 2

	Mum	Dad	Sister/Brother
Leisure activities			
Time spent			
Cost			

Figure 1

104

Homework ideas

Make a list of all the jobs that you can think of that depend on people's leisure time. For example, pop star, coach driver, ticket seller, hot-dog seller and so on.

5 Make lists of the 'top 10' most popular activities in your class (a) for boys and (b) for girls.
6 Look at Figure 2 which shows a typical town centre.
   (a) How many leisure facilities can you spot in the picture?
   (b) Make a list of all the leisure facilities you can think of in your area.
   (c) How much do they cost?
   (d) How easy are they to get to?
   (e) What are the differences between those that are close to home and those that are further away?
   (f) Do the leisure facilities that are further away attract larger numbers of people and are they more expensive?
   (g) Why do you think it is important to have plenty of leisure facilities provided in a town or village?

Figure 2   Leisure facilities in a town

7 (a) For one pastime that you know well, write down all the equipment and facilities you need to be able to take part.
   (b) How far do you need to travel to take part?
   (c) How much does it cost you?
   (d) How many other people are involved in the activity?
   (e) How many people's jobs depend on your chosen pastime?

49 Recreation in towns

Figure 1   Leisure activities in towns

Figure 1 shows three different leisure activities that take place in our towns and cities.

Things to do

1 Write down the activity that each picture shows.
2 Can you think of any other leisure activities that take place in towns?

It is often difficult for a person who plans new buildings—a *planner*—to build facilities for recreation because fashions often influence what people want to do. Can you think of recent crazes that require space or special tracks in your area?

Some play areas are used everyday by a few people and so are scattered throughout a town, close to people's homes. Other sites for recreation need to be where large numbers of people can visit them from far away.

Which of the activities in Figure 1 fall into each of these groups?

──Homework ideas──

See if you can find out more about your local parks and recreation facilities. Who uses them? How often are they visited? How could they be improved?

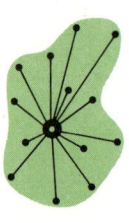

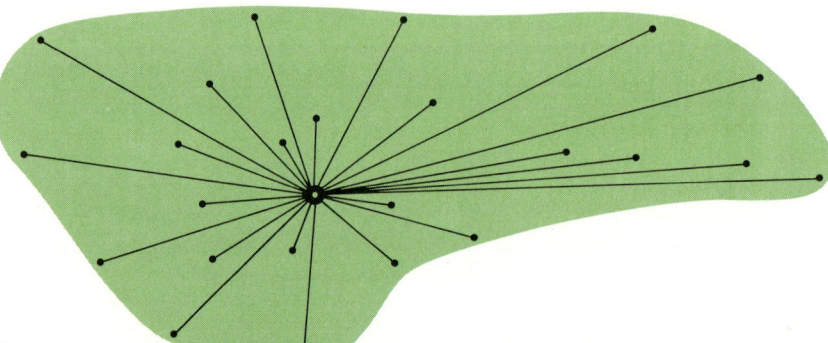

0 km 1

Figures 2 and 3   The catchment areas of a pub and a football ground

3 Look at Figures 2 and 3. The straight lines join people's homes to (a) a pub and (b) a football ground. Can you suggest which diagram represents the football ground? Why? We call the zone represented by the shading the *catchment area* or *market area*. Can you suggest why?

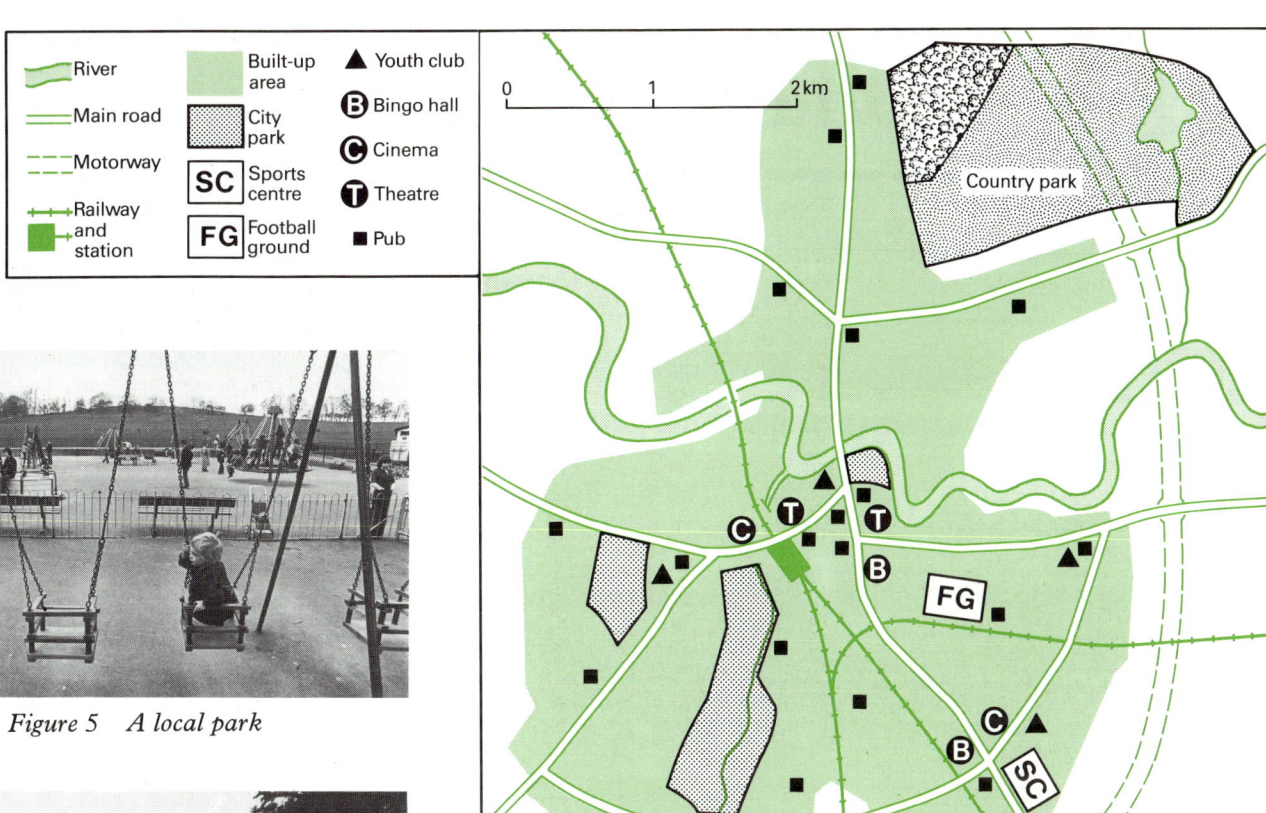

River		Built-up area	▲	Youth club
Main road		City park	Ⓑ	Bingo hall
Motorway			Ⓒ	Cinema
Railway and station	SC	Sports centre	Ⓣ	Theatre
	FG	Football ground	■	Pub

Country park

Figure 4   A map of recreation facilities in a typical British city

Figure 5   A local park

Figure 6   A country park

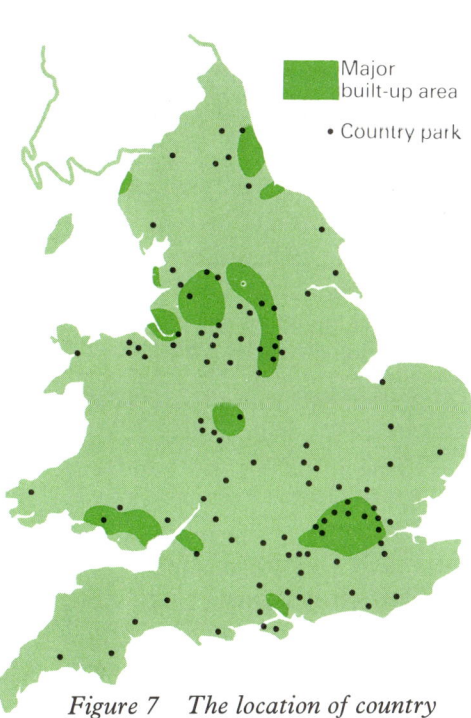

Major built-up area

• Country park

Figure 7   The location of country parks in Britain

4 Look at Figure 4 which shows a map of recreation facilities in a typical British city.
   (a) What do you notice about the space taken up by facilities (i) near the centre? (ii) towards the outskirts?
   (b) Why do you think that cinemas and theatres are usually found near the centre of towns?
   (c) What do you notice about the position of the football ground?

5 Arrange your list of leisure activities from questions 1 and 2 into three groups.
   (a) Those you would expect to find in a city centre.
   (b) Those you would expect to find in a less important district centre, suburb or small town.
   (c) Those you would expect to find in a local neighbourhood or village.

The placing of leisure areas in order of importance like this we call a *hierarchy*.

More people today own cars, earn more money and work shorter hours than ever before. As a result there has been an increase in the demand for new recreation facilities. Land is now being set aside around the outskirts of cities for recreation. One example of this sort of facility is the *country park*.

Look at the two photographs, Figures 5 and 6. One shows a local town park, the other a country park. Figure 7 shows the location of country parks in Britain.

6 Write a comparison between the two sorts of park. You should mention size, amenities, visitors, length of visit, how often visited, transport used to get there, distance travelled, and pursuits followed in the parks.

107

50 Holiday choices

Where people decide to go on holiday depends upon a large number of factors.

Things to do

1 Look at Figure 1 which shows the Smith family discussing their holiday plans.
   (a) Make a list of all the different things that the Smith family take into account when deciding on the type of holiday they want and where to go.
   (b) Look at a selection of holiday brochures and see how many different sorts of holiday are catered for.
   (c) What would be your idea of a perfect holiday and why?
   (d) Find out what sort of holidays the rest of your class enjoy.

Figure 2   Rock climbing in the Lake District

Figure 1   The Smith family's holiday choices

Although it would be difficult to think of one place that would satisfy each member of the Smith family, some areas do offer many of the things that they want. These areas have become important holiday centres and their towns and villages cater for tourists in many different ways. We shall be looking at some of these areas in the next few units.

2 Look at the two maps (Figures 3 and 4) which show the areas of high land and the areas that have the most sunshine each year in Britain.
   (a) Which areas have the best weather for holidays?
   (b) Which areas have the best scenery?
   (c) Which areas would suit each member of the Smith family best?
3 What do these maps tell you about the main holiday areas in Britain?

Homework ideas

1 Try and think of as many places as you can in Britain that are famous as holiday centres.
2 Make a list of all the places thought of by your class.
3 Try and find all the places in your atlas and mark them on a map of Britain.
4 Have a look through British holiday brochures. Are there any areas or places that do not appear on your map?

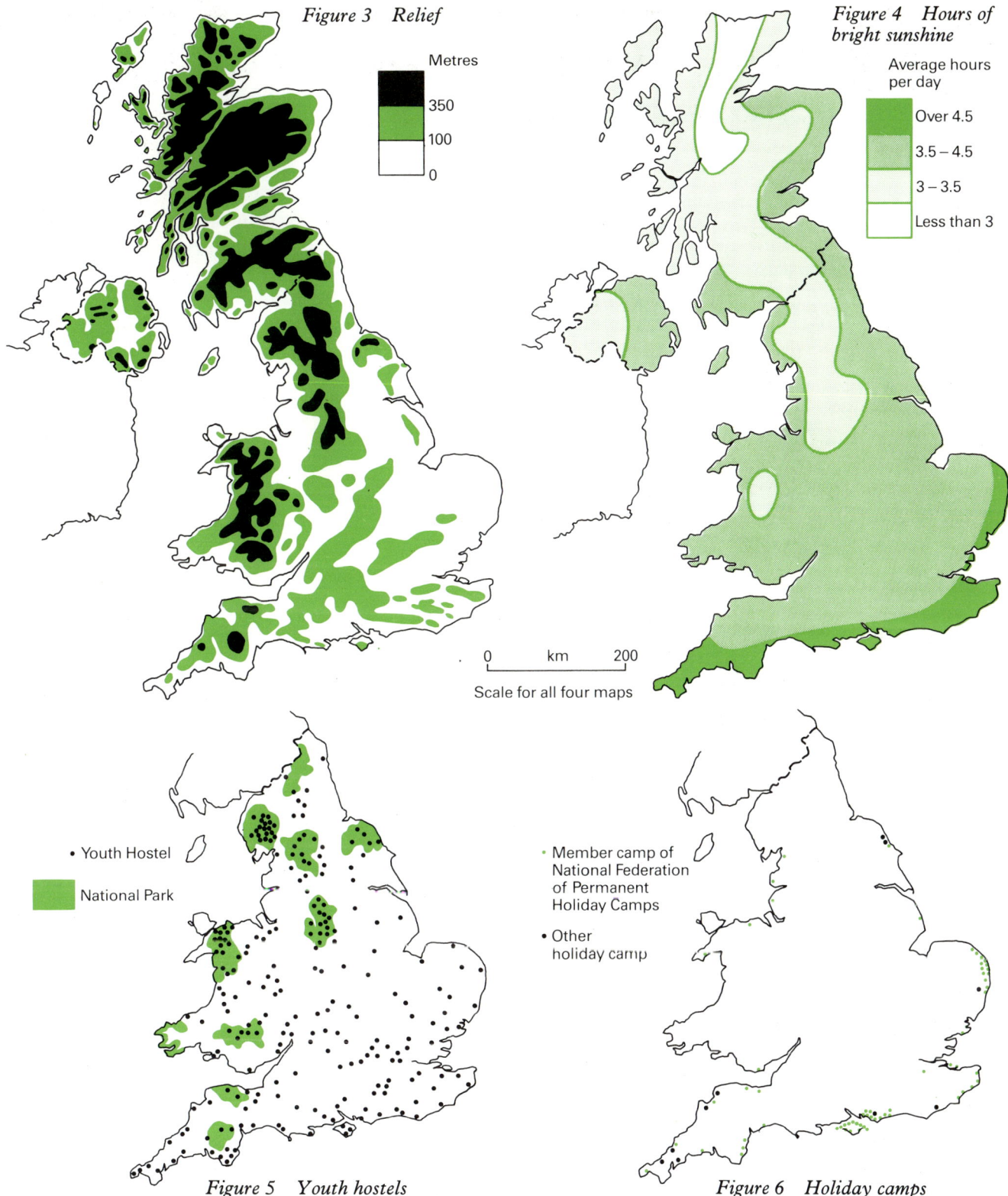

Figure 3   Relief

Metres

350
100
0

Figure 4   Hours of bright sunshine

Average hours per day

Over 4.5
3.5 – 4.5
3 – 3.5
Less than 3

0   km   200
Scale for all four maps

• Youth Hostel

National Park

• Member camp of National Federation of Permanent Holiday Camps

• Other holiday camp

Figure 5   Youth hostels

Figure 6   Holiday camps

4 Look at the two maps (Figures 5 and 6) which show the distribution of Youth Hostels and Holiday Camps in Great Britain.
   (a) Can you think why the Youth Hostels are scattered all over the country?
   (b) Use your atlas to name the National Parks shown on Figure 5.
   (c) Are Youth Hostels concentrated in any of these areas?
   (d) Where are most of the Holiday Camps situated?
   (e) Why do you think there are more Youth Hostels than Holiday Camps?
5 From the two maps can you tell where the main holiday areas are in Great Britain?

51 Tourism—a blessing or a curse?

There are many areas in Europe that are unsuitable for manufacturing because they have no natural resources or have poor communications. There are also many areas, especially in the south and around the Mediterranean, that are unsuitable for agriculture because they are so dry and hot. As a result, these areas are often the poorest in Europe. The very things, however, that make such areas unattractive for industry or unsuitable for farming, may make them ideal for tourism.

Figure 1   The problems facing people in remote areas

Figure 3   Blackpool illuminations

Things to do

1 Look at Figure 1. How might the tourist industry help each of the people in the diagram?
2 Look at Figures 2 and 3.
   (a) How many services for the tourist can you see in both the photographs?
   (b) What jobs do you think these would create for local people?

Figure 2   A windswept pier in winter

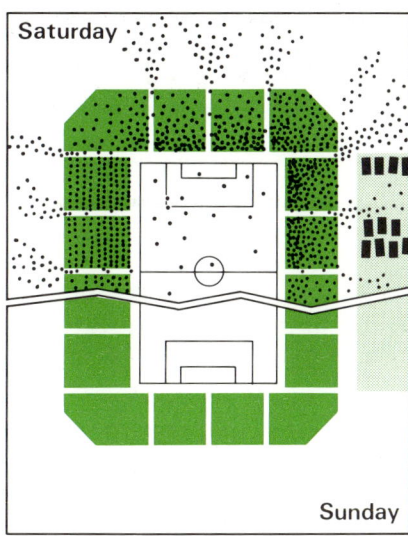

Figure 4   A football pitch at two different times

3 Look at the list of people below whose jobs are linked to tourism.

souvenir seller	aircraft crew	tour guide
car rent person	travel agent	customs official
hotel staff	bank staff	insurance seller

Make a similar list of jobs for a leisure activity that you know well. You could draw a diagram to show all the people involved.

One of the main problems with leisure activities is that they only take place at certain times. Look at Figure 4. What do you think the diagram shows? Places that are used for recreation or tourism may be crowded at certain times, under-used at others and perhaps not used at all at other times. Try and think of some leisure activities that we take part in several times a day, several times a week or only at certain times of the year. What are the problems this may cause for the people whose jobs depend on these activities?

4 Look at Figure 5.
  (a) What do you notice about the numbers of people staying in hotels at different times of the year?
  (b) What do you think is the problem with relying on tourism in an area? (You should think about jobs, costs of keeping open hotels, and the effects on other businesses in the area.)
5 Look at Figure 6 which shows several ways that holiday resorts can help to solve the problems of a quiet season.
  (a) List the ways shown in the figure.
  (b) Are there many other ways that you can think of?

Figure 6   How resorts can help to solve the problems of a quiet season

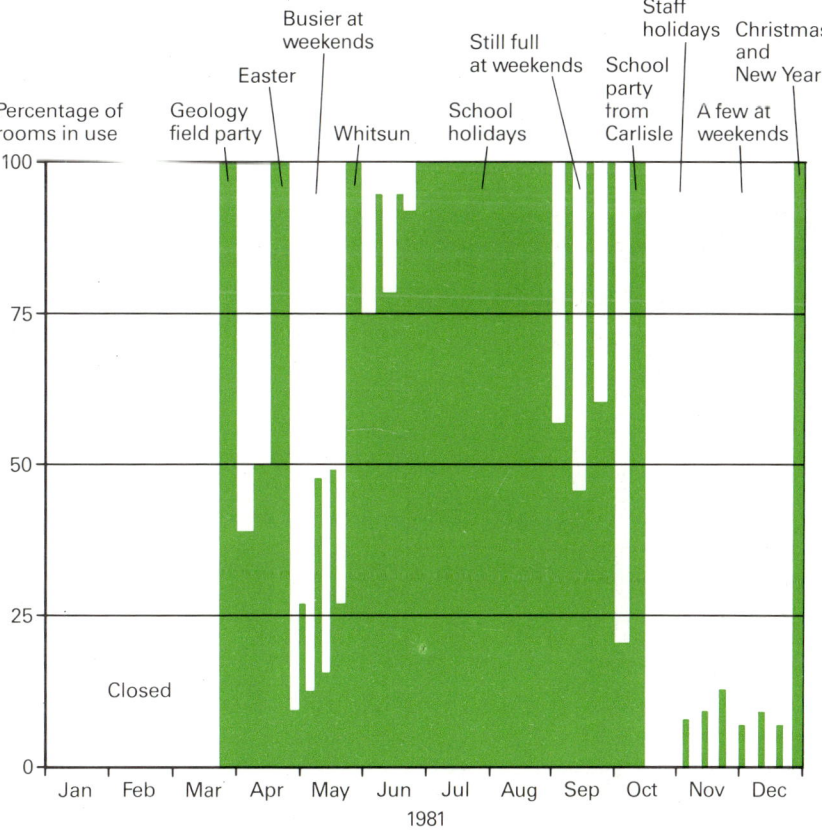

Figure 5   The number of people staying at hotels at different times of the year

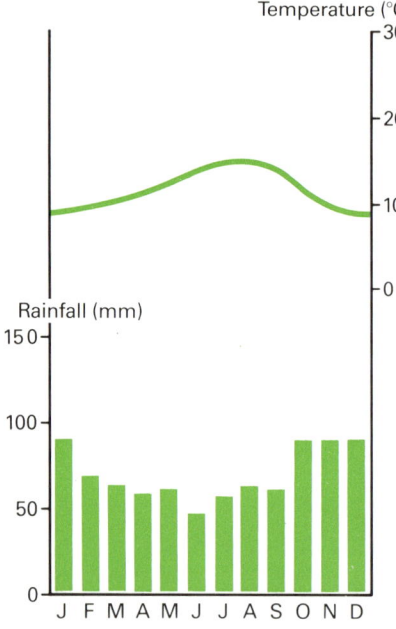

Figure 1   Climate graphs of three different places in Europe

Figure 1 shows three climate graphs for different places in Europe. The three places are the Scilly Isles, Athens and Berlin. How can we tell which graph is which? You may need to look back to unit 11 to revise climate graphs.

Temperature

Let us first try to understand why temperature differs from one place to another. Look at Figures 2, 3, 4 and 5; they should help you.

Figure 2 shows that it gets colder higher up. So, mountain tops are much colder than the bottom of valleys.

Figure 3 shows two places, one near the sea, the other far inland. The sea does not change in temperature by very much all through the year. But the land gets hot in summer and cold in winter. So, the nearer a place is to the sea the less difference there will be between its summer and winter temperatures. We call this type of climate *moderate*. Places a long way from the sea have hot summers and very cold winters. We call this an *extreme* climate.

Homework ideas

Choose four areas of Europe which experience very different climates. Try and find out how these areas cope with their climate. What clothes do the people wear? Do the buildings look different?

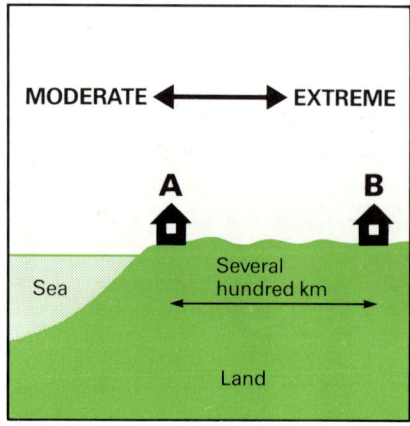

Figure 2

Figure 3

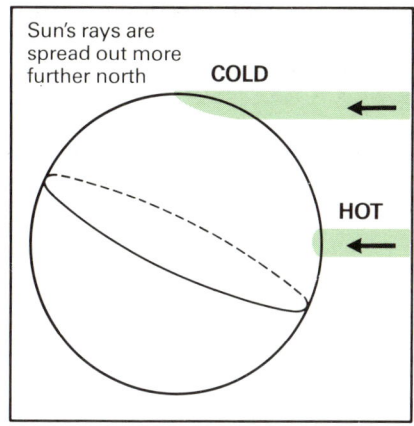

Figure 4

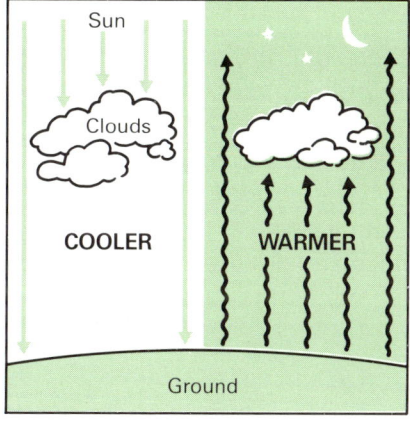

Figure 5

Figure 4 shows the reason why the further north a place is, the colder its climate is. The earth is round, shaped like a football, and the sun's rays only glance across its surface towards the top and bottom—the North and South Poles. This means the sun's rays are weaker and so the earth is colder towards those places.

Finally, in Figure 5, one place may be colder than another on a summer's day because clouds can shade the ground from the sun. In the winter or at night the clouds can have the opposite effect; they can keep a place warmer by stopping heat escaping.

Can we solve the puzzle of the graphs yet?

Rainfall

We still have to understand why some places get more rain than others. There are two main reasons. In Europe, winds usually blow from the west and bring rain with them. By the time these winds have reached the east they have lost most of their rain. So places towards the east of Europe tend to get less rain. The other reason that an area may get more rain is if it is on high ground, because if winds are forced up over hills they often produce rain.

Now, by looking at where the Scilly Isles, Berlin and Athens are in Europe, you should be able to tell which climate graph belongs to which place. Look at the maps of rainfall and temperature in your atlas, can you understand the patterns a little better now?

Things to do

1 Copy Figure 6 and in place of the letters A-J add the correct labels from the following list.

air loses its rain as it moves east; sea water evaporates; sea water circulates and stays the same temperature in summer and winter; moderate climate; low rainfall; clouds form due to condensation; moist air rises and cools; extreme climate; high rainfall; warm air blows over the sea.

Figure 6   Europe's climate

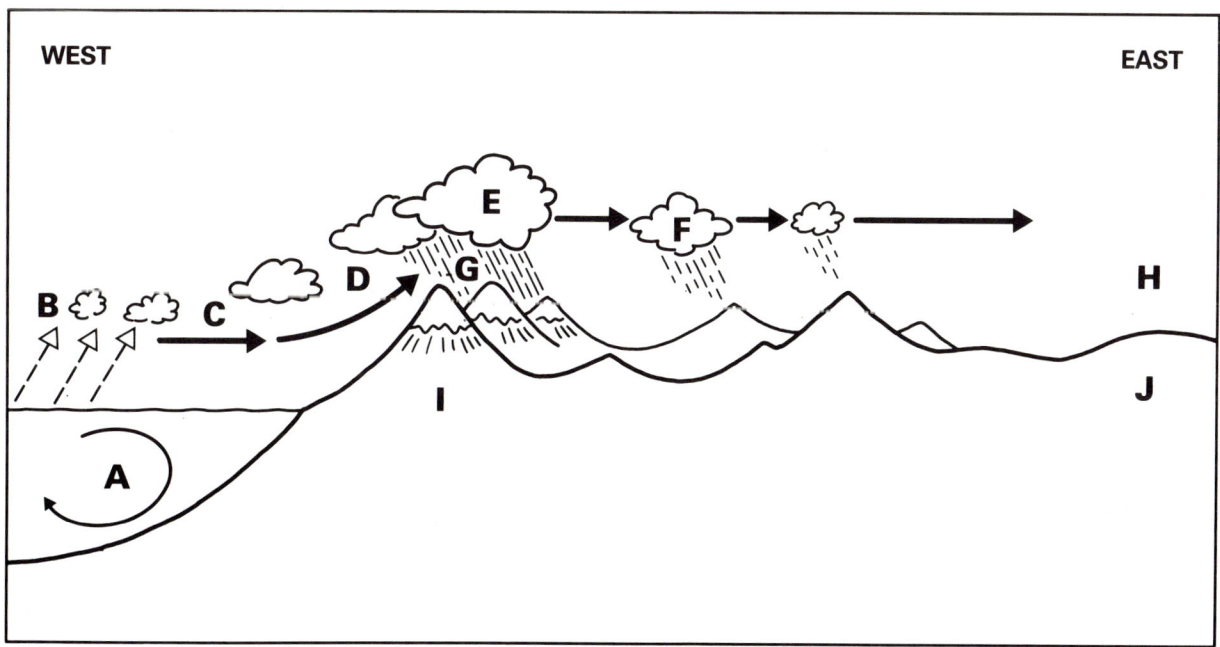

113

53 The sunshine coasts

One of the main things that people think about before they decide where to go for their holiday, is the climate. What sort of climate do most people want a place to have for a summer holiday? What sort of climate do they look for if they want a winter skiing holiday? A good place to start finding out where most people go for their holidays is in a travel brochure.

Things to do

Look at Figure 1. It shows an outline map of Europe on which many of the places mentioned in a typical holiday brochure have been plotted with an **X**.
1 Use an atlas to find out the names of as many of the places as you can.
2 Use a brochure of your own to produce a similar map by marking each place mentioned with a small **x** on an outline map of Europe.
3 Along which coastline are the main concentrations of places?

Figure 1   The main holiday resorts covered by a typical travel brochure

Figure 2   A Mediterranean holiday beach

Figure 3   The Acropolis, Athens, Greece

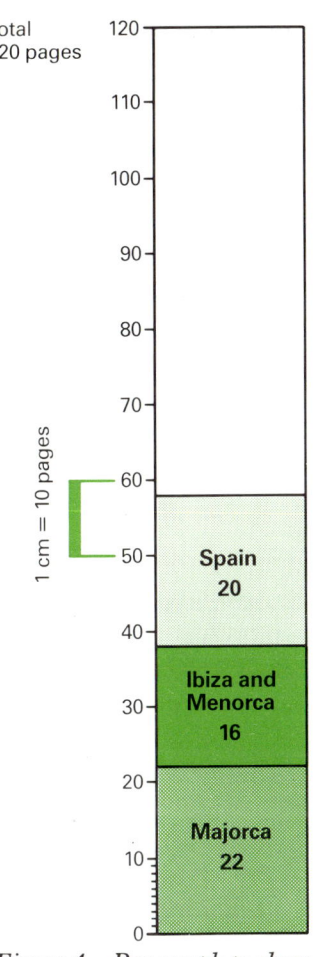

Total 120 pages

1 cm = 10 pages

Spain 20

Ibiza and Menorca 16

Majorca 22

Figure 4   Bar graph to show the number of pages given to different Mediterranean areas in a typical holiday brochure

Let us now look a bit more closely at the brochure and find out how many pages are given to each area. For example, if your brochure has 120 pages you might find that 20 are given to Majorca, 16 to Ibiza and Menorca, 20 to Spain, 6 to Tenerife, 14 to Italy, 6 to Corfu, 12 to Crete, Rhodes and Malta and 24 to other places. One way to make this information easier to understand is to show it as a bar graph.

Look at Figure 4. The height of the bar represents the total number of pages in the brochure (120). A suitable scale might be 1 cm = 100 pages or 1 mm = 1 page. Since there are 120 pages in the brochure altogether the bar must be drawn 12 cms long. Now the bar can be divided up according to the number of pages given to each area.

4 The bar graph has been partly completed. See if you can plot the information for the remaining places or produce a bar graph from your own brochure.
5 What are the main attractions of the Mediterranean coast —sunshine, warm sea, cheap wine? Make your own list from a study of your brochure.
6 What jobs can you see in the photographs in Figure 5 which have been created by tourism?

Homework ideas

Tourism is very important in earning money for the countries of the Mediterranean area. Make a list of any disadvantages you can think of, both for the area and for the population whose jobs depend on tourism.

Figure 5

115

54 Atlam—two viewpoints

Figure 1   Three typical Mediterranean views

A poor farmer in a Mediterranean country sees his environment in a very different way from the way a tourist sees it. Clear skies and rainless days can mean disaster to a farmer whose crops will not grow. Traditional farming methods and quaint customs that the tourists like to see can hold back progress. Natural forest and grassland areas cannot be exploited for timber and grazing. Rugged natural scenery is difficult to farm. Clean sandy beaches with shallow water are not ideal for fishermen who need deep water and a new port. Low wages and a low cost of living keep people poor.

However, these problems for local people are some of the most important things which attract tourists. A dry season with good swimming beaches close at hand, a different kind of scenery and wildlife, a different lifestyle which can be seen in comfort at low cost, all add up to a perfect holiday.

Things to do

1 Explain in your own words how each of the following could be both a problem for a poor farmer and an attraction for a tourist in the Mediterranean.
   (a) A dry, hot summer.
   (b) Old-fashioned farming methods, traditional housing styles and quaint local culture.
   (c) Low wages for local people.
   (d) Rugged natural scenery.

Atlam is an imaginary island situated in the Mediterranean. The island experiences all the problems of this area of Europe. Two main groups of people are concerned with the development of the island—the inhabitants and the travel companies (representing the tourists).

Look carefully at the map of Atlam, Figure 2. You must decide to which of the two groups you belong. If you decide to be an inhabitant of the island, you should try and answer the following questions in the way you think that person would. The notes about the inhabitants of the island should help you. The same thing applies if you decide to be an employee of a travel company.

2 Use the map (Figure 2) and all you know about the problems of the Mediterranean area to write a paragraph on each of the following.
   (a) How you would like to see Atlam develop.
   (b) How this development would take place and the effect it might have on transport, settlement, agriculture or tourism.
   (c) What you think would be the major objections to the plan.
   Remember, use the actual places and information from the map to make your suggestions.

Homework ideas

Produce your own holiday brochure for the island of Atlam. You might like to cut up old brochures and use suitable pictures to show the various resorts on the island.

116

The inhabitants

The people who live on Atlam lead a hard life. Most of them are farmers who earn very low wages. Imagine you are a farmer on the island. What problems do you face? How would you like to see things improve? Some of you might feel that better irrigation on the farms, or more jobs in industry are good ideas, others may prefer to see more jobs in tourism.

The inhabitants are worried about the numbers of young people leaving Atlam to live abroad. They also want to preserve the beauty of the island and its culture.

The travel companies

These companies want to invest money in Atlam in order to make a profit for themselves. Many large travel companies are interested in developing the coastline of the island by creating holiday resorts, building large hotels, shops, swimming pools etc.

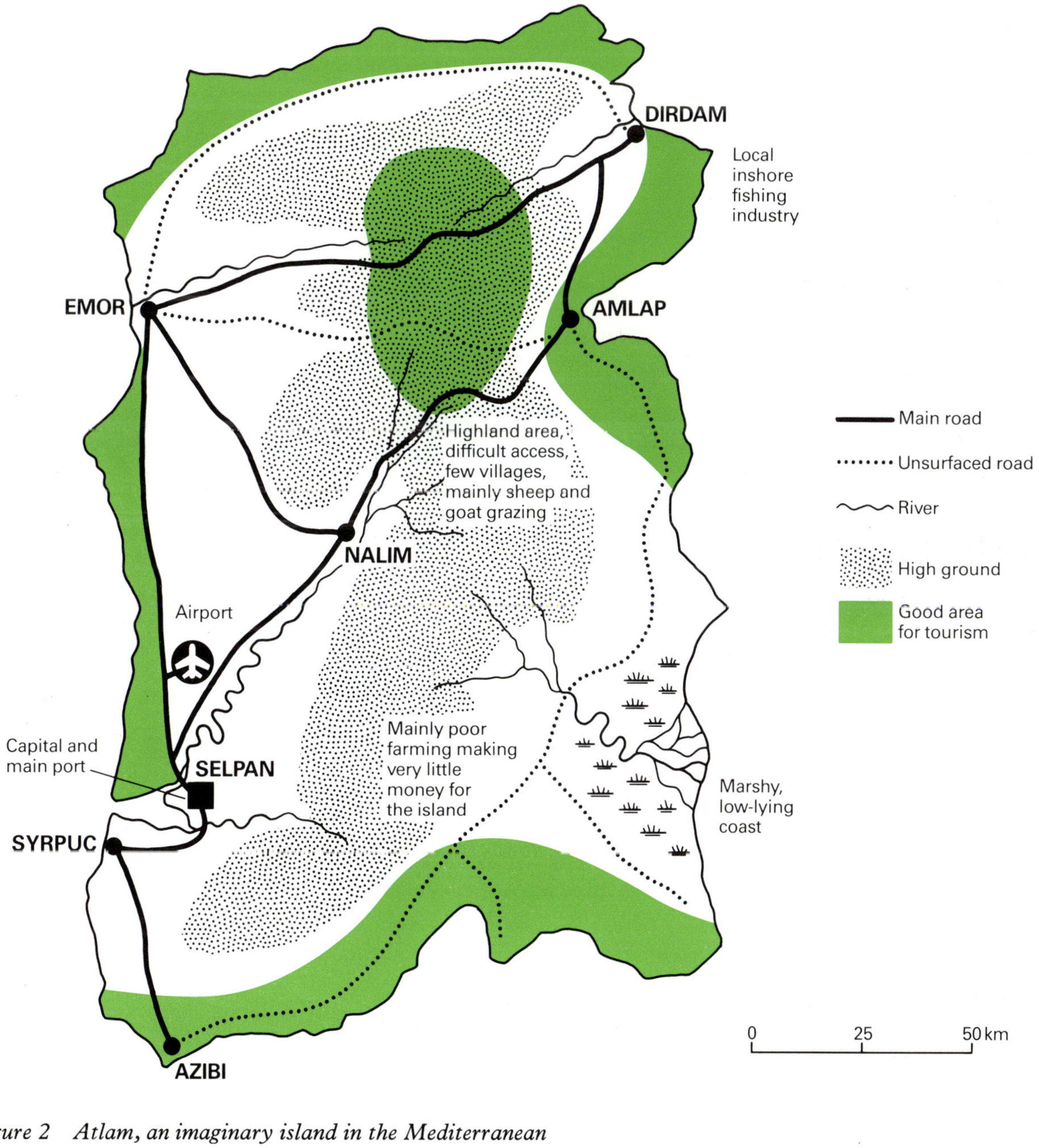

DIRDAM

Local inshore fishing industry

EMOR

AMLAP

Highland area, difficult access, few villages, mainly sheep and goat grazing

NALIM

Airport

Mainly poor farming making very little money for the island

Marshy, low-lying coast

Capital and main port

SELPAN

SYRPUC

AZIBI

——— Main road

········· Unsurfaced road

∿∿∿ River

High ground

Good area for tourism

0   25   50 km

Figure 2   Atlam, an imaginary island in the Mediterranean

117

55 Sun, sea and sand?

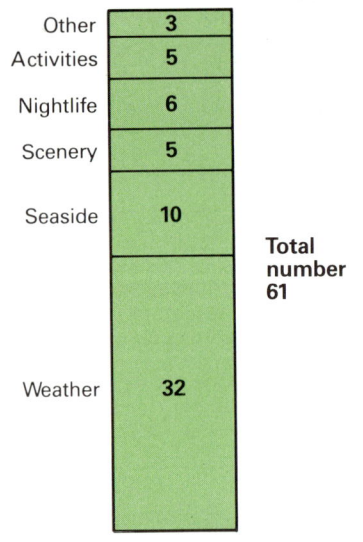

Other	3
Activities	5
Nightlife	6
Scenery	5
Seaside	10
Weather	32

Total number 61

Figure 1 A divided bar graph to show the importance of different things when choosing a holiday

Things to do

1 (a) Write down three things that you think are important when choosing where to go for a holiday.
   (b) Make a list of all the class's suggestions.
   (c) How many times was the weather mentioned?
   (d) How many times was the sea mentioned? What about scenery and mountains?

2 Draw a divided bar graph like that in Figure 1 to show the results of your class survey.

3 Places with high temperatures and lots of sunshine always seem to attract tourists.
   (a) What are the advantages to the tourist?
   (b) What are the disadvantages for the people who live in the area?
   (c) What other types of weather also attracts tourists?

4 The seaside has always been a favourite place to go for holidays. Write down as many different things as you can think of that holiday makers could do at the seaside. Figure 2 may help you.

Figure 3 A highland area in summer

Figure 2 A seaside view

There are areas, however, which are very popular with tourists but are not near the sea. Look again at Figure 6 in unit 49. The National Parks in Britain are found mainly in highland areas. Look at Figures 3 and 4. What sort of activities can people enjoy in highland areas in summer and in winter?

Switzerland is also a very popular country with Europe's tourists. Its snow-covered mountains, forests and lakes provide beautiful scenery suitable for winter holidays. There are many sports which can be enjoyed in the healthy mountains and glittering snow of the Swiss Alps.

Figure 4 A highland area in winter

5 Make a list of as many alpine sports as you can.
6 (a) Make a copy of the map, Figure 5, and shade the land 700 metres or more *above* sea level in brown and the land *below* 700 m in green.
 (b) Use your atlas to name the countries which border Switzerland. Also name the large lakes, the River Rhine and the Alps.
 (c) Now mark on the map the important tourist resorts of Davos, Interlaken and San Moritz

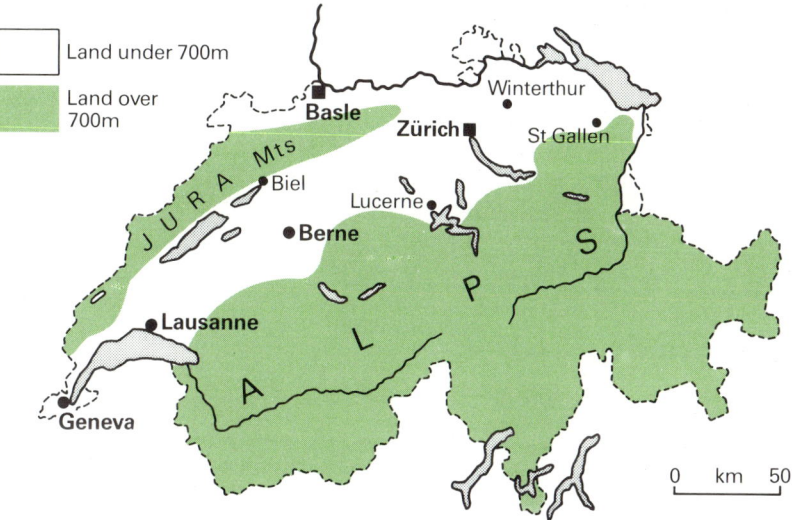

Figure 5   Switzerland

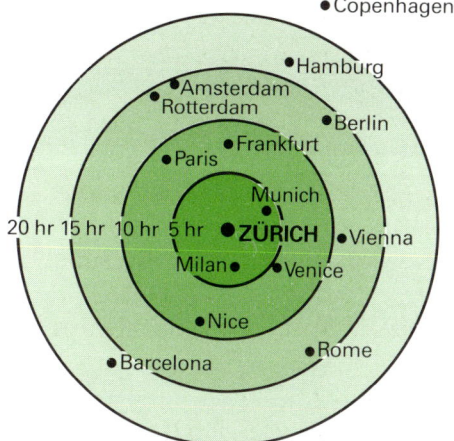

Figure 6   Road journey times to Zurich

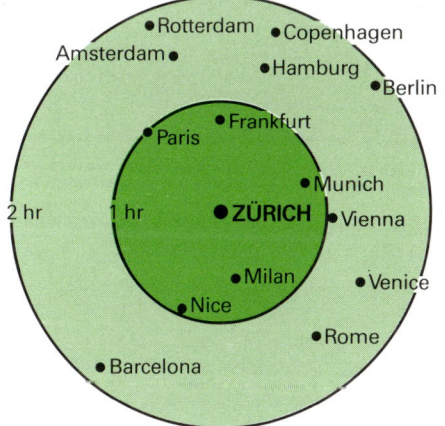

Figure 7   Air journey times to Zurich

Table 1

Country	Visitors to Switzerland per 1000 population
Austria	71
Belgium	97
Denmark	30
Finland	22
France	47
Greece	23
Italy	31
Irish Republic	17
Luxembourg	267
Netherlands	71
Norway	23
Portugal	15
Spain	23
Sweden	43
UK	33
West Germany	120
Yugoslavia	10

7 Look carefully at your map. What do all the biggest towns in Switzerland have in common?
8 Why do three-quarters of Switzerland's people live in the area you have shaded green on your map?
9 Although Switzerland is almost at the centre of Europe, it is not very easy to travel there by car. Can you suggest why?
10 Look at Figures 6 and 7 which show journey times by road and air from European cities to Zurich in Switzerland.
 (a) How many cities lie within 10 hours drive of Zurich?
 (b) How many cities lie within 2 hours flight time?
11 Air travel has made it almost as cheap and easy for Londoners to visit Switzerland as it is for those living in the countries which border Switzerland. Imagine you live in the Swiss Alps. What changes do you think you will have experienced since air travel has increased the numbers of tourists visiting the area?
12 Look at Table 1 which shows the number of people who visited Switzerland for a holiday from other European countries, expressed as a proportion of every 1000 people living in each country. Colour in an outline map of Europe using the following key. The information comes from Table 1.

 Visitors to Switzerland from other countries (per 1000 population)
 Less than 25 visitors – yellow
 25–75 visitors – orange
 over 75 visitors – red
 Switzerland – black
13 Why do you think West Germany and Luxembourg have such a high score and Italy and France have such a low a score, considering how close they are to Switzerland?

119

56 National Parks

In 1949, the government created ten National Parks to try and preserve some of Britain's most beautiful scenery and help people to enjoy the countryside. The idea was that each National Park would be kept as open countryside and people could come to the area to admire the views, to walk, picnic or study nature.

Industry and housing eats up more and more land in Britain each year and large numbers of people use the National Parks to get away from the cities in their spare time.

Look at Figure 1 which shows how long it takes to get to the Lake District National Park from a number of large cities in Britain. Over 20 million people live within three hours car journey of the Lake District.

Things to do

1 What do you think would happen on a national holiday if most of the people living near the Lake District decided to spend the day in the National Park?
2 Look at Figures 2 and 3. How do too many tourists damage the area and spoil its potential for a peaceful country walk?

Figure 2   A crowded picnic area in summer

Figure 3   A traffic jam on a country road

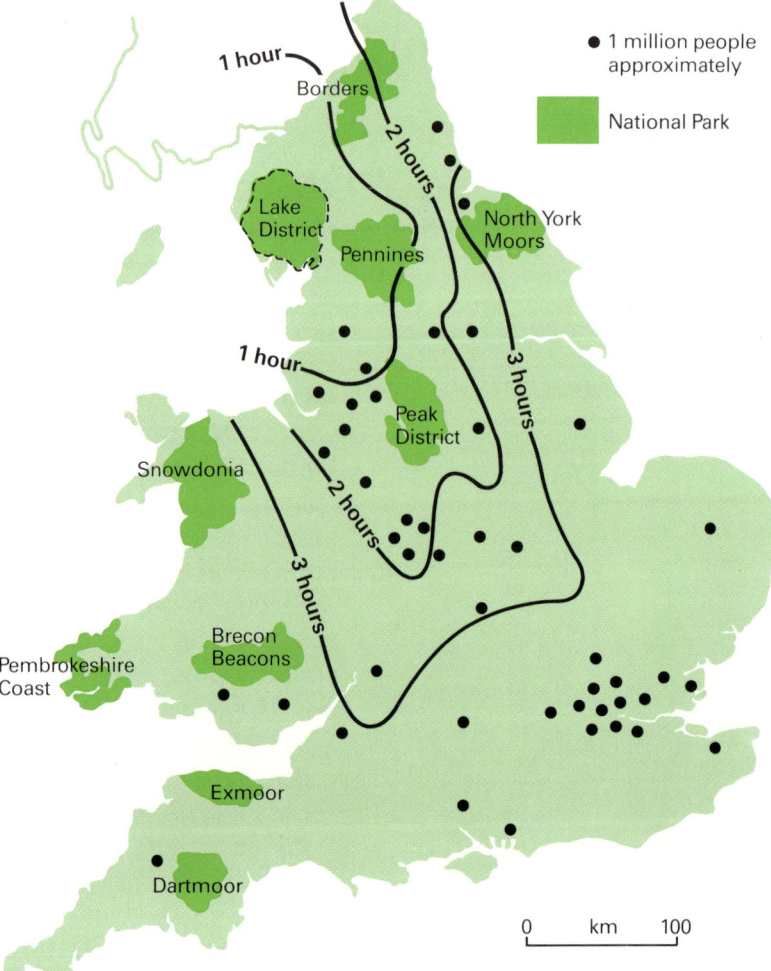

Figure 1   Journey times to the Lake District National Park

Figure 5　The industrial
landscape of the Ruhr

Figure 4　(left) The Lake District

Most of the land in the National Parks is farmed or grazed by sheep. Although visiting the Parks is free, some of the land is fenced off from the public and wildlife is protected. Scenery is the main attraction. Many people live and work in the Parks.

3 Do you find the scenery in Figure 4 attractive? if so, say why?

The Ruhr is an area of West Germany in which about five and a half million people live. It is an area of heavy industry and closely-packed housing. This ugly, industrial landscape is now being 'turned green' by the government which is concerned about providing leisure facilities for the people of the Ruhr and about improving the environment.

4 Look at Figure 5.
  (a) How old are most of the buildings in the area?
  (b) Are the buildings in a good state of repair?
  (c) Do you think there would be much traffic in the area?
  (d) What sort of pollution would be a problem in the area?
  (e) Why do you think improving the environment in the Ruhr is thought to be important by the government?

Look at the map, Figure 6, which shows how the government has planned green strips or belts of land between the cities of the Ruhr to stop them joining together and to provide open space for the people who live in the area.

Large nature parks have been created on the outskirts of the towns and six free-time leisure centres have been built to provide games facilities, water sports and open countryside. There is also work going on to clean up the area by landscaping and reclaiming derelict land and stopping pollution.

5 Draw and label a diagram to show the ways the government of the Ruhr is trying to improve the environment.
6 In what ways do our British National parks differ from the nature parks and free-time leisure centres of the Ruhr?

Homework ideas

Try and find out as much as you can about one of our National Parks.

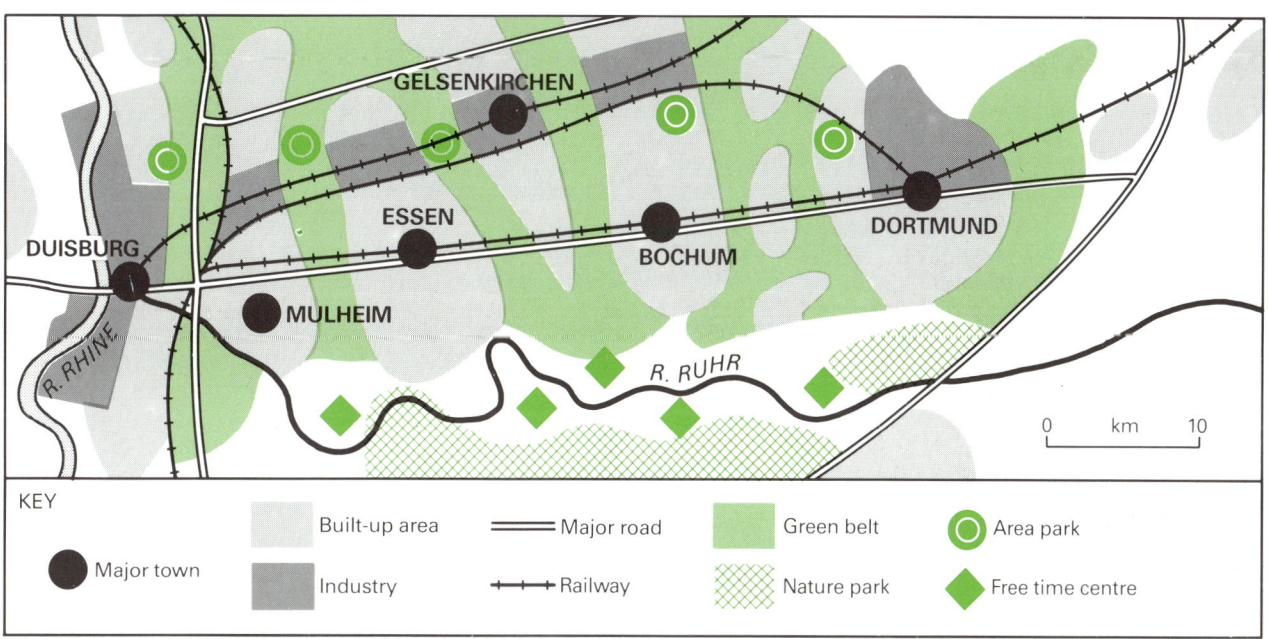

Figure 6　Plan of the Ruhr area

121

57 Conflicts in the Parks

The National Parks in England and Wales cover about one tenth of the land surface. Around 100 000 people live in them and 10 000 000 visit them each year. Obviously the sorts of things that tourists want from the National Parks may not be what local people like to see. Farmers get angry when tourists disturb their sheep or leave gates open. Tourists can destroy delicate plants and spoil the area for wildlife. Sometimes the National Parks are in areas where valuable rocks, like limestone, are found and so mining and quarrying companies want to dig them out. The Army often wants to use such wild, remote areas for military exercises. The Forestry Commission wants to plant large areas with trees. The big cities need more and more water and so reservoirs are often needed in the mountains of the National Parks. Figure 1 shows three of these problems.

Let us have a look at one proposal that could cause conflicts between the various interested groups in the Parks.

The Proposal

The traffic congestion in the small town of Denton has been so bad in recent years during holiday periods, that a new motorway has now been proposed that will cut across the surrounding National Park and bypass the town. This proposal has produced some strong feelings both for and against the plans, from people interested in the area. How do you think each of the people in Figure 3 view the proposal?

Figure 1

Figure 2   Things that put the parks in danger

Simon Kinna

Murray Clayson

Jeremy Jenkins

Nigel Thorn

Nick Wood

Victoria Slonims

Lucy Mawson

Christine Aplin

Simon Kinna, Sales Representative lives about three hours drive from the Park and the new road would cut about half-an-hour off his journey. He feels he would see more of the area, spend less time in the car and avoid traffic jams.

Murray Clayson, Lorry Driver, finds driving his lorry along the narrow lanes in the Park difficult and sometimes dangerous. In the holiday season things get really bad and he is often caught up for hours in queues.

Jeremy Jenkins, Company Director, finds it a time-consuming and expensive business getting the raw materials to his factory across the Park and transporting the finished products away. Although the area is really beautiful it's difficult to attract good managers when it takes them so long to get to work.

Nigel Thorn, Local Doctor thinks it would be nice to have less traffic passing through Denton, especially since his little girl has to cross the busy road each day on her way to school. He could certainly do without the noise and fumes too. It would also be easier for him and his wife to get to work each day. But like others in the town he is worried that more people will come and live in the area and so make it difficult for local people to buy houses.

Nick Wood, Farmer, thinks that there would be a chance to earn extra money by offering bed and breakfast accommodation at the farm house or by selling farm produce or even setting up a camp site in one of the fields. He is worried about the increased noise and air pollution though. The motorway would also use up some of his precious land and he is worried about tourists trampling the crops and letting their dogs worry the sheep.

Victoria Slonims, Retired Nurse, feels that the noise and fumes are bad enough for the local residents, but the increased numbers of people will destroy the wildlife. The road will spoil the view across the Park and cars and feet will trample the ground and increase erosion. There is even a chance that litter bugs may cause fires in summer. She is very concerned about the effect of the new motorway on the natural beauty of the area.

Lucy Mawson, Shopkeeper, is worried about losing business when traffic that originally passed her shop will bypass the town.

Christine Aplin, Solicitor, is worried that the atmosphere of quiet beauty that exists in the area will be lost forever and the character of the area completely destroyed.

Figure 3

Homework ideas

Think up your own set of characters who would have strong feelings about the plan for a new open-cast mine in a National Park, or the plan to flood a beautiful valley for a new reservoir. Produce a radio programme of the ideas you have discussed on a cassette recorder.

Things to do

1 Hold a public meeting about the proposal in class. Divide the class into two groups: FOR and AGAINST. Each member of the group can pretend they are one of the characters in Figure 3, and you can probably think of some more. When you have discussed the proposal fully, put it to a class vote.
2 Can you suggest ways that some of the objectors to the scheme could be satisfied?
3 Now look at the cartoon, Figure 2. Some factors that are putting the Parks in danger have been included in the cartoon. How many of them can you identify?
4 Now write up what happened in the enquiry and what decision was taken in the end.

58 Too many visitors

Figure 1   The Norfolk Broads

Table 1

	Motor Craft	Sailing Craft
1950	3000	2000
1955	3500	2100
1960	4000	2200
1965	4500	2300
1970	5000	2400
1975	5500	2500
1980	6000	2600

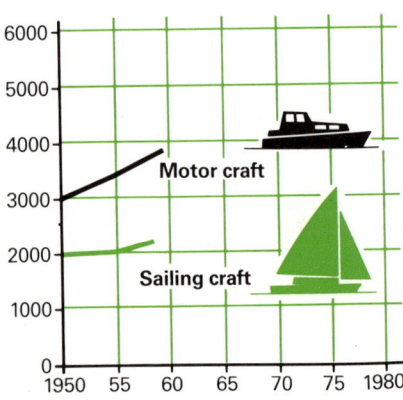

Figure 2   Relative numbers of sailing and motor craft on the Broads, 1950–80

Sometimes tourists can over-use an area and disturb the natural balance that exists there. One such area lies in east Norfolk. It is an area of shallow lakes and rivers called the Norfolk Broads. The shallow lakes were formed 500 years ago when the local people dug peat from the area and the hollows they left eventually filled with water and become home for a rich variety of fish and bird life (Figure 1).

However, during the last 70 years or so this beautiful wilderness has become a holiday centre, and many holiday shacks and motor cruisers have appeared along its quiet waterways. Sewage from nearby towns and fertilizers from nearby fields have begun to pollute the water. Motor boats create waves that break up the banks and stir up mud and silt.

Things to do

1 Look at Table 1. Plot the information as two line graphs, as shown in Figure 2. What do the graphs tell us? Why is this a bad thing for the Broads?

2 Look at Figure 3 showing the Broads before and after over-use.
  (a) Explain in your own words what the two diagrams show.
  (b) Can you suggest ways to improve the situation?

3 Look at Figure 4. Imagine you are concerned about the damage that is being done to the Broads by farmers, tourists and local industries and cities. Write a letter to your MP explaining the problems of the area, and suggesting ways they might be solved.

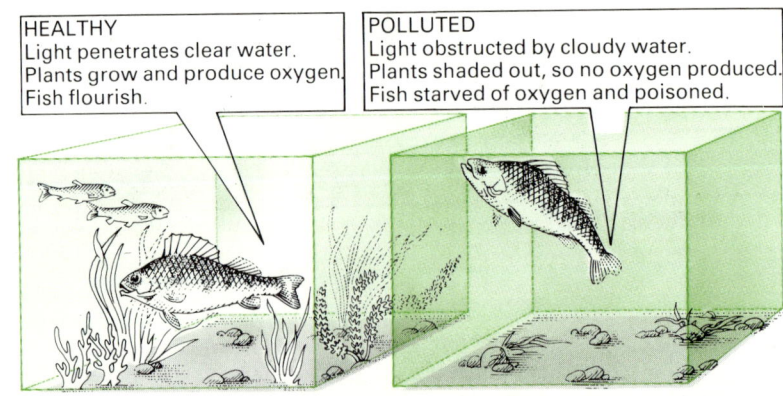

Figure 3   The Broads before and after over-use

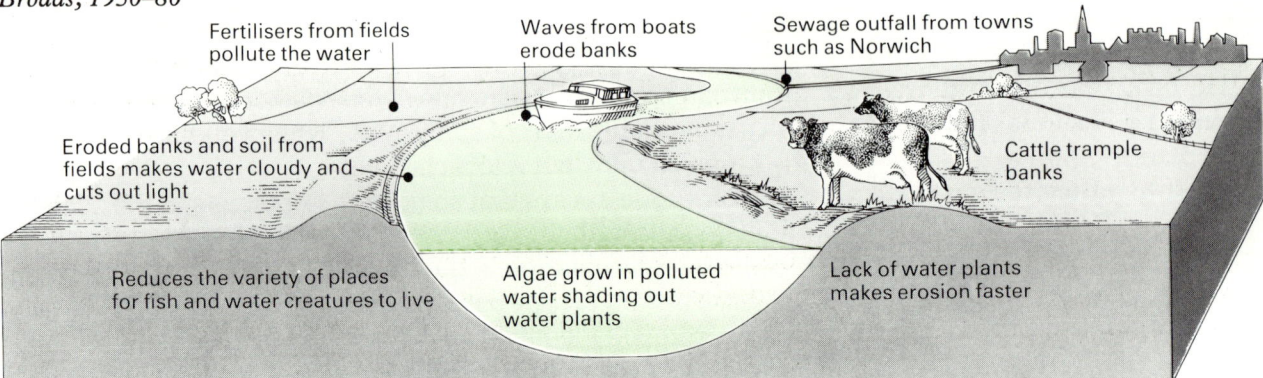

Figure 4   Threats to the Broads

Figure 5   A polluted beach in Spain

Problems in the Mediterranean

We have seen in earlier chapters how popular the Mediterranean is as a holiday area. Over 100 000 000 tourists visit the Mediterranean each year. But so many extra people in the area causes problems. They go there for the golden sand, hot sun and clear, blue sea. But is the sea really so clear and blue?

4 Look at Figure 6 which is a map of the Mediterranean showing some of the reasons for pollution in the area.
   (a) Where does water enter and leave the Mediterranean sea?
   (b) What do you think that the size of this opening means for the pollutants discharged into the Mediterranean?
   (c) From the section on the Norfolk Broads (Figure 4), what pollutants other than oil, sewage and industrial waste do you think are being discharged into the Mediterranean?
   (d) Several large rivers flow into the Mediterranean. What might these do to pollution levels?

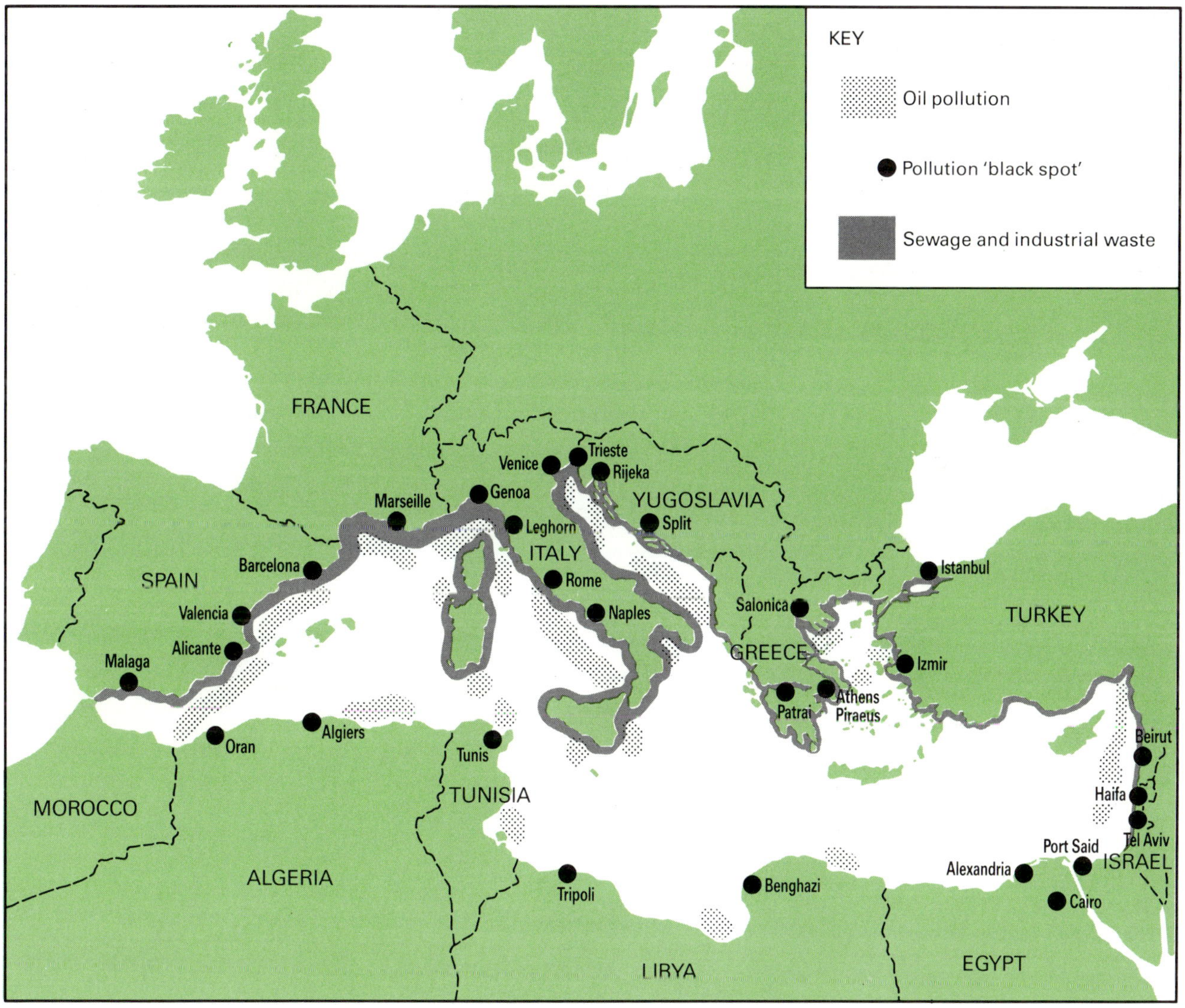

KEY

Oil pollution

● Pollution 'black spot'

Sewage and industrial waste

FRANCE

Trieste
Venice
Rijeka
Genoa
Marseille
Leghorn
YUGOSLAVIA
Split
ITALY
Rome
Barcelona
Istanbul
SPAIN
Valencia
Naples
Salonica
TURKEY
Alicante
GREECE
Izmir
Malaga
Athens
Patrai
Piraeus
Oran
Algiers
Beirut
Tunis
Haifa
MOROCCO
TUNISIA
Port Said
Tel Aviv
Alexandria
ISRAEL
ALGERIA
Tripoli
Benghazi
Cairo
LIBYA
EGYPT

Figure 6   Pollution in the Mediterranean

Homework ideas

Design a poster or write a letter to persuade a Mediterranean country to spend money on preventing pollution.

In 1976, eighteen countries around the Mediterranean produced *The Blue Plan* to try and control pollution. But it isn't working very well. The trouble is that all the countries want to develop more industry to earn more money and none wants to spend money on reducing pollution. If they don't agree soon, the Mediterranean may die.

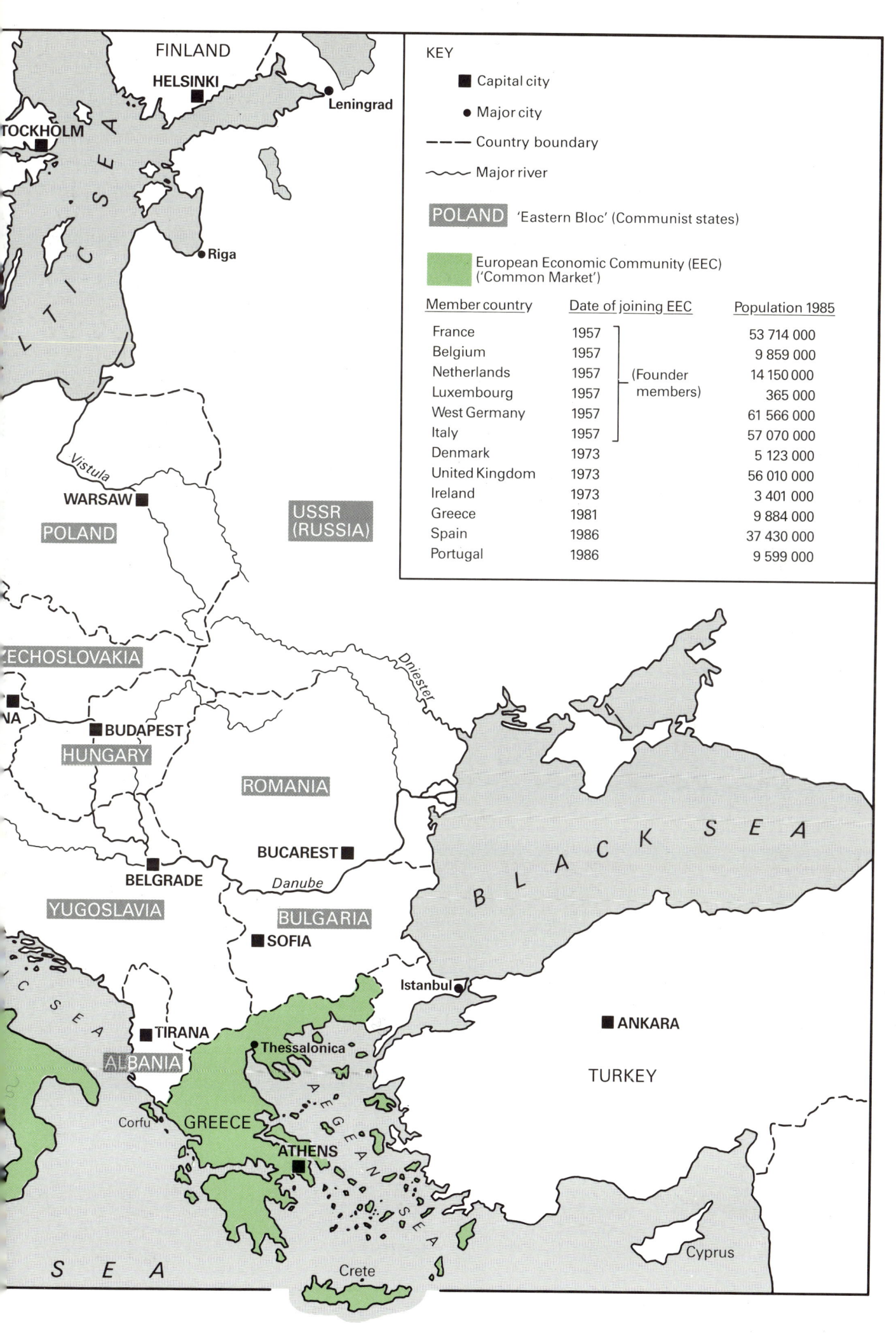

KEY

■ Capital city

● Major city

--- Country boundary

〜 Major river

POLAND 'Eastern Bloc' (Communist states)

European Economic Community (EEC)
('Common Market')

Member country	Date of joining EEC	Population 1985
France	1957	53 714 000
Belgium	1957	9 859 000
Netherlands	1957 (Founder	14 150 000
Luxembourg	1957 members)	365 000
West Germany	1957	61 566 000
Italy	1957	57 070 000
Denmark	1973	5 123 000
United Kingdom	1973	56 010 000
Ireland	1973	3 401 000
Greece	1981	9 884 000
Spain	1986	37 430 000
Portugal	1986	9 599 000

FINLAND

HELSINKI

Leningrad

STOCKHOLM

BALTIC SEA

Riga

Vistula

WARSAW

POLAND

USSR
(RUSSIA)

CZECHOSLOVAKIA

VIENNA

BUDAPEST

HUNGARY

ROMANIA

Dniester

BUCAREST

BELGRADE

Danube

YUGOSLAVIA

BULGARIA

SOFIA

BLACK SEA

ADRIATIC SEA

Istanbul

ANKARA

TIRANA

Thessalonica

ALBANIA

TURKEY

Corfu

GREECE

AEGEAN SEA

ATHENS

Cyprus

IONIAN SEA

Crete

Index